OVERSIZE

ACPL ITEM
DISCARDED

S0-EBU-776

The Great Showbusiness Animals

THE GREAT SHOW BUSINESS ANIMALS
BY DAVID ROTHEL

San Diego • New York
A. S. BARNES & COMPANY, INC.
In London:
THE TANTIVY PRESS

The Great Show Business Animals copyright © 1980
by A. S. Barnes Co., Inc.

All rights reserved under International and Pan American Copyright Conventions. No part of this book may be reproduced in any manner whatsoever without written permission from the publisher, except in the case of brief quotations embodied in reviews and articles.

First Edition
Manufactured in the United States of America

For information write to:
A. S. Barnes & Company, Inc.
P.O. Box 3051
La Jolla, California 92038

The Tantivy Press
Magdalen House
136-148 Tooley Street
London, SE1 2TT, England

Library of Congress Cataloging in Publication Data

Rothel, David, 1936-
　Great show business animals.

　Includes index.

　1. Animals in moving-pictures.　2. Animals in television.　I. Title.
PN1995.9.A5R67　　　791.43'09'0936　　　80-16891
ISBN 0-498-02519-5

1 2 3 4 5 6 7 8 9　84 83 82 81 80

To Nancy
 without whom . . .

Proprietary Notice

Lassie Television, Inc. and Lone Ranger Television, Inc., subsidiaries of Wrather Corporation, are the owners of all rights to the *Lassie, Lone Ranger* and *Sergeant Preston of the Yukon* properties. Permission has been granted the author by the above-named corporations for inclusion of certain pictorial and literary material in this book, which material is protected by copyright. Such permission does not convey any interest in the material to the author, publisher, or any other person or firm. The above-named corporations assume no responsibility for the accuracy of the facts and statements contained in this book, and the opinions expressed herein are solely those of the author.

Contents

Acknowledgments	ix
Preface	xi
1 Monkeying Around on the Sets	
J. Fred Muggs	3
Cheetah	23
Bonzo	29
Kimba	31
Tamba	33
Judy	35
2 Our Friend from the Deep	
Flipper	38
3 Man's Best Friends	
Rin Tin Tin	66
Lassie	87
Benji	128
Asta	142
Bullet	148
Chinook	150
Cleo	164
Daisy	167
Rusty	171
Yukon King	176
4 The Gentle Giants	
Gentle Ben	184
Ben	196
5 Daktari	
Clarence the Cross-eyed Lion and Judy the Chimp	202

Thundering Hoofbeats
　　A Visit with Glenn Randall 208
　　Champion 214
　　My Pal Trigger 222
　　Tony the Wonder Horse 226
　　Black Beauty 231
　　My Friend Flicka (and descendants) 237
　　Fury 244
　　National Velvet 251
　　The Lone Ranger's Silver 261
　　Thunder 266
　　Francis and Mr. Ed — the Talkers! 269

The Cockatoo of the Walk
　　Fred the Cockatoo 280

Epilogue
　　The PATSY Awards 283

Selected Bibliography 285

Index 287

Acknowledgments

I wish to extend my sincere thanks and deep appreciation to the following individuals and organizations which provided me with information and photographs that helped to make this book possible.

The Individuals:

Gene Autry
Bobbie Brooks
Rand Brooks
James Brown
Ricou Browning
Carolyn Camp
Joe Camp
Mario DeMarco
Ted Donaldson
Kirby Grant
Luke Halpin
Dr. James Lanier
Charles D. Livingstone

Myrna Loy
Buddy Mennella
Roddy McDowall
Jock Mahoney
Carmelita Pope
Jerry Preis
Glenn Randall
Roy Rogers
Margaret Scully
Stanley Stunell
Zoë Todd
Roy Waldron
Rob Word

The Organizations:

American International Television, Inc.
Columbia Pictures Corporation
Filmways, Inc.
Florida Stories, Inc.
Freemantle International, Inc.
Fries/Marcum Productions, Inc.
Heritage Enterprises, Inc.
Independent Television Corporation
Lassie Television, Inc.
Lone Ranger Television, Inc.
Metro-Goldwyn-Mayer

MGM Television
Miami Seaquarium
Mulberry Square Productions
Screen Gems, Inc.
SMF Media Service Corporation
Sunn Classics Pictures
Telewide Systems, Inc.
20th Century-Fox Television
Worldvision Enterprises, Inc.
Wrather Corporation

Preface

I think perhaps it's appropriate to establish what this book is and what it is not. It is, I believe, a book for people who have loved the many animals in motion pictures and on television over the years, or who have delighted in the comic and/or tender moments provided by supporting animal performers—performances which have often outshone those of the human actors who have had to share the camera with these notorious scene stealers. This is also a book for film aficionados and animal lovers who wish to enjoy a behind-the-scenes visit with many of the actors, trainers and directors who have worked with the animals to create some of our most memorable films and television series.

This is not a book on animal training, although training techniques are mentioned quite often. It is not an encyclopedic indexing of all the animal performers who have entertained us over the years, but probably most of your favorite show-business animals will be found on the pages which follow.

The title of the book proclaims that these are the *great* show business animals—thus you can gather that this is a subjective book. The animals included are or were stars of motion pictures and/or television series or else they were major supporting players in a series that would have been seriously diminished in charm and overall appeal if the animals had not been there. Lassie, Flipper and Benji are good examples of the animals that fall into the first category; Fred the cockatoo from *Baretta,* Cheetah of the *Tarzan* films and Daisy in the *Blondie* series are good examples of the second category of supporting star animals.

The animals that appeared in individual films and television programs but did not establish an ongoing public identity are not included; therefore, such animals as Tonto the cat in *Harry and Tonto* and *Namu the Killer Whale* are not included. Whatever the criteria used for selection, ultimately you get to the point where personal judgments regarding the inclusion or exclusion of certain animals must be made, otherwise the list would just go on and on. Consequently, such fairly popular animals as Tramp on *My Three Sons,* Scruffy on *The Ghost and Mrs. Muir,* most of the multitude of cowboy horses, and many other lovable, talented, supporting pets are not included among the "greats."

I trust, however, that the reader will agree with me on the selection of most of the animals and will enjoy getting to know them a little better through the information I've been able to gather.

1
Monkeying Around on the Sets

J. Fred Muggs

Monkeying Around on the Sets

Dave Garroway and J. Fred Muggs during an early *"Today Show."*

". . . that wretched little ape did more to put *Today* over the top than *Today*'s news coverage."

—Richard Pinkham, producer of *Today*

"He was acting up so badly that it was a constant concern. He knocked a girl off a desk, injuring her, and he bit me not once but many times. I made numerous visits to the NBC infirmary for a tetanus shot."

—Dave Garroway, host of *Today*

Joe Culligan, who headed the sales force and should know the figures, said that J. Fred Muggs' publicity value coupled with star Dave Garroway's appeal got the show the necessary momentum: "The net result was we returned from a loss of $1.7 million a year to a profit of $2 million on a gross of $10 million on the first full fiscal year—after six months of getting organized."

—from . . . *The Today Show* by Robert Metz

J. Fred, Buddy and Roy

Sylvester "Pat" Weaver, NBC's vice-president in charge of television in the early 1950s, was the man responsible for creating the *Today Show*. Weaver had first built his reputation in radio, producing Fred Allen's *Town Hall Tonight* comedy program. Later he was responsible for the prestigious *Command Performance* radio series. In the infant medium of television, his support and executive nurturing helped to establish the early video landmark, *Your Show of Shows* with Sid Caesar and Imogene Coca.

Television in those pioneering years was not an early morning medium. People listened to the radio during the day and watched television at night (if they happened to own one or had a close neighbor who had made the television plunge). Weaver carried the belief, however, that audiences could be lured from their radios to the viewing tube early in the morning while they were dressing or eating breakfast. His cohorts at NBC were dubious, but Weaver was the boss, so plans were drafted for an early morning show.

Once the basic concept for the *Today Show* had been laid out and approved, the problems really began. For one thing, affiliate stations on the extremely limited 1952 network would be left daily with an hour of non-network programming when *Today* shut down after its two-hour, seven-to-nine o'clock stint—the next network program not being telecast until 10:00 A.M. This meant affiliate stations had to fill the time with *something*—a movie or a local show, whatever, but expensive nonetheless. And since local television advertisers were few, even at prime time in the evening, they could be expected to be scarce as worms in a chicken yard at ten o'clock in the morning. It's enough to say that the fledgling *Today Show* met with considerable resistance from the video hinterlands.

Weaver persevered, however, and on Monday, January 14, 1952, at seven A.M. *Today* premiered on NBC with Dave Garroway as host. Early reviews ranged from cool to frigid and the show limped along on its daily schedule searching seemingly in vain for the half-awake, bleary-eyed home constituency that Weaver maintained was there but still unaware. Rumors abounded that the show would momentarily vanish from the network—little noted nor long remembered.

Luckily Pat Weaver was at the helm while the storms of threatened cancellation roared in coaxial swirls around him and his hearty crew. Weaver, both Columbus and Ahab-like, stood resolute in his search for that whale of a rating (and resultant sponsors) that would ensure the continuation of his daily two-hour news and information voyage into the uncharted world of morning television.

The program survived for a year, adding nine additional television markets to the original thirty-one. Then in late January 1953 a fluke occurred—the proverbial accidental meeting of people, time, place and luck from which show-business legends are made and from which hope is encouraged to spring eternal. A *Today Show* staff member on his way to a meeting passed a baby chimpanzee sipping formula from a bottle as it sat upon the lap of its young owner. The *Today Show* staffer, wise beyond his knowing, immediately envisioned the possibilities for the baby ape in the network television jungle for the *Today Show*. Baby J. Fred Muggs and the *Today Show* would never be the same again.

I had to make only two phone calls to locate Buddy Mennella, the young man who had sat in the NBC hallway with baby Muggs on his lap in January 1953. The intervening years had been good and then not so good for the two of them and the other member of the team, Roy Waldron, the co-owner of J. Fred Muggs. I had heard that they had been working for several years at Busch Gardens in Tampa. When I called there, however, I learned that their contract had expired some time back, but that they still resided in the Tampa area—out in the country. The Busch people passed along Buddy's telephone number.

The phone rang twice before a male voice answered. I asked to speak with Buddy Mennella. The voice on the line asked who I was and what I wanted. When I had supplied the proper information, he acknowledged that he was in fact Buddy and was amenable to an interview about Muggs. We agreed to meet the following Saturday morning.

During the interim I did some research and reflected on Muggs and his contribution to the *Today Show*. If the *Today Show* could be viewed as a sort of electronic newspaper, then J. Fred Muggs was certainly the comic page. Muggs, dressed as a little boy, would do cute, comic things naturally and unaffectedly on the program. On a typical day J. Fred could be found sitting on host Dave Garroway's lap or, as Fred grew older and larger, next to Dave. Garroway, in his laid-back, casual manner, would treat Muggs (at least on the air) like a little boy who was visiting the show or as a regular guest on the show. He might try to interview Muggs who could always be counted on to be unpredictable. As Garroway would ramble on amiably to him, J. Fred might stare at Garroway in stony seriousness; he might make goofy faces at his inquisitor; he might leap about, spilling coffee cups, upsetting table mikes and generally creating havoc—offsetting the frequent lethargy and stuffiness of the program. The important thing was that Muggs always appeared to the viewing audience as cute, not a little precocious, and loveable—especially loveable.

As time passed, Muggs began to do impressions of famous people or characters. He would do Popeye the Sailor Man in a sailor suit or Jack Benny's famous take, appearing in costume as a DeMille-like Hollywood director complete with beret, plaid jacket and cigarette holder.

An audience delight was something they called "the chase" on the program. Basically, this consisted of J. Fred running amuck on the set, performing every form of high jinks that came into his head. With time he learned that when the little red light on the camera was on he could pretty much do as he wished; nobody could scold or punish him as long as that red light glowed. For Muggs red meant "go," not stop. Also, as he grew older, it was reported that he frequently had bad days when, apparently without provocation, he would take nips at people. Sometimes the nips were full-fledged bites that required tetanus shots and other treatment.

J. Fred in director's garb.

Finally his monkeyshines became too much for the NBC staffers and brass. J. Fred Muggs was relieved of his duties; *Today's* and J. Fred's infancy had passed and they were no longer compatible.

I didn't realize from Buddy's directions just how far out in the country they lived. Consequently, I was running a few minutes late as I turned into the drive and approached the fashionable upper middle-class Florida ranch-style home. The house was fairly new and seemed a little out of place in this secluded farming area. Next to the house was what appeared to be a small barn or oversized three-car garage. I learned later that this building is the home of J. Fred and the other animals owned by Buddy and his partner Roy Waldron.

Buddy and Roy greeted me warmly and introduced me to the third member of their J. Fred Muggs Enterprises, a strapping young man named Jerry Preis who was clad only in skin-fitting swim trunks. Jerry's duties were not defined to me, but he appeared to be responsible for taking care of the animals and performing small roles and backstage duties during Muggs' performances. I was also introduced to Panky Glamsch, the official biographer of J. Fred Muggs as well as a feature writer for the *Tampa Tribune*. Panky seemed very pleasant and forthright considering that I was about to gather Muggs material for a chapter in my own book.

Buddy, dressed only in cut-off shorts, escorted me into the living room which overlooked the adjoining pool area. Buddy is short and possesses what can only be called a round little beer belly. Roy, who appears to be slightly older than Buddy, is taller and was dressed in boxer swim trunks with a matching top. Roy has a dignified air about him at all times and seems almost courtly in manner. We all sat around an octagonal table with the exception of Jerry who, in restless caged-animal fashion, roamed to different locations in the room as the interview progressed.

Buddy did most of the talking for the team with Roy or, occasionally, Jerry throwing in a line or two, or reminding Buddy of an incident or name that briefly slipped his mind. A couple of times during the lengthy interview when I struck a sensitive nerve regarding Muggs' alleged misbehavior during his *Today Show* years or mentioned *Today* host Dave Garroway, Buddy would ask me to stop the tape. At these tapeless times the three of them would vent the anger and frustration which still hangs like a black cloud around the fringes of their memories—a litany of sorts that they have practiced over the years, perhaps not without cause. But much of the time the remembrances were pleasant, the tape rolled and Buddy relived the good times with J. Fred and Roy.

David Rothel: How did you happen to acquire Muggs originally?

Buddy Mennella: Roy and I were pages at NBC. At that time NBC was just getting into television which was in its infancy. Our boss at NBC wanted us to go along with the television office, but we decided to tour with a road company. I was the stage manager and singer, getting fifteen dollars a week. Roy was dancing with the show. So we did that. Eventually we got tired of one-night stands and we came back to Jersey to see his grandmother—actually we had two weeks off.

One day we went into Jersey to buy some birdseed for Roy's grandmother at a pet shop. The lady in the shop said, "I hate this place. My husband keeps me here and I want to get out." Roy and I decided right then that we were going to buy that pet shop. We didn't have the money, so we ran to the bank and borrowed money for the shop. We talked the man at the bank into thinking we knew a lot about animals. We only had two English bulldogs and a couple of parakeets; that was the extent of our animal training. The bank loaned us the money, so we bought the pet shop and proceeded to build it up.

Business profits went from ten to three hundred dollars a day. Often I would go into New York to buy the stuff for the shop. I used to invariably end up in the chimp room at Henry Trefflich's in New York. I loved the apes, you know, and I couldn't wait to own one. Our first in the monkey family was a Rhesus monkey. We bought that one and kept him at the shop. So I kept going back and finally Henry Trefflich grabbed me one day and said, "Buddy, I've got two of the sweetest chimps. They just arrived, and if you don't grab one right away, you're losing out—you're missing the chance of a lifetime." Little did he know that it really was the chance of a lifetime (laugh).

I had only eleven dollars in my pocket and he wanted six hundred dollars for one of the apes. So I gave him a ten dollar deposit; I needed a dollar to get over the bridge home (laugh). I knew that if I went to Roy he'd be sore as the dickens at me, so I ran directly to the banker. I told him I'd like to have some more money. Now this was way back, mind you. Nobody loaned you money for apes (laugh). I told him I needed some money. He asked me what for. I said that I wanted to buy a chimpanzee. He said, "WHAT!" When he calmed down, he said, "You boys did such a nice job in that shop that I'm going to let you have that six hundred dollars providing you sign this insurance paper."

Now I knew I had the money, but I still had to convince Roy. The only way I could do that was to run back to the pet shop and say to Roy, "Would you please pick up the ape?" I knew he loved animals, and there was no way he was going to turn down this poor little thing. And that's how we got Muggs.

David Rothel: How old was Muggs at the time you got him?

Buddy Mennella: He was about thirteen weeks old. He weighed three and a half pounds. When we brought him home, I set the box on the table and I said, "Oh my God, what have I done?" I began to picture some day in the future this three hundred pound ape killing me (laugh). But he soon became one of the family. He went everywhere with us. He went to the drive-ins with us. When we crossed the bridge, he'd hand the coin to the guy in the booth. It got so that no matter where we traveled with Muggs, the people adored him. At first when he was in the pet shop, people used to bring in clothes for him. His first clothes were hand-me-downs that were brought in. [Muggs was eventually costumed in some 450 outfits for his television and personal appearances.]

David Rothel: Did you name him Muggs right away?

Buddy Mennella: No. That came later. While we had him in the shop, we decided to have a contest to name the chimp. The prize was that we'd give the winning child, aged six to fourteen, anything he wanted from the shop—except Muggs, of course. A boy finally gave him the name of Mr. Muggs, which we chose as the winner. Later on, we added the J. Fred to give him an air of distinction.

David Rothel: Was that at the time of the *Today Show* that you added the J. Fred?

Buddy Mennella: Right.

David Rothel: When did Muggs make his first show-business appearance?

Buddy Mennella: When we had our pet shop in New Jersey, Ray Forrest, a television personality, lived locally and wanted to do a film story on Muggs joining a group of kids for a day. Actually the film was shot at Ray's home and we had about twenty or thirty kids there. The kids gave Muggs a bath, a haircut, they shaved him,

Monkeying Around on the Sets

they scrubbed him, they played with him until he fell asleep in their arms. Ray filmed all of this. It ended up being a sixteen minute film which he showed on his Saturday morning television program. The program was called *The Children's Hour* and was sponsored by National Shoes, I think. That was the first program Muggs appeared on.

As I mentioned, Roy and I were pages at NBC many years ago—way back— and Perry Como was a good friend of ours. So the day we locked up the *Today Show,* we decided to go down to see Perry. When we went backstage, he grabbed us and brought us on the stage as he was warming up the audience for his television show. He talked about Roy and me and the services we had rendered him as pages and how much he liked us. He built us up until we got all flushed in the face. Then he took Muggs and used him in one of his songs. He sang a song called "Jambalaya," and he held Muggs in his arms as he sang it. That was actually the first network show on which Muggs appeared.

J. Fred is about to make his TV debut with Perry Como.

(Left to right) Roy Waldron, The Fontanne Sisters, Buddy Mennella. Perry Como and J. Fred Muggs are sitting.

David Rothel: How did you happen to place Muggs on the *Today Show*?

Buddy Mennella: When Roy and I were pages at NBC, we were favorites of the people in the studios. We got to know Uncle Jim Harkins, who was Fred Allen's manager. He used to call us the "gold dust twins"—he always did. Then we left NBC and eventually started the pet shop. Well, one day we went into New York to visit my dad who was in the hospital. We were too early to get into the hospital, so we decided to stop in at NBC and see Uncle Jim. Muggs always traveled with us, so he was there, too.

We discovered that after Fred Allen had died, Uncle Jim had been placed in charge of all talent at NBC. He was busy, but his secretary said, "I'm sure he'll want to see you, so why don't you wait a few minutes?" At that time NBC had an office in the RKO Building for the *Today Show* and across the hall was Uncle Jim's office. We were waiting outside his office and during that time somebody from the *Today Show* spotted us and said, "Don't leave." Well, we weren't going anywhere anyhow. After a few minutes they came back, grabbed us and rushed us into an office. I don't remember who we saw then; I guess it was Mort Werner and Richard Pinkham of the *Today Show* and some other producers and associate producers. Mort Werner told us they wanted to use Muggs the following Monday on the show and that they would give us twenty dollars. Having been a page and knowing a little about NBC's ways, I said, "No." So then he came out and offered us fifty. I said, "Okay, we'll do it."

So we went back home and waited for Monday. It was February, I remember that. Roy set the alarm clock for four o'clock, but it never went off. Also it had snowed that night and turned to ice on the highway. We were supposed to be there at six in the morning. We didn't get there until ten—the program was already off the air. The producers said, "Well, forget about it. If we need you, we'll call you."

Feeling rather dejected, we went down to the drugstore to get a cup of coffee. Muggs was sitting there with us. Within ten minutes the *Today* people were searching that whole building looking for us. They grabbed us bodily—poor Muggs never got to finish his donut—and rushed us upstairs to an office. Before that day was over, we had a five-year contract.

As an interesting aside, there had been a young fellow sitting by the window in the drugstore. He came over and asked if we minded if he looked at the chimpanzee. I said we didn't. When the NBC people rushed in, the poor guy got shoved aside. He was James Dean, who later became the famous actor. They shoved him completely aside.

David Rothel: When did Muggs first appear on the *Today Show?*
Buddy Mennella: In February of 1953.
David Rothel: It's apparent that the years on the *Today Show* weren't always terribly happy years—that there were ups and and downs during those years for Muggs on the program. What is your comment on that?
Buddy Mennella: Well, I'd say this: that over the years a lot of derogatory things were said against Muggs. Unfortunately, an animal can never speak for himself—he has no voice to defend himself. You see, little did we know that the chase—they used to have a thing called "the chase"—was started because someone on the show—and I won't even mention the name—was hoping that Muggs would get on top of all those monitors and get electrocuted. This was what was in his mind—to fry Muggs up there. It was going to be considered a good news item. They said it would be the biggest funeral New York had ever seen with David Sarnoff as a pallbearer.
David Rothel: Were you always just off camera on the set with Muggs during the *Today* program?
Buddy Mennella: Always under a table, in the wings, places of that sort. That was one of the difficulties, because once you turned the animal over to the star, the

Today host Dave Garroway readies J. Fred for a little excursion through the NBC Studio. Buddy Mennella looks on from off camera.

star did what he pleased and there was always the possibility of the star doing something wrong to the animal and hurting him—not necessarily on purpose, but because of a lack of knowledge. We were actually at the mercy of whoever was handling Muggs.

All the hours they worked Muggs, it was a wonder he wasn't irritable, snappy and biting everybody. He was on camera three hours and he had to be there three hours before he went on camera. Then he had to pose for magazines and NBC photograhers who had to take pictures to flood out to the markets all over. An animal has to be an angel to go through all of that. We had to get up and start our day at four o'clock in the morning so that we could be there at six o'clock. It was all against the rules of animal life.

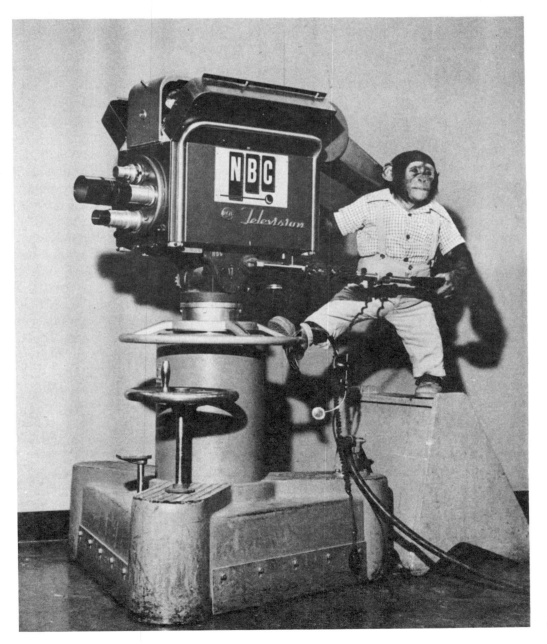

J. Fred Muggs, cameraman.

Today on tour. (Left to right) Buddy Mennella, Jack Lescoulie, Frank Blair, unidentified woman and two men. Dave Garroway is squatting, looking at Muggs.

David Rothel: How long was Muggs on the *Today Show*?

Buddy Mennella: Four and a half years—from 1953 to 1957.

David Rothel: Was he ever a regular on any other television series?

Buddy Mennella: Well, *Howdy Doody* wanted Muggs. You see, NBC wouldn't let Muggs go on any other network shows except for two shows a year. They limited him. The thing that really put the crimp on us was that in those days AFTRA couldn't figure out how to classify an animal. You see, Muggs was the first animal in television. I wish they had classified us as the act, not just Muggs. Had it been that way, NBC would have had to pay us something fantastic—like maybe two thousand dollars a week to start with. Whereas we only got two hundred dollars a week. That's two guys traveling with an ape back and forth from Jersey to New York. The expenses ate up most of that money. Here we were working, I don't know how many hours a day. [Author Robert Metz in his book, *The Today Show*, states that "In no time Muggs was earning upwards of $500 a week...."] After the *Today Show*, we had our own show, you know, *The J. Fred Muggs Show*, out of New Jersey. This was a local program.

David Rothel: It's amazing to me what you were able to accomplish with Muggs considering that you really didn't have any background in animal training.

Buddy Mennella: Well, we had these English bulldogs, you know, and we had monkeys in the shop. It just sort of mushroomed. We liked the animals and we started getting exotic animals—nice ones, you know.

David Rothel: When did you give up the pet shop?

Buddy Mennella: We kept it all those years we were on the *Today Show*, but it just got to be too much. We were never there and it was kind of difficult.

David Rothel: When did you get the idea of training Muggs to perform?

Buddy Mennella: We really never trained him to perform at that time. When we were on the *Today Show*, he was never a trained champanzee. He was brought up to understand words, and he had that little different spark about him that other apes will never have. When you see a baby picture of him, you can tell right away. He had the spark and those big, big eyes—tremendous eyes. He would partake of everything that happened—he learned everything. He became part of our family.

I'll tell you how smart he is. You could put thirty pieces of different fruits and vegetables in front of him and ask him for each one of them individually by name and he'd give them to you. He *is* amazing. I keep hearing people say that porpoises are smarter than apes, or that orangutans are smarter than apes. But I have never seen anybody show me another animal do what Muggs does. I'm inclined to believe a chimpanzee is the most intelligent animal.

David Rothel: Were you able to toilet train Muggs?

Buddy Mennella: When we used to do the *Today Show,* we lived on an old farm which had the chain type toilet. We'd sit him on the commode—he'd be half-asleep—and we'd wash his face, shave him, wash his hands. I'd say to him, "Okay, do number one." Eventually, it got so that when I said, "Do number one," he'd do it. And then I'd ask him if he went "poopy"? And he'd look underneath to see if he had (laugh). And he learned to pull the chain. The only thing he'd never do is use the toilet paper himself; he'd always hand it to me (laugh). "You do it!"

David Rothel: But he did get so that you could trust him in public with his toilet training—you could trust him on the set on the *Today Show.*

Buddy Mennella: Oh, yes, sure. We always took security anyway. We always put diapers on him and rubber pants. But he was good.

David Rothel: How easily does a chimp take to wearing clothes?

Buddy Mennella: The only thing Muggs doesn't like is sleeves—long sleeves. He will tolerate them for a certain period and then he will take them off. Otherwise, he's worn clothes all his life. He was brought up in clothes, so it was natural for him to wear them.

David Rothel: Was your training of Muggs a sort of hit-and-miss kind of thing—he lived with you and, therefore, as you wanted him to do certain things, you worked with him to do it—or was the training a studied thing?

J. Fred on his first birthday.

Buddy Mennella: No, I never planned it. In other words, I would talk to him the way you would to a son or daughter. This was the only way we approached it. We never even thought of doing it any other way. I'll give you an example. On stage we do a physical fitness thing. In one part of it Muggs and I touch toes together. My eyeglasses are loose and sometimes they fall off when I'm doing this. One time my glasses fell off and Muggs caught them before they hit the stage; he handed them to me and then went right back into the act of touching his toes. Now is that reasoning? Okay, that's one example. Another: I always see that Muggs' hands are washed right after he comes off stage. Now this just happened by accident. One day I took him into the dressing room and I said, "Muggs, open the water tap." So he opened the water tap. I said, "Take some soap and wash your hands under the water." So he did. I said, "Put the soap back into the dish." He did. I said, "Now rinse your hands and turn the water off." He did. I said, "Take the towel and wipe your hands and put it back." He did, and put the towel on a metal ring, but not neatly. I said, "Fix it right!" He pushed the towel around until it was neat. Now you tell me if that's not intelligence!

J. Fred on the set with Bob Hope during the filming of *The Seven Little Foys*.

David Rothel: Is the Muggs that appears now the original Muggs that was on the *Today Show?*

Buddy Mennella: Yes. You know, we did three-and-a-half years at Busch Gardens here in Tampa. We went there for six weeks work to open the amphitheater and ended up being there three-and-a-half years. Muggs worked loose on stage. He weighs 175 pounds now and the comments from the audience to the Busch Gardens' administration were that love showed through the act. It showed through that the trainer and the animal had a great love for each other. That speaks for itself. In other words, it's not an act where the animal fears the trainer.

David Rothel: Give me a rundown on the type of act Muggs was doing at Busch Gardens.

J. Fred with (left to right) Roy Waldron, Jerry Preis and Buddy Mennella during their three-and-a-half-year engagement at Tampa's Busch Gardens.

Buddy Mennella: We'd do a sort of intelligence act. We started doing this act when we went on tour with Bob Hope. It's an offbeat type of thing where Muggs' understanding of words comes into play. Let me just tell you about the finale of the act. We have a set of octave bells—one octave. Whether it be an orchestra or taped music in the background, he'll put his arm out when he's ready. I say, "Maestro," and then I say, "Muggs." At that time the music is started. Muggs plays "The Bells of St. Mary's" and concludes with three sustains. This is with no commands, no talk, no nothing. It only took me about four hours to do this; that's how smart he is. He would pick up each individual bell that was a different note to play the melody of the song. He had to pick up the right bell in the proper sequence, of course, for each note of the song. And it is not just remembering the right notes, he's got to remember that a phrase of music ends at a certain point and then begin at another point in time. He would pick up the new bells at the right time in the music phrase. That really tears the house down. We did this act for Totie Fields at the Steel Pier years ago and she told us, "Buddy and Roy, use this as your finale because this *is* your finale. No animal does this!"

Muggs also does impressions of celebrities. He does Jackie Gleason, Jimmy Durante, Ed Sullivan, Richard Nixon, Jack Benny and Popeye. He has little mannerisms of each person down pat, just as if he had studied them. We do a half-shour show, which is unusual—most animal acts do six or eight minutes. He used to do Groucho Marx; he had the walk down pat. The thing about Muggs is that he is so good that you almost don't appreciate him because you just think, well, he's another person rather than an animal.

The biggest compliment we get is that there is a bet going on that it's a midget in costume. They make a bet and then they have to come to me and we have to show them that he is really a chimp.

David Rothel: Does Muggs work for a reward motive?

Buddy Mennella: No, no.

David Rothel: He works to please you, then, for affection?

Buddy Mennella: Right, right. At the end of the show he'll look up at me and his *eyes* will pierce my *eyes*; he'll put his arms around me and seem to ask, "Did I do good?" And if he's done something *his* way—not as planned in the act—I won't look at him. I'll just walk out with him. From the time we leave the amphitheater until we get to the dressing room, he's going (whine sound) and putting his arms around me. I'll indicate, "Don't bother me." He'll get very upset because he wants me to be pleased.

David Rothel: Do *you* always work with him on stage?

Buddy Mennella: Yes. Roy is the emcee of the show. You see, we have a little production type of thing. It's different from most animal acts; it's a produced show where Muggs has to be accurate in everything he does to keep the show moving. We do offbeat things in the act like fencing, and there's a complete manual of arms that he does.

You know he's been a cover artist. He was once the cover artist for *Mad* magazine. He also did two pages in *Look* and a cover for *Relax* magazine a few years ago. That sold for five hundred dollars. We have to laugh because in the book *The Naked Ape* the author states that Muggs has done a few paintings. Well, little does he know that Muggs has finished ten thousand finger paintings. Muggs has probably painted more than any ape in the business (laugh). He's been a cover artist twice; even humans don't usually get that privilege.

J. Fred is seen here doing his Jack Benny impersonation.

David Rothel: Are there days when Muggs just says, "No, today I'm off. I'm not going to do the act.?"

Buddy Mennella: No. Would you believe we never have lost a show?

David Rothel: Are chimps very sickness prone?

Buddy Mennella: Yes. You have to be careful of diseases that people get—colds and pneumonia. We try to stress to all our friends to let us know if they have a cold because there have been times when one chimp would get a cold and it'd run through all of them and cost us four or five hundred dollars at a time for doctor bills. We have a rule ourselves that if we have a cold and go into the chimp room, we wear a mask. Muggs had pneumonia three times while on the *Today Show*. That was because they put him in snow and other elements that would hurt the poor thing.

David Rothel: How long does a chimp normally live?

Buddy Mennella: Around forty-five years.

David Rothel: Have you thought about raising some Muggs Juniors?

Buddy Mennella: No. I'll be honest with you. We love our apes. Most ape people get rid of their apes within a few years, but we can't bring ourselves to do that. As a matter of fact we adopted two apes to save them from going for research. It makes a hardship on us because when we go some place, we have to take all six apes. That's very difficult because they're all big. But we did this because we love the apes and we'll never get rid of them. The building next to this house is a good example of our love and concern for the animals—the money we spent on that thing! It would have been much easier on us just to have Muggs.

David Rothel: But Muggs is mortal like all of the rest of us and could drop dead tomorrow. Shouldn't you have another one ready to take his place?

Buddy Mennella: My reason for not getting any more apes is that my thoughts on apes have changed over the years. I really think it is unfair for apes to be made available to trainers anymore. Would you believe that? I'm including myself, even though I love them very much.

David Rothel: In the wild, though, a chimp probably wouldn't live as long as Muggs.

Buddy Mennella: Sure, but they're doing their thing. You have to realize that he's like a child in *every* way. If you were to keep him in the house all the time, you'd be constantly after him to keep his foot off that, don't touch that, put that down. You'd quickly make him a neurotic. And, too, chimps have to have a time where they are in their own place. They look forward to that, to get away.

David Rothel: I take it that you would not recommend a chimpanzee for a pet, then.

Buddy Mennella: Never! Only because of my feelings for the ape. Most people buy an ape because they can afford it and want it as a novelty. The novelty wears off within three or four months and within that same time the poor animal is spoiled because the people didn't know how to handle it. Secondly, the poor animal will then probably not work with another trainer. They've ruined him and so the animal probably will end up in research somewhere. This is why I'm against any individual owning an ape.

David Rothel: Has Muggs had to spend a great deal of time without any other chimps around?

Buddy Mennella: Well, we had Phoebe B. Beebe on the *Today Show* with Muggs. We still have Phoebe who's really a big girl—a big, fat mama (laugh). So he

Phoebe B. Beebe is seen here smooching with *Today* host Dave Garroway in a mid-fifties program.

has her to play with, but he prefers to be with humans. And he has likes and dislikes with humans. We were once at the Copacabana with the Copa Girls. Muggs didn't like one of them and he pushed her away. So I sort of scolded him. I said, "Now look, you be nice and give her a kiss and a hug." He pushed her away again, but he hugged every other Copa Girl. So he has likes and dislikes, but he is *not* a vicious animal. He could *not* be and be on that show for four and a half years, five days a week, and travel every weekend promoting the show in every city in the United States, and go around the world.

There are so many things that have happened to him, funny things. One day Anita Ekberg was on the *Today* program. She was wearing earrings that just slipped on; they weren't through her ears. Of course, she's built! Muggs was sitting on her lap. He admired beautiful women; he always admired beautiful women. He was looking at her and then he touched her earring and it dropped down into her bosom. The camera was on a tight shot so it was right on top of the whole thing. The natural thing for Muggs was to get it out of her bosom and give it back to her. As Muggs tried to retrieve the earring, we heard the director from downstairs scream, "Get off that shot!" Muggs finally got that earring out and gave it to Anita Ekberg and she just adored him. Twenty years later we heard Frank Blair (longtime *Today* newsman) on a program saying that they had to get off the shot because they heard Anita Ekberg scream. That was his interpretation of the situation. Muggs was only just a baby then; he wasn't as big as a one-year-old child. There are so many stories about Muggs. One time he soul kissed with Kim Novak (laugh).

David Rothel: But chimps do have a reputation for being mean.

Buddy Mennella: True, but you have to hurt them first; they only act mean when they are put in bad situations. If you put a wild animal in a circumstance where he's going to have to protect himself, he's *going* to protect himself. You just don't put him in those circumstances. You can't treat animals today the way they did in those early days of live television. It was pandemonium in the first place because it was a new business. You had to hand the animal over to a person who had no knowledge of animals or animal training, and you had to teach the person to be a trainer in five easy lessons—which is almost impossible. And then you couldn't be there to be part of it, because you couldn't be on camera, otherwise they had to pay you. And they didn't want to do that!

David Rothel: I asked my vet about chimps, if he treated them. He said he did when he first started his practice, but he told me he had an awful time trying to treat them. He said, "I swear that their heads can swivel all the way around and nip you. It just got to the point where it took two or three people to hold them for treatment."

Buddy Mennella: When you force any animal to do something against his will—I don't care what it is—you are going to get the same reaction. You'll get the same reaction from a house cat. We trained our animals in the beginning to accept a rectal thermometer and to put their arms out for a shot, so they know when they are being taken care of. It makes a big difference.

David Rothel: Was Muggs allowed in the passenger compartments of airplanes?

Buddy Mennella: When we went on a world tour, he rode in a seat on the plane with us. The airlines made the exception to the rule with him because he was so good on a plane. A while back we went to New York for the *Good Morning America* show to celebrate Muggs' birthday. One hundred four photographers, magazine, newspaper, radio and television reporters were at the airport to meet us. The remark was made that Muggs got more coverage than the President of the United States. You're talking big time now; you're not talking baby stuff. If he's that important years later, then, by God, there's something in this animal that people remember and never forgot.

David Rothel: You were on the *Good Morning America* program, *Today's* competition?

Buddy Mennella: Variety came out and said that Muggs was going to be on that show permanently. They wrote a big article about it. Then we got a call—we were still appearing at Busch Gardens—from a company called Leisure Concepts. They had heard that we were going to be regulars on *Good Morning America* and said that this was going to be such a tremendous thing that they wanted to be the first ones to merchandise Muggs. That's how fast they're going to jump in if Muggs gets a vehicle again. [Muggs never became a regular on *Good Morning America*.]

David Rothel: What's in the works for Muggs now?

Buddy Mennella: His life story in a book, for one thing. There are quite a few other things in the air now, you know. If I tell you now, you know, other acts may get in on it, so I can't talk about it now.

And suddenly I was aware of a funereal scent of desperation shrouding the room.

Buddy, Roy and Jerry took me into an adjacent bedroom/office where they kept Muggs' memorabilia—plaques, dolls, awards, photos, etc. They let me select some photos for this Muggs chapter from the hundreds of stills they had stacked in piles. We sat crosslegged on the carpeted floor, thumbing through the various stages of Mugg's career. He *was* a photogenic creature, no doubt about it!

J. Fred as General Patton.

Buddy suddenly remembered Muggs' famous finger painting and told Jerry to get some of them so that I could select one as a gift from them and Muggs. Jerry returned with probably twenty-five different paintings from which I could take my choice. I thought about the color scheme in our home and finally selected one that I thought would be appropriate. I noticed that the painting was autographed by Muggs and inquired. Buddy explained that he had held Muggs' hand (paw?) and helped him to write his name. From that original signature a stamp was made which was then used for all the paintings.

I asked about seeing Muggs. Looks were exchanged between Buddy, Roy and Jerry. Jerry indicated that, being Saturday, he was running late and had not as yet taken care of the housekeeping duties in the chimp room and that another time would be better. Buddy suggested I visit another time when they could have Muggs ready for company. I didn't push the matter; I guess I really didn't want to visit the home of J. Fred Muggs that day.

J. Fred Muggs today.

"Me Tarzan, You Cheetah"

Next to J. Fred Muggs, the most famous chimp in show business has probably been Cheetah, Tarzan's monkey friend, who has swung through the African jungles with the "Lord of the Jungle" on most of his multimedia adventures—novels, motion pictures, radio, comics and television.

Cheetah in the Tarzan movie and television adventures served generally two purposes: to provide comic relief between action scenes or during slow periods in the plot and to be a "go for" in times of trouble. As comic relief—let's face it—Cheetah was often a bore except in very brief doses. Generally, the tendency was to have him do cutesy things for the juvenile contingent in the audience who were particularly fond of his escapades. When Cheetah was held to a bit of monkey business near the beginning of the story, with a booster shot of high jinks midway and then a final bit of pranksterism as the closing titles came up on the screen, the Cheetah monkeyshines were fun for all, kids and adults. Unfortunately, too often when jungle-script fever set in, Cheetah's antics were sometimes tedious.

When Cheetah was involved in legitimate plot action, however, he could be appreciated by everyone in the audience. Cheetah could be counted on to go for help when Tarzan was trapped and in danger. Other times he might go for a knife to cut the ropes that bound the helpless Tarzan and his mate, Jane. He might also go for other animals, such as Tonda the elephant and his friends, who would then come to Tarzan's rescue. In situations such as these Cheetah the chimp had his finest screen moments.

Unlike the one and only J. Fred Muggs, there have been a multitude of Cheetahs over the years. Animal trainers on the Tarzan films generally did not like to use a chimpanzee for more than a few years because of their tendency to become ill-tempered and dangerous—a situation especially difficult for actors untrained in handling animals.

Johnny Weissmuller, undoubtedly the most famous Tarzan and the actor to play the part longest (twelve films between 1932 and 1947), was known for his ability to work well with most animals on the Tarzan set. It was reported by Gabe Essoe in his book *Tarzan of the Movies* that when Weissmuller met his first Cheetah in 1931, "The chimp bared his teeth, his sly eyes searching for a sign of weakness or fear. Drawing his hunting knife, Johnny held it close to Cheetah's nose so he recognized the object, then knocked it hard against the chimp's skull. After replacing the knife in its sheath, he offered Cheetah his hand. Momentarily, Cheetah glared at him in anger, then the inscrutable grin returned and he took Johnny's hand. From that instant there was a lasting friendship between them."

Johnny "Tarzan" Weissmuller and Johnny "Boy" Sheffield with Cheetah and an unidentified horse in a scene from *Tarzan's Desert Mystery* (1943).

Most of the screen Tarzans that preceded Johnny Weismuller had their little Cheetahs. And the "bronzed white sons of the jungle" who succeeded Weissmuller in the 1950s—Lex Barker, Gordon Scott and Denny Miller—also had their simian scene-stealers. But in the early 1960s when Jock Mahoney signed to play the loin-clothed jungle lord, he was delighted to learn that producer Sy Weintraub was not planning to include a Jane or Cheetah in the new movie episodes. Mahoney commented, "I'm glad the chimp's gone. They're the dirtiest, meanest animals to work with." Mahoney had other problems, however, during location filming for his two Tarzan films—*Tarzan Goes to India* (shot in the jungles of Mysore Province, in Bangalore, and Bombay, India) and *Tarzan's Three Challenges* (which was filmed in Bangkok, Thailand). Soon after production on the *Three Challenges* film began, Mahoney contracted amoebic dysentery, dengue fever and, finally, pneumonia. His weight plummeted from 220 pounds to 175 pounds. For days his temperature soared, but trouper-like, Mahoney saw the film through to completion. He commented to me in an interview that during his illness the only time he was left alone on the set was when the camera was rolling; otherwise, there was always someone at his side in case he collapsed. Jock laughed as he recollected the final indignity he faced in the *Three Challenges* film. He had lost so much weight that his "diaper" kept falling off. But he reempahsized, he was grateful that he didn't have to contend with a chimp, too.

Brenda Joyce (Jane), Cheetah and Lex Barker pause for a picnic in this scene from *Tarzan's Magic Fountain* (1948).

Gordon Scott, Cheetah (played by Zippy) and Rickie Sorensen appear rather disconsolate in this quiet moment from *Tarzan's Fight for Life* (1958). When shown on TV the film is called *Tarzan and the Trappers*.

Jock Mahoney had many problems to contend with during the filming of his two Tarzan films, but he was very happy that Cheetah wasn't one of them.

Mahoney's successor was not so fortunate. Mike Henry acquired the role in 1966 for *Tarzan and the Valley of Gold* in which Cheetah returned, played by an especially temperamental chimp called Dinky. From their first scenes together on the Acapulco jungle locations, it was obvious that the two of them were not going to get along well together. When Henry's second Tarzan film, *Tarzan and the Great River,* began location shooting in Brazil, the relationship between chimp and Tarzan became even more strained. Finally Dinky turned vicious. As Henry recalls, "I was to run over to the chimp and pick him up. When I did, he lashed out at me and ripped my jaw open. It took twenty stitches to put my face back together. I was in a monkey-fever delirium for three days and nights. It took me three weeks to recuperate."

Dinky was destroyed after the incident and a new chimp was brought in for the final scenes of the picture. Mike Henry eventually filed two lawsuits against the Tarzan production company—asking $800,000 for "maltreatment, abuse and working conditions detrimental to my health and welfare," and an additional $75,000 for the chimp bite which "resulted from human error." Henry claimed that "although the chimp chittered nervously just before that particular shot and I cautioned the director about it, he instructed me to do as I was told and go ahead with the scene. And that's when I got bit."

Henry made one more feature, *Tarzan and the Jungle Boy* (1968) and was slated to go from the three features into the NBC television series. He was so distraught from his experiences on the features, however, that he withdrew from the video series.

Mike Henry and Dinky during one of their happier moments during the filming of *Tarzan and the Great River* (1967). Manuel Padilla, Jr. (who later went into the Tarzan television series) and Jan Murray are also in the scene.

Ron Ely became the television Tarzan for the two-year run of the series on NBC from 1966 through 1968. Ely also suffered much from encounters with chimps and other wild animals during the filming of the series—probably more than any other actor who played Tarzan, because he generally insisted on doing his own stunts. The unintimidated Ely seemed to hold the philosophy that bites, scratches, sprains and battle scars went with the territory. Ely was a source of great worry for producer Sy Weintraub, who resignedly insured his star for three million dollars and groused that the actor "just doesn't listen. . . . He actually believes that in a fight to the death with a five-hundred-pound lion he could win."

Ron Ely and the Cheetah used for the NBC television series.

Bonzo

Back in early 1951, long before he was to seriously embrace the Republican elephant as a candidate, Ronald Reagan briefly cavorted with a chimp named Bonzo in a film the later California governor and presidential hopeful would probably like to forget ever happened—or at least would like critics and television comedians to forget. It isn't that the film *Bedtime for Bonzo* was bad (in fact, it was good family fun for 1951 film audiences), it is just that Ronald Reagan, today's statesman, appears rather silly at times as he competes for laughs with a chimp and loses.

In *Bedtime for Bonzo* Reagan is a psychology professor who takes a chimp named Bonzo into his home to raise as a real child to prove his theory that environment and human treatment, not heredity, mold a person's character. Diana Lynn is cast as Reagan's housekeeper and loving nursemade to Bonzo, thus winning Reagan's heart by the time the film winds to a close. Portly Walter Slezak is also in the cast as a professor friend of Reagan. For all the winning characteristics of the human cast, they don't stand a chance when Bonzo joins them on screen. There are such scenes as Bonzo in baby sleepers gulping down his breakfast cereal just like any human juvenile and Bonzo causing havoc with a vacuum cleaner when housekeeper Lynn is otherwise distracted. Monkey mugging prevails throughout, but for the most part the movie possesses a beguiling nonsense that makes it all work niftily as a film comedy.

Bonzo was played by a charmer named Peggy. When she wasn't Bonzo for Universal Pictures, Peggy was over at Columbia Pictures playing Tamba with Johnny Weissmuller in his Jungle Jim adventures.

With the success of *Bedtime for Bonzo,* Universal decided a sequel was in order. The result was *Bonzo Goes to College,* released in 1952, a year and a half after the original entry. Ronnie Reagan is nowhere to be found in the cast—only the chimp was retained for the follow-up.

This time Bonzo takes up residence in a college professor's home, passes the college entrance exams and (Get this!) becomes a football player on the college team. He, not unexpectedly, wins the team's big game with only seconds to spare (plot credibility was not one of the long suits of the two Bonzo features).

Human cast members fared as well as possible under the simian circumstances. Maureen O'Sullivan (late of the Jane role in the Tarzan features—what must have been going through her mind during the filming of this movie!) plays professor Charles Drake's wife in the film. Edmund Gwenn (who had in earlier years spent considerable time with Lassie) and juvenile Gigi Perreau are appealing in granddaughter/grandfather roles. Irene Ryan (Granny years later on TV's *Beverly Hillbillies*) steals a few laughs from Bonzo in her role as the family's long-suffering maid.

Bonzo Goes to College was a successful sequel, but Universal apparently felt there were just so many features to be gotten out of the chimp before audience ennui would set in—and in this case the number was two.

Bonzo and his friend Ronald Reagan embrace in this tender scene from *Bedtime for Bonzo*.

Other Monkeying Around . . .

Johnny Sheffield appeared as "Boy" in the Tarzan series of films from 1939 (*Tarzan Finds a Son!*) through 1947 (*Tarzan and the Huntress*), when it was decided that he had outgrown the role, since he had gotten almost as tall as Johnny Weissmuller, his Tarzan father. (Sheffield had, however, *just* grown up; he had not acquired the bulk that Weissmuller was displaying in greater and greater quantities with each Tarzan film, and which would be one of the reasons for Weissmuller leaving the Tarzan series the year following Sheffield.)

Sheffield, a handsome, athletic eighteen-year-old, was signed in 1948 by Monogram Pictures, a B-movie factory, for a series of low-budget features in which he played Bomba the Jungle Boy, based on the popular Roy Rockwood novels. The series was an appropriate vehicle for the limited but already familiar abilities of the young actor.

Sheffield as Bomba was made to suffer the same monosyllabic dialogue that Tarzan actors were cursed with for many years. In the first few Bomba episodes the jungle boy's speaking was very limited and fell into the "Me Bomba, you white hunter" vein. As the series progressed, however, he acquired the ability to speak more fluently and lost most of his lingual limitations. The jungle boy's "civilizing" was noted in a couple of the episode's scripts, perhaps to assuage the concerns of anthropologists in the audience who might have been troubled by the temptations of civilization being thrust upon the innocent jungle youth.

Sheffield's plain leather loincloth from the Tarzan films was swapped for a leopard skin one, he was given a spear for a weapon and a chimp for a friend— otherwise, he was still basically "Boy" minus a father, mother and adequate budget.

Bomba's chimp was named Nakimba or, occasionally, just Kimba. An animal by the name of Kimbbo played the role for some of the episodes. Bomba's chimp played a much smaller role in these quickie jungle films than Cheetah did in the Tarzan films. Occasionally the chimp was eliminated altogether, as in *The Lost Volcano* (1950) and *Killer Leopard* (1954).

The lackluster Bomba series was rather a comedown for Sheffield when compared with his work in the generally exciting and big-budget Tarzan films. The eleven Bomba films made between 1948 and 1955 were each slapped together in a few days with an overly generous amount of stock animal footage from the 1930 documentary/travel film, *Africa Speaks*. Bomba or other cast members were frequently required to point off camera and say, "Look!" Then the film editor would insert a few dozen feet of ancient animal footage. Usually it would pertain to some element of the plot line, but often the irrelevancy of the stock footage could cause one to suspect that it was just filler to get the film up to feature length. Occasionally the same stock footage would be used in more than one of the episodes in the series. Volcano footage which included a bubbling lake spewing molten lava was used in both *The Lost Volcano* and *Safari Drums* (1953). Scenes of Bomba swinging Tarzan-like through the jungle, vine to vine, were reused regularly.

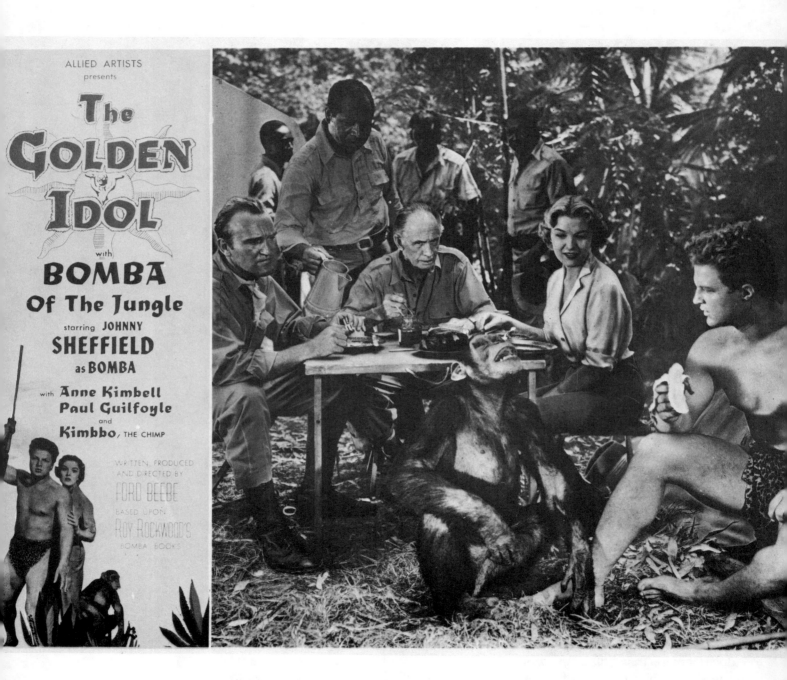

Kimbbo is seen here playing Bomba's chimp pal, Nakimba.

Even though Johnny Sheffield was a pleasant enough Bomba and several of the episodes were fairly exciting (and they were certainly harmless jungle stories for the juvenile audience), the feeling persists when viewing a Bomba film today that Monogram (later known as Allied Artists) and the individuals responsible for the series could have striven for a higher level of accomplishment, even given the obvious budget restraints. B-movie specialist Ford Beebe was the person most responsible for the Bomba series, directing all eleven films, writing most of the screenplays and adding the chore of producing for the last four pictures in the series. The obvious assessment would have to be that he spread his talents too thin trying to do all of those tasks.

Johnny Sheffield retired from show business when the Bomba series succumbed with *Lord of the Jungle* in 1955. He entered U.C.L.A. and ultimately graduated with a B.A. in business administration. His Tarzan and Bomba salaries had been well-managed during the intervening years, primarily through shrewd real estate purchases in Pacific Palisades, Santa Monica and Malibu. The word is that Johnny Sheffield can now afford to swing in any tree he chooses.

* * *

During the same time Johnny Sheffield was donning his Bomba loincloth, Johnny Weissmuller was forsaking his Tarzan one for the Khaki "white hunter" look of comic-strip hero, Jungle Jim. In 1948 when the first Jungle Jim feature was made, Weissmuller was in his mid-forties and overweight—both factors having accounted for his switch from loinclothed swinger to land-lumbering jungle guide/white hunter.

Serial and B-feature producer Sam Katzman hired Weissmuller for the low-budget Columbia Pictures series and gave him a piece of the financial action. The series, for all its faults (a bored-looking, overweight hero; excessive stock footage; absurdities of storyline—one episode dealt with supposed pygmy moon men, for example) was popular and very profitable for all parties concerned. When the feature series ended in 1955 (sixteen episodes in all with Weissmuller playing himself in the last three), a twenty-six episode television series completed the Jungle Jim stanzas and concluded the film career of Johnny Weissmuller.

Jungle Jim had a number of animal friends in the series—the most frequent ones being Caw-caw the crow, Skipper the dog and Tamba the de rigueur chimp for anyone claiming jungle-hero status. Tamba functioned in the stories in the same manner as Cheetah and Nakimba in the other jungle series. By the time the *Jungle Jim* television series rolled, Tamba's comic antics were a demanded story ingredient by young viewers and almost a stock closing for each episode, with Jim and the other cast members laughing uncontrollably at Tamba's high jinks.

* * *

Johnny "Jungle Jim" Weissmuller and Tamba study the script for one of their adventures.

About ten years after the *Jungle Jim* television series disappeared from first-run view, a new jungle series featuring a chimp named Judy was launched on the CBS television network. *Daktari* was another in the series of Ivan Tors' productions which proliferated during the 1960s. Judy the chimp was greatly overshadowed most of the time in the *Daktari* series by a cross-eyed lion named Clarence. When she did capture a few moments of screen footage, Judy performed the same sorts of monkey-shenanigans as her counterparts in other movies and television series. She and her friend, Clarence, will be discussed in a later chapter.

Judy the chimp embraces fellow *Daktari* performers Ross Hagen and Erin Moran.

2
Our Friend from the Deep

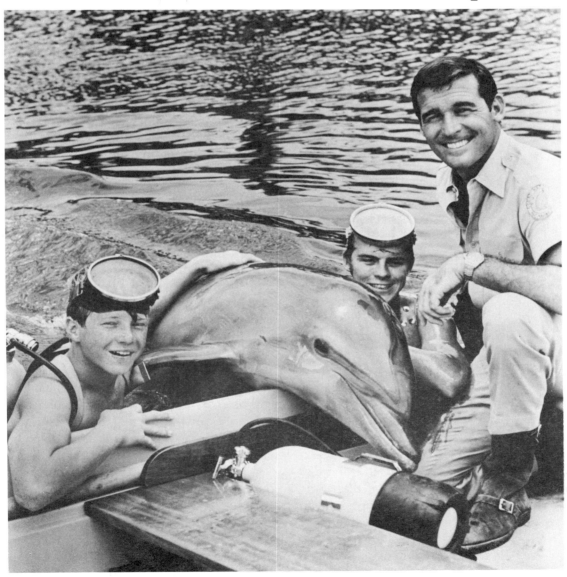

Flipper and his television family (left to right), Tommy Norden, Luke Halpin and Brian Kelly.

Flipper

A flippant *TV Guide* writer of some years back tossed off the line that Flipper, the dolphin star of the popular Ivan Tors produced television series of that title, was really Lassie in a wet suit. For aficionados of television animal-adventure shows, the riposte was probably not as far from the mark as one might originally think. Certainly the scripted adventures for either of these popular stars could be transposed from land to water or the reverse (with minor alterations in the dialogue of the human supporting cast members) and work equally well for either the canine or aquatic star—the basic plot lines generally calling for the animal stars to save the humans from some hideous fate established during the first fifteen minutes of each episode.

As a matter of fact, Ricou Browning, the creator of Flipper, acknowledges that Lassie provided much of the inspiration for his creation of the aquatic star. As Ricou recalls it, "As I was watching *Lassie* on television with my kids, I thought, wouldn't it be great to do an animal show similar to *Lassie* with a kid and a dolphin? So I got with a young man who worked for a radio station, Jack Cowden, and told him about my idea. We sat down over a period of three or four months and wrote a story about a boy and a dolphin, and we entitled it *Flipper*. When we had it finished, I went to New York to see if I could get it published as a book. I walked the streets for weeks. I finally got it to some readers and one publishing company was somewhat interested, but I ran out of funds and came home.

"Now prior to all of this, I'd just finished doing stunt work in a television series called *Sea Hunt* for producer Ivan Tors. When I got back from New York, I got the bright idea that if I had a movie producer say, 'I'm interested in making *Flipper* into a movie,' the book company might be more interested in publishing it. So I called Ivan and said, 'Ivan, we've written a book and I've taken it to New York to try to get it published. I'd like you to read it to see if you'd be interested in doing it as a TV series, or at least *say* you're interested.' He said, 'Send me a copy of it.' Several weeks passed and one day I got a phone call from Ivan. He said, 'Let's make a movie of *Flipper,* that story of yours.' So I pulled the book from the publisher and we spent a year preparing for the movie."

The consensus at the time (1962) was that nobody but an idiot would think of making a picture starring a dolphin. (A twist on the line was that nobody but Ivan Tors would have the guts to try.) At that time little was really known about dolphin behavior or whether they could be trained to perform in front of a camera in a predictable manner.

Flipper and his young friend Sandy (Luke Halpin).

But Ivan Tors was not the sort of man to be put off by the mere fact that something had not been done before. This hardworking, super-inquisitive, Hungarian-born producer had come up the ranks in filmmaking, arriving in Hollywood in 1940 with the title "writer" appended to his name. Eventually he became what they call in Hollywood a hyphenate—writer-producer-director. The result was a string of credits for such films as *Song of Love* (1947) (writer), *The Forsyte Saga* (1949) (writer), *Storm over Tibet* (1952) (writer-producer), *The Magnetic Monster* (1953) (writer-producer) and *Riders to the Stars* (1955) (producer). He got his director credit years later in 1963 for *Rhino*.

By the mid 1950s Ivan Tors had acquired a justified reputation as a more than competent producer of science fiction films—*Gog* and *Riders to the Stars* being minor classics of his genre.

With the rapidly expanding television industry clamoring for products to feed this always-hungry electronic monster, Tors turned his talents to the new medium, first grinding out the highly praised (for its time) *Science Fiction Theatre* starting in 1955, an anthology series with Truman Bradley as host. Seventy-eight half-hour episodes were produced in the series.

In 1957 Tors began *Sea Hunt,* the series that first introduced him to the underwater world that was to fascinate him from that time on. *Sea Hunt,* starring Lloyd Bridges, was in production from 1957 until 1961 and ultimately resulted in 155 episodes, making it one of the most successful television series of all time.

While *Sea Hunt* was riding its tide of popularity, Tors attempted another water series, *The Aquanauts* (also briefly entitled *Malibu Run*). The stars of this 1960-61 series (32 films) included Keith Larsen, Jerome Slate and Ron Ely (later television's Tarzan).

Other television series Tors produced prior to *Flipper* included *The Man and the Challenge* and *Ripcord*. *The Man and the Challenge* (36 half-hour films produced during 1959 and 1960) starred George Nader as Glenn Barton, a scientist assigned to testing survival problems. The series had a clever premise that, unfortunately, faltered for some reason in execution. *Ripcord* (76 half-hour films produced from 1961 until 1963) starred Larry Pernell (a regular years later on *Lassie*) and Ken Curtis (later Festus on *Gunsmoke*) as two sky divers who dropped out of planes to rescue people in distress, or to trap saboteurs and smugglers.

And then underwater stuntman and aquatic-filming expert Ricou Browning dropped the idea for *Flipper* into the lap of Ivan Tors, firing his imagination and re-stirring his love for the sea and its creatures.

Ricou, like Ivan Tors, had always had a love for the sea and a desire for a career in some area of show business. It is humorously ironic that Ricou's first major show-business job was as the creature in Universal Pictures' *The Creature from the Black Lagoon* (1954).

"I lucked into it," Ricou remembers. "I was going to Florida State University in Tallahassee and I'd done some stunts locally for the Grantland Rice sports films. I was known as a water sports kind of guy—I used to do tower dives and that kind of stuff. When I was in high school I had done a water show with a man named Newton Perry at Marineland Studios in St. Augustine. Later I worked as Newton's assistant at the Weeki Wachee Springs attraction which he started in 1946. That's where they have the underwater-ballet shows. We developed hose breathing at Weeki Wachee for the ballet girls before the aqualung was invented.

"Anyway, one day I got a telephone call from Newton. He said that some people from a movie studio had called him and said they were looking for a location where they might shoot underwater scenes for a movie they were going to do. Newton was busy and asked me if I could take these people to see Wakulla Springs, up near Tallahassee. I said, 'Sure, I'd be glad to.'

"So I met them at the airport and took them to Wakulla—there were several people, including a director and cameraman. While I was showing them Wakulla Springs, the cameraman, who was shooting some film, asked me if I would swim in front of the camera so that when they looked at the [test] film later, they could judge the size of logs, the height of underwater grass, and other such things. I said to the cameraman, 'Look, if you want to get some deeper stuff, you wear your lung and I'll hose breathe and swim around in the deeper water.' So I did, and they photographed it and paid me something like twenty-five dollars for helping them that day. I went home and thought nothing more of it.

"Then some time later I got a call from Universal Studios and was asked if I would be interested in playing the part of the creature in the picture. I said, 'Sure, why not?' I was told that they had looked at the test film they had of all the swimmers and they liked my style of swimming best (I had a different way of swimming from most people). Then I was asked, 'By the way, how tall are you?' I said that I was six feet. 'Well, I don't know,' the man from the studio said. 'We're looking for a big, gigantic guy to do the role. Anyway, we'd like you to come out to California.'

"So, dissolve, I went out there and met all the people and they decided they would use me for all the underwater shots of the creature despite the fact that I was only six feet tall and that they would use a different guy topside [on land] to be the creature. They would also double the other actors for the underwater scenes with shorter people so that I would appear larger — if the actor was six foot on the surface, they'd get a guy five-two to double under water.

"I spent three months at the studio fitting the creature outfit. Bud Westmore was doing all the molding and everything on the creature design. We went through two different creature suits before he got the right look for the suit. During this time I would also do swim tests in the tank on the back lot. When we were finally ready, we did the first picture. We shot topside in California on the back lot—most of it, and we shot the underwater scenes at Wakulla Springs near Tallahassee. *The Creature from the Black Lagoon* was so successful dollarwise for Universal that they made two more after that. I was involved in all three of them. It was a ball; I really enjoyed it!"

From the *Creature* films Ricou went on to do stunt and underwater work in such films as Disney's *Twenty Thousand Leagues Under the Sea*, Esther Williams' *Jupiter's Darling* and the Jerry Lewis film, *Don't Give Up the Ship*. In the late '50s and early '60s Ricou did some stunt and underwater work for Ivan Tors on the *Sea Hunt* series—a fateful assignment, for it was at that time the idea for Flipper came into Ricou's head and shortly thereafter he took it to Ivan Tors.

Producer Ivan Tors is seen here at his Miami studios during the time *Flipper* was in production.

Producer Stanley Colbert has said of Tors, "Ivan always starts from fact rather than gimmick. Example: Francis the Talking Mule was a gimmick—mules can't talk and never will. Flipper, an animal which responds to man, is a fact. Ivan can jack up a fact and slip thirty-nine episodes of a series under it."

And a lot of Tors' fascination with the Flipper idea was based upon the fact that dolphins *do* respond to man. As Tors commented, "It is a mystic experience for a normal human being to make contact with a dolphin. It makes me feel humility. Man is supposed to be on the top of the heap, but when you reach the dolphin, you are forced to recognize a superior creature."

Tors, of course, had heard the ancient stories of the dolphin's friendliness to man and he was intrigued by them. Plutarch wrote that the dolphin "is the only creature who loves man for his own sake. Some land animals avoid man altogether, and tame ones such as dogs and horses are tame because he feeds them. To the dolphin alone, nature has given what the best philosophers seek: friendship for no advantage." A dolphin is supposed to have saved Ulysses' drowning son by pushing him ashore with its nose. Pliny the Elder, the Roman scholar, wrote of a boy named Hermias who often was seen taking rides on the back of a friendly dolphin. One day during a sudden storm the boy lost his balance while riding the accommodating dolphin and was drowned. The story goes that the grief-stricken dolphin brought the body of the boy ashore and there cast its own body on the beach to die with its friend.

Shakespeare comments in *Twelfth Night* about the legend of Arion who, thrown into the sea by pirates, is saved by a passing dolphin and is carried back home to Greece. In more recent times a Florida woman who fell overboard while on a cruise in the Bahamas was nudged to shore and safety by a friendly dolphin. Stories of this sort fascinated producer Tors and caused him to want to produce this modern-day story about a boy and a dolphin called Flipper. He gave Ricou Browning the go-ahead to find a dolphin suitable for the role of Flipper and to begin to train him. And now the full enormity of the project came rushing home to author, soon-to-be-dolphin-trainer Ricou Browning.

As I began to research this chapter on Flipper, I quickly realized that I was dealing with a completely different kind of animal from those usually trained for show business. I knew if I intended to get some close-up insight into the business of training and working with these animals, I must locate and talk in some depth with Ricou Browning about his experiences with the dolphins that were to play Flipper over the years.

Since the Miami Seaquarium advertises that it is the home of Flipper, I started my search for Ricou there. It was a good start because Zoe Todd of Seaquarium's public relations department just happened to have Ricou's telephone number handy. I dialed it; Ricou answered; I explained; he agreed. A few days later I was sitting in a back corner of a Howard Johnson's in North Miami talking with the original Creature from the Black Lagoon, only now he was in the guise of a ruggedly masculine human who exuded warmth and intelligence as he related the events of his years with Flipper.

"My only real experience with dolphins before Flipper was what I'd done with fresh-water dolphins at Marineland Studios some years before," Ricou related to me. "To begin our effort to get a dolphin to work as Flipper, I went to aquariums all over Florida and the rest of the United States. I found at that time that no one was working *in* the water with dolphins. Trainers were putting on shows, but they were outside the water and the dolphins were in the water. In our *Flipper* story we had to have a boy riding a dolphin, and to my knowledge no one had ever really ridden a dolphin, although we've all seen ancient pictures and Grecian coins of a boy sitting on the back of a dolphin.

"On my travels to various aquariums I tried to get into the water with dolphins. As soon as I did, they just spooked, took off; they were afraid. Finally, we heard that there was a man on the Florida Keys who had a dolphin that would eat out of your hand and that you could get into the water with. So Ivan and I went down to investigate and found that it was owned by a man named Milton Santini. He captured dolphins and sold them to aquariums in the United States and abroad. He kept one dolphin named Mitzi in a pool so that when he got new dolphins in, they would see Mitzi eat and they would begin to eat sooner. He kept Mitzi as a sort of pet. She would play with a ball and stick and would retrieve. As soon as I got into the water, the dolphin swam over to me. I held her in my arms for a few minutes, then she swam off. We decided immediately that this was the animal we were going to use for Flipper and negotiated a deal with Santini.

"Now we got down to the business of training Mitzi to do the things the script called for. Most of the trainers I'd talked with at the aquariums had told me it would take a year to do this, a year to do that, and six months to do something else. Some tricks or behaviors they didn't think we could ever get. I think their pessimism was based on lack of knowledge from not having ever gotten into the water with the animals. I took my son, Ricky, who was nine years old at the time, and moved to the Keys in Marathon. We got a cottage right near the pool where Mitzi was kept, and we began training her. It was a hit-and-miss type of training. I'd try something and if it didn't work, I'd try something else. For the next two or three months we trained the animal and the animal trained us.

"Mitzi would retrieve sticks and balls and most anything that you'd throw that she was used to. She'd bring back anything that was small enough or shaped well enough so that she could physically carry it. But after weeks of training, we were not able to accomplish one of the major tricks we needed in the film—the boy riding the dolphin. Ricky would get into the water with Mitzi and they would become very playful with each other, and it looked good and was cute, but it still wasn't what we wanted.

"Finally I got the bright idea that maybe I could use the retrieve behavior to get the effect we wanted. I picked up Ricky on the dock and, as Mitzi came there, I said 'Fetch!' and I threw him into the water. Ricky landed in the water only about three or four feet from the dock. Mitzi went right to him. The water was clear enough so that I could see that she was trying somehow to get a hold of him. On the back of his cutoff blue jeans he had one of those little buckles. Well, the buckle was open and the two ends were hanging down—one with the buckle and the other with the strap. She would grab the strap and pull a little way, but it would slip out of her mouth because of his body weight. Then Ricky's arm hit over the top of her fin and she pushed him until he was back at the dock. I fed her for it, which was a reward for doing what she did. I threw Ricky in again and this time she swam to him and immediately put her fin right into his arm where his elbow bends. I yelled to him, 'Grab her fins!' He did, and she immediately pulled him back to me. As far as I know that's the first time a trained dolphin had ever done that. I was getting awfully excited about what we were accomplishing. I sent Ricky around the lake to the other side—it was only about fifty yards. I took a ball in my hands and said, 'Fetch!'

and threw it across the lake, but it went over the water and landed in the woods. I yelled, 'Ricky, jump!' He jumped into the water and made the splash that the ball would have made. When he splashed, Mitzi swam over to him. He grabbed her fin and she pulled him to me immediately—all the way. I was so excited over accomplishing this that I wanted to break open a bottle of champagne or something.

"I went to downtown Marathon and looked for a photographer because I wanted to get pictures for Ivan. I couldn't find one. Finally, some man from the chamber of commerce came with his camera and we shot a bunch of stills—we didn't have a movie camera—of various rides that Mitzi gave Ricky.

"The training of a dolphin is a matter of being able to communicate what you want the animal to do. Once you're able to communicate with the animal, you'll get the tricks or behaviors you want. Once it learns one thing, then it's easier for it to learn the next trick. We began to train Mitzi to do various other things. We'd make mistakes many times while training her, but eventually we would succeed.

"When we had Mitzi trained to do the tricks and behaviors needed for the movie, we then got ready to do the actual filming. Shooting a movie with a dolphin is quite different from doing an aquarium show, because in a show you don't have all the outside interferences. In filming a movie you have so much activity and noise taking place with the crew setting up the lights, reflectors and cameras. The first day

On location for *Flipper*. (From left to right) Luke Halpin, Flipper and production crew. Ricou Browning is the man with the hand up to his face. Photo courtesy of Miami Seaquarium.

we tried to film Mitzi with an underwater camera, the buzz of it under water spooked her and she took off to the other end of the pool. We didn't see her for the rest of the day. So I learned something else: you've got to familiarize the animal with everything that you're going to do ahead of time. What we did was have a little motor made up which made a sound similar to the camera and put it down into the water. It took about a day for her to get used to it, but she was never afraid of that sound again. To get her used to outboard motors running, we put a cage around the propeller so the animal wouldn't hit it, and then just ran the engine all day until she got used to it. We took reflectors and bounced the sun on her body and into her eyes. When a hot reflection off the sun hits you, it can startle you. Pretty soon Mitzi got used to it.

"We filmed both Flipper feature films, *Flipper* and *Flipper's New Adventure,* in Nassau—both the topside and the underwater shots. The three-year television series was shot in Miami at Key Biscayne, Virginia Key and Miami Seaquarium—really, the whole Miami area. The underwater scenes were shot in Nassau. You see, in Nassau you have one great advantage over Florida for underwater work. Miami is on the East Coast, and when you get bad weather coming out of the East, it's impossible to do any underwater filming. In Nassau the island is shaped such that when you have bad weather in one direction, you can go to the lee side of the island and find some clear water and a smooth place to work. We found it much better working over there for water shots because we were assured of filming something every day on the water.

"When we decided to do a television series of *Flipper,* it was to our benefit to have our own animals. We went to the Miami Seaquarium and made a deal with them that they would capture five dolphins that we would train and use in the *Flipper* television series. They would furnish a veterinarian, food and a place to house the dolphins. In return, they would have the right to say that Seaquarium was the home of Flipper. When we finished the series, the dolphins would revert back to them. It turned out to be very successful for them as far as their attraction was concerned, and very successful for us.

"Milton Santini, the man who owned Mitzi, started an attraction in the Keys called 'Flipper's Sea School.' He kept Mitzi there and advertised her as the animal that was used in the first *Flipper* feature. Milton was successful with the little attraction. I understand that Mitzi died several years ago.

"It took me about six months to train Suzy, the first dolphin from Seaquarium. Then I got pretty much out of training the dolphins and into directing. Over the period of the series, I guess I must have hired three or four trainers. My head trainer, Ric O'Feldman, began training the other dolphins, which were named Cathy, Scotty and—I forget the other names. During the filming of the television series, however, we only used two animals: Suzy, first, and then Cathy. These animals were so highly intelligent that they soon could do thirty-five to forty behaviors, and that was all that we needed for just about any script circumstance."

But Ricou and his trainers were to discover that the necessary rigidity of the training could lead to unexpected trouble—in the case of Suzy, trouble serious enough to force her early retirement. As Ricou recounted, "Everything that a dolphin does during filming is a trick, it is a behavior done for a reward, and the reward is fish. You give her a signal to go get a person; then you give her a signal to bring the person back to you; then you reward her.

"Well, over a period of months we filmed the boys in the program riding the animal from one place to another or from the bottom up or from the surface of the water down and then back up to the trainer for a reward. Then one day the script called for a scene where the boy is riding the dolphin down to the bottom of the sea, he sees something, lets go and swims off. What we didn't realize at first was that if the boy did this, he would be interfering with the trick the animal knew. The animal knew to take the boy all the way to the trainer for a piece of fish.

"We were filming in the Bahamas in about thirty-two feet of water. Tommy Norden, the younger boy in the program, was riding Flipper down under the water and, as the script indicated, he let go and started swimming down alone. Suzy politely circled Tommy at first to give him a chance to hold on again. Then she came over to him and nudged him. Tommy kept going alone so Suzy nudged him harder, hard enough to hurt the boy. When Suzy hit him again, Tommy stopped swimming away, held on, and Suzy took him to the trainer—and the trainer fed her. What Suzy now knew was that if she hit the boy, he would hang on. Not too much later the incident happened again with Luke Halpin, the older boy, and the hit was harder, much harder. When it happened, the trainer saw the hit and immediately threw a fish off to the side to get the dolphin away from the boy so she wouldn't hurt him. Now the dolphin had learned that if she hit somebody, she'd be thrown a fish. What we were doing was screwing up the dolphin's training and we didn't know how to correct what we'd done.

"This went on for a month or so and Suzy got so rough that we were afraid for the boys on the show. We finally had to switch animals and go to Cathy, and we made sure that we didn't make the same mistake with her. We had to retire Suzy to the Seaquarium.

"During training and work with the dolphins, we found that when dolphins got mad they would often hit with the nose. It's not a ram, it's an upward or sideways hit, and it hurts. But the vicious thing is the tail which is as hard as a board. When they swing that tail sideways and it hits you, it's like somebody swung a baseball bat and hit you with it. One of our trainers got hit in the head and received a slight brain concussion. One of the other trainers and I got broken ribs when a dolphin got angry.

"A wild animal is a wild animal and all wild animals are unpredictable. On occasion you can get into trouble with any wild animal. I've had accidents, nothing serious. It's strange; you have a good pet, a good animal like a chimpanzee, for example, and it suddenly bites somebody. You don't really know why it bit, but it bit. I trained two otters which I raised as house pets for three or four years. I could do anything with them. My children could play with them and never get bitten. One day my godson was bitten in the mouth by one of the otters and had to have a lot of stitches. Another boy was bitten in the back. I don't know why the otters bit them. I don't know whether a person shows a fear through a chemical odor or a look in the eyes or what.

"One Sunday my daughter and I went out to Seaquarium where I had housed the otters, a baby bear and a raccoon. I was cleaning out the pen with a hose when my young daughter came inside and suddenly screamed. When I looked over to where she was, all I could see was blood coming from her foot. The raccoon had bitten her on top of her instep. I rushed over to her as the raccoon started attacking her again. I got in front of her, but the raccoon tried to find a way to get around me to get to her. I hit him with my foot to keep him away from her. I hit him and knocked him across the pen, but he kept coming back. I finally grabbed my daughter and held her up so that she could grab a pipe and hold on until I could get the raccoon. I grabbed him by the scruff of the neck and put him in a second pen and closed the gate. I have no idea why he bit her. I know she didn't do anything to the raccoon. It must have been something that said, 'Bite her!' to the raccoon. He had never made any effort to bite me.

"Whenever I work with wild animals, I'm as careful as I can possibly be, and I would include dolphins in that. Most people want to believe that dolphins love people because they have been known to save sailors and they have that natural smile built into their faces. When they are in the wild, they don't bother anybody, so people want to believe that they are an affectionate animal. Well, I don't think this is true. I think on occasion they are affectionate; they can be.

Brian Kelly as Porter Ricks on the *Flipper* series.

"I was born in Florida. My grandfather was a fisherman so I heard about porpoises all my life—the myths or legends that they save overboard sailors from sharks by ramming the sharks with their noses. In the first *Flipper* feature we created a battle between a shark and Flipper. We had a scene where a shark was after the boy, and to save the boy, the dolphin killed the shark.

"We had a fiberglass shark made which was about nine feet long. It was a stiff, hard, good-looking shark. Then we made some fiberglass dolphins—six feet long and about the size of Flipper. They were hard, rigid, real-looking dolphins. Now we were ready to start filming. As we had a live shark swim in front of the camera, we would shove a fiberglass dolphin at the shark, hitting it. When it was hit, the shark would take off. We rammed it a number of times for the camera in close-up where you just saw the head of the dolphin and part of the shark.

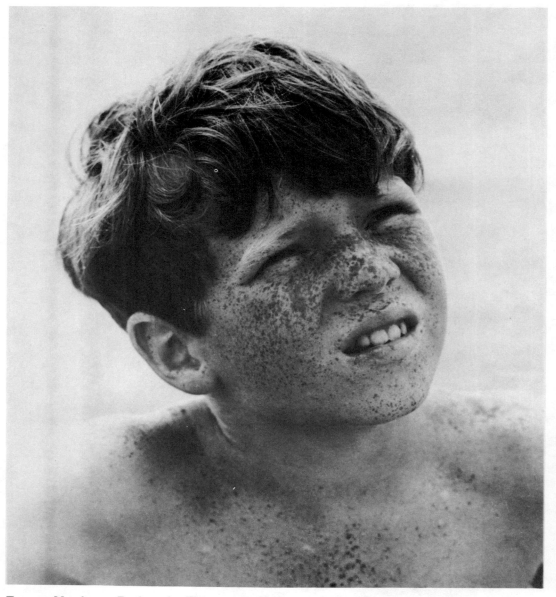

Tommy Norden as Bud on the *Flipper* television series.

"Then we reversed the scene and used the fiberglass shark. We had the live dolphin swim by and in close-up we shoved the fiberglass shark at the dolphin like it was going to bite it. As soon as the dolphin saw the fake shark, it swam off. So those two things were filmed. Then we filmed a dolphin with a live shark, swimming, making fast passes at him. When we edited all of that film together, we had the damnedest fight you ever saw and we made it appear as if the dolphin killed the shark. That was in our feature and we did variations of that ten or fifteen times in the television series.

"We created the impression of a dolphin killing a shark for the film, but we didn't really make it happen. I think, however, that you could train a dolphin to kill a shark. I think you could train a dolphin to kill anything in a very short period of time. For example, you could take a piece of paper and put it into a hoop and train a dolphin to go through that paper for a reward. Then you could keep changing that paper until it became cardboard, until it became plywood, with the dolphin ramming and smashing through it with its tail for a reward. (You can train a dolphin to hit a ball with its tail as hard as a soccer player kicks a ball, or harder.) When you had the dolphin trained to do this, all you would have to do is replace the object with whatever you wanted the dolphin to hit, perhaps a live something. You could train him to hit that live something for food. I think in a very short period of time you'd have a killer on your hands. I don't think the animal would do it thinking, 'I'm killing somebody.' He'd do it just as he would retrieve a ball or jump into the air for a piece of fish. He'd do it for you, for the reward you'd give him. It wouldn't be that difficult to do. I'd sure hate to see it done. The animals we used, however, were disciplined, controlled, and when they were working for food, you had very little trouble with them, other than the exceptions I told you about where the training screwed them up."

Ricou feels very strongly that memory rather than just conditioned reflexes played an important role in the response he got from dolphins. "I definitely think there was memory," he stated. "I believe they can also think and make decisions. I'll give you one example. One time when I was training Suzy, I had various-sized balls in a bucket. I threw a ball and she'd bring it back. After a few minutes of this, I thought I'd try something different on her to see what she'd do. I threw a ball for her, it hit and she went to get it. Then, immediately, I threw a second ball to see what she would do with it. What I didn't realize was they were two different-sized balls. One was about the size of a tennis ball and the other about the size of a golf ball.

"She picked up the big ball and then went to the little ball. But when she opened her mouth to get the little ball, the big ball came out. So she picked up the little ball, but when she went to get the big ball, it was too big to fit in with the little ball. It took her about two minutes to figure out her problem. She finally picked up the big ball, scooped the little ball in behind it and brought both of them back to me. Now that's thinking! That's realizing a problem, solving it and carrying the solution through. From that minute on, when you threw the two balls, she would immediately pick up the big ball and then scoop up the little ball. If she got to the little ball first, she would ignore it, go to the big ball and then return to the little ball.

"It was possible to train the dolphin to bring back as many items as she had a way of physically carrying. If you threw a stick, she'd pick up the stick in her mouth. Toss out a rag and she'd scoop the rag over the stick. Throw another rag and she'd put it on her tail. Then another stick; she'd put it under her fin. She'd bring all of these items back at one time. From a training standpoint, the trick was for me to throw the items so that she knew in which order to get them—to help her organize the items. For example, if at the beginning of the training you threw a rag first for her nose, then she couldn't pick up the stick. Eventually you could throw them all into the water at once and she'd pick the right items up in the correct order and bring them back to you.

"Whatever you threw into the water, no matter what position the dolphins were in—they could be over there facing away and you could throw a penny in over here—when you gave them the signal, 'Fetch!,' they'd go get it. They have some kind of sonar that finds anything you throw into the water."

Luke Halpin played Sandy throughout the Flipper movies and the television series.

I mentioned to Ricou the research being done to try to decode dolphin communication and wondered if in his work with them he ever suspected that they were attempting to communicate with him. He indicated that he found this in only the most simplistic way—such as the way a dog or cat would indicate that it wanted to be fed. But then that sort of mystical look that would occasionally overtake Ivan Tors when he talked of the dolphins seemed to creep into Ricou's response: "I think two-way communication with these very intelligent animals could be developed. We never got into trying to develop a communication between us—we never had the time. My feeling is that someday someone will do this. There's only one thing it takes—money. If a person had enough money to support himself and the animals, and a nice place to work and no given period of time to accomplish his work, I'm sure that some kind of communication could be developed. I know the Navy is trying to do this. How successful they've been, I don't know. A number of people have written books indicating they've worked on it. I think the people on the right track are the ones who are recording dolphin sounds and playing them back to the other dolphins. They're also trying to mimic the dolphins. Eventually they will hit upon something the dolphins say that says, 'Do this.' I think gradually they might find a way of communicating with a language of some kind."

Domesticated animals like dogs and cats show affection and a desire to please human beings, and Ricou feels that Flipper's tricks or behaviors were many times done for the purpose of pleasing rather than just as a response to a command for the fish reward.

"I can only speak of dolphins and sea lions (Ricou also trained "Salty the Sea Lion" for the feature and short-lived television series) because they are the only two animals that I've gone into detailed training with, but I would say their affection is very much like that of a cat rather than a dog. The dog, I think, is affectionate at almost all times, where the cat is affectionate when it wants to be affectionate. I think a dolphin and sea lion are both the same way. When they want to be affectionate, they are very affectionate. They do things to make you know they are being affectionate, but you can't cause them to be affectionate. You can't say, 'Hey, I want you to be affectionate because we're going to film it on the camera.' There's no signal, there's no way of doing it on cue.

"One day while we were on lunch break from the filming of the *Flipper* feature, Luke Halpin got into the water with Flipper and suddenly the dolphin started being affectionate—playing and rolling, the boy crawling on her and she laying on him. We quickly broke out the camera and filmed it, because it's not something you can command, it's something that just happens. We did develop tricks that looked like affection, but they were done for a food reward; they weren't true affection."

There was no male chauvinism when it came to selecting the dolphins to play Flipper—they were all females. Ricou explained that he had heard that it was better to work with females rather than male animals for this kind of work, and that's why they got females. "The females are thought to be gentler to work with and they don't get as aggressive or high-strung," he pointed out. "I don't know where I had heard that, but I used females because of it."

Being Flipper the dolphin was no life of ease for the chosen aquatic animal. She went through a rigid set of workouts to keep in training for upcoming script demands. Ricou explained, "I developed a method of training for myself that I adhered to and I had my trainers adhere to. None of the animals ever got a free meal. They worked for *every* piece of fish or whatever they ate—every day, every

52 Our Friend from the Deep

feeding. The reason for this was that these animals in captivity were in a smaller area than when they were in the ocean. In the ocean they swam continuously and they exercised. The more the trainer worked the animals, the more exercise they'd get, the healthier they'd be, the more muscular they'd become and the more endurance they'd build up. I found the animals didn't resent working as long as you didn't cheat them. When we ran out of food, we didn't ask anything of them. We wouldn't ask them to do anything without a reward. If we went in to play with them without food, we wouldn't ask them to do a trick, we'd just play with them. They knew that

Flipper, Pamela Franklin and Luke Halpin enjoy a few quiet moments together in this scene from the second Flipper motion picture.

when they did something, they'd get food for it. As a result, when we were filming, we always knew beyond a shadow of a doubt we'd get the trick.

"It's like people. If a person works for you for two-hundred dollars a week and this week you don't pay him the two hundred, you might give him an excuse. If next week you don't pay him the two hundred dollars, you probably won't have the guy working for you any more. The animals were the same way. If you didn't reward them, they were going to quit on you and say goodbye.

"But I must say, however, that I was impressed with the dolphin's ability to remember training for long periods of time. When we retired Suzy, we just put her into a pool at the Seaquarium and didn't work her, just fed her. We put a little male in with her and they just had fun. Finally, they traded her for some white-sided dolphins from California. The guy that bought her put her into a show. I didn't see her for about a year and a half. Then I heard that she was down in the Keys, so one day I took a drive down to see her. She looked good and was in good shape. They had used her in shows and had done tricks with her, but I had no idea what commands they had developed. The guy who now owned Suzy let me go through my old routine with her. She did every trick that she'd done a year and a half before except one. I couldn't get her to do the tail pop, which they do by popping their tail on the surface. Our command was to push the hands straight down. I don't know why I couldn't get her to do the tail pop, but she immediately took every other command; I mean without even a hesitation—she remembered all of them. That's a pretty good memory, I think. Whether the commands they were giving her were similar or not, I'm not sure, but she responded just that quickly to my hand signals. I was amazed that she was able to retain so much."

Time is money on a film set, and to hear Ricou tell it (nothing against the human actors, of course), Ivan Tors could have saved a lot of money with an all-animal cast. "I guess I'm bragging a little bit," Ricou smiles, "but the comment by the producer was that he wished the actors were as good as the animals."

* * *

The first appearance by Flipper was, of course, in the 1963 MGM feature-film release. Chuck Connors (of television's *Rifleman*-series fame) played Porter Ricks, the father role that Brian Kelly would take over for the sequel, *Flipper's New Adventure* (1964), and the television series which quickly followed. Connors' Porter Ricks character was quite different from the Brian Kelly version as written. In the *Flipper* feature Connors is a poor but honest, hardworking fisherman whose concerns are primarily to provide for his wife and son's simple needs and to be able to make enough money fishing to avoid a "wages" type of job. His life is a constant struggle to keep ahead of bill collectors because of the empty nets that he bears home evening after evening—that is, until a friendly dolphin named Flipper guides Porter and his son Sandy to some bountiful fishing grounds and they all live happily ever after—or at least until the second feature film and its adventures.

Brian Kelly's Porter Ricks is a widower (with one son in *Flipper's New Adventure* and two sons in the television series—figure that one out). He works as a marine preserve ranger, patrolling and protecting the series-created Coral Key Park in Florida. Kelly's character provided for more adventure and was a far more glamorous character than Connors' simple fisherman. But Kelly's assignment in *Flipper* was not exactly an adult actor's dream role, playing opposite two freckle-faced boys, a dolphin and two family pets—Pete the pelican and Spray the

Labrador retriever. Considering the competition, it's to Kelly's credit that his father-figure character came across so forcefully to viewers.

The younger son/brother, Bud, played by Tommy Norden, didn't appear on the scene until the television series was created—his maternal parentage was left a question mark by the screenwriters. Tommy began his career as a photographic model at the age of five, appearing in the pages of such magazines as *Life* and *Look*. He did over one hundred television commercials, including Polaroid, Gleem toothpaste, and Palmolive soap. On Broadway he was featured in Frank Loesser's musical, *Greenwillow,* and Meredith Willson's *The Music Man*. In films he performed with Sophia Loren and Anthony Perkins in Anatole Litvak's French-made *Five Miles to Midnight*.

From 1960 to 1963 Tommy was a regular on television's *Sing Along with Mitch* series and guested on many of the major series during those years. When the call from Ivan Tors came for *Flipper,* Tommy was already a total professional and ready for the responsibilities of a major role in a television series.

Young Luke Halpin played the son Sandy in both features and throughout the television series—the only cast member, human or otherwise, to continue with Flipper from the two feature films through the entire television series.

Both Flipper feature films received good marks from the critics who were as intrigued as everyone else that a dolphin could be trained to work with humans safely and comfortably—even with a youngster of Luke Halpin's tender years. The underwater color photography came in for special mention in both films. One critic noted that producer Ivan Tors had done so much subaqueous filming by this time that he undoubtedly worked out his budget with pens that wrote under water.

If so, Tors was writing in black ink, because the first Flipper feature grossed over two-and-a-half-million dollars in the United States and Canada, with many more dollars accrued in the foreign markets. *Flipper's New Adventure* showed similar vigor at the box office during the spring and summer months of 1964, and served to prepare its audience for the television series that would premiere on NBC that fall.

On Saturday, September 19, 1964, *Flipper* swam into living rooms across America—the first of eighty-eight first-run visits he would make between then and May 14, 1967. His competition over at CBS was their "Great One," Jackie Gleason—

high-powered rating competition for the friendly dolphin and his human friends.

"Flipper's success was a surprise to us," Ivan Tors exclaimed later. "So many other shows had failed in that spot opposite Gleason." Tors felt that two elements contributed greatly to the success of the television series: children had a new animal friend with a built-in perpetual smile to entertain them, and they got the chance to identify with a beautiful father-children relationship. "The father image in the United States is in dreadful shape," Tors told a *TV Guide* reporter. "A stronger image is needed and we provide it."

* * *

Flipper, Brian Kelly, Luke Halpin and producer Ivan Tors exchange happy greetings in this picture taken at the Miami Seaquarium.

Ricou Browning (left) watches as Flipper receives the PATSY Award from a representative of the American Humane Association.

Luke Halpin poses for the author's camera.

Ricou told me I should get in touch with Luke Halpin who was still living in the Miami area. Ricou thought Luke could provide me with some behind-the-scenes Flipper material from the actor's standpoint that might be interesting. A phone call was made, a time set and a week or so later Luke and I met in a little outdoor marina in south Miami to talk about the Flipper years.

Luke in adult life is much like his character of Sandy on *Flipper* only grown up. Physically, of course, he has changed considerably from the teen-age boy we remember on the television series. He is now, after all, around thirty years of age. Luke is shorter in height than one might expect, having almost an Alan Ladd build—perfectly proportioned for the camera, but slight in build in person. Luke is modest, almost shy, and speaks very softly.

David Rothel: Luke, how did you happen to get cast in *Flipper*?

Luke Halpin: Ivan Tors had been interviewing children for a long time looking for a child actor to play the part of Sandy in the *Flipper* movie. Around this time I was working as an actor in New York City on Broadway with Jackie Gleason in a musical called *Take Me Along*. When Ivan came to New York, he saw *Take Me Along* and called for an interview with me.

He talked to me, liked me and knew I had a good track record as an actor—I'd been working since I was about seven years old, acting. We went to the pool so he could see me swim. It seemed that he had interviewed lots of kids who could swim and dive and were outdoor types, but they didn't have the acting background that he needed, or was wanting. I guess he wanted someone that he could be absolutely sure would get the job done. He finally hired me, and away we went!

David Rothel: Yours isn't the classic tale then of the pushy stage mother who strives to make her son a star of stage and screen.

Luke Halpin: No, my mother wasn't like that, but she did encourage me as I got into it more and more. My acting career started more as a necessity. My father had had a bad accident working for the railroad in New York. My piano instructor arranged for me to go into New York City to audition for some acting on live television. The first time out I got away with it, so I just kept going.

David Rothel: You just went into New York one day and auditioned for a television program?

Luke Halpin: Yes, I did!

David Rothel: And you got a job! You know there are probably thousands of hungry actors who would like to murder you for doing it that easily.

Luke Halpin: I was only seven or eight years old at the time and really had no idea what any of that competition was all about. I just lucked out. The first person I had as a director was Franklin Schaffner, who was (and is) a very successful director in the film business. I'd like to run into him again now and tell him that I'd like another job (laugh). So, I started doing live television out of New York. I did *The United States Steel Hour, Armstrong Theatre, Studio One* and religious morning shows—things like that. Then I started doing Broadway and road shows. I worked in California with Mary Martin in *Annie Get Your Gun.* I did the *Peter Pan* special with her and a bunch of other children actors, singers and dancers.

David Rothel: This must have been during the late 1950s.

Luke Halpin: Yes, and after that I got into *Flipper.* That really helped me a lot, you know, doing *Flipper* the dolphin for a few years. I was going through the teen-age times of my life then and probably wouldn't have been working [acting] had I been in New York, or at least it probably would have been a lot more limited. So I love Flipper the dolphin.

David Rothel: Did you ever have any formal acting training?

Luke Halpin: No. The live television acting was a sort of on-the-job training, though, when I was a child. I took some speech lessons after that so that I would always be understandable. I learned more about projecting and what I needed to keep working.

David Rothel: Many former child actors look back upon the years when they were performing in pictures, whatever, with some bitterness—a sense of lost or stolen youth, all that sort of thing.

Luke Halpin: Well, there *were* things that went wrong and things I didn't like about the way it was at times. You know, there were times I just wanted to be a kid and go out and play, and I couldn't. There were times like that, but what I eventually got out of it makes me very happy that it went that way. Otherwise I would have been hanging around the streets of New York, and going out to play in New York City isn't too great!

David Rothel: So occasionally you'd want to be out playing baseball with the guys and you'd have to get your lines for tomorrow's shooting on *Flipper.*

Luke Halpin: That wasn't so during *Flipper.* During *Flipper* I wanted to be doing *Flipper* all the time because we were playing in the water, we had the animals with us and we were having a wonderful time. What could be better?

David Rothel: For a city kid you seem to have taken to the outdoor character of Sandy very naturally.

Luke Halpin: I took some ribbing from the crew to begin with. When I first went out to row a boat for a scene, they asked me if that was the way people did it in Central Park (laugh).

David Rothel: How did the other kids that you knew react when you became a movie and television star? Were you a hero to them or did you get kidded a lot?

Luke Halpin: Some of them really liked it. I guess I was like a hero to them for doing something, for doing *anything*. They thought that being on the television was kind of fantastic. But some thought I was a fool and would try to make me feel that way, and sometimes I did *feel* somewhat silly at some of the things I had to do later in the series. You know, being sixteen and doing a film where I had to respond like a fourteen-year-old. Here I was sixteen and I thought I was so much older, when I really wasn't that much older, but . . .

David Rothel: But at *that* time . . .

Luke Halpin: Yes, at that time it made me feel a little bit silly. I guess, overall, I handled it all right. And most of the kids I grew up with in New York, the ones I hear from occasionally, they still think it was pretty great.

Luke and Flipper. "They're like a torpedo with the brain of . . . a ten-year-old kid who loves to hang out in the water." Photo courtesy of Miami Seaquarium.

David Rothel: How did you get your schooling during those years that you were working steadily on live television, then on the stage, and, later, *Flipper?*

Luke Halpin: When I started doing my first television work in New York, I left the school I was in and went into a school for the kids who were doing shows on Broadway or who were on television or doing similar work such as commercials and modeling for catalogs. We would get instruction mainly in what we had to know to pass the New York State Regency Test for high school. We didn't have sports or a shop class or subjects of that sort, of course. When I was working on *Flipper,* we had a teacher on the set, whether it was here in Florida or in Nassau.

David Rothel: You had a couple of hours of school a day?

Luke Halpin: Yes. As long as we were up-to-date, there was no problem. Have you interviewed Flipper yet?

David Rothel: (laugh) I'll have to get down to Miami Seaquarium to visit with her, find out what she thinks about the series, how happy she was with it.

Luke Halpin: Absolutely. Anybody who writes anything about a dolphin should get a good close look at one. Jump into the water and examine one up close. See what it looks like, observe it, listen to it. They are really fantastic to observe. They're sleek; they're like a torpedo with the brain of, I don't know, a ten-year-old kid who loves to hang out in the water. You know, they just play tag, eat fish, run around and do all kinds of incredible feats in the water.

There were moments during the filming of the series when I thought the dolphin had a special understanding of me. For instance, once I was diving, just taking a breath from the surface and free diving for a shot we were filming. When I went under the water, I held on to the dolphin and she would swim underwater. I had been diving a lot so I'd built up to where I could hold my breath for a pretty long time. But whenever I would get hungry for air, the dolphin would start going toward the surface with me. I wondered how she knew to do that. One day while this was happening, I determined that she was listening to my heart rate. You know, of course, that they have very keen hearing and incredible sonar ability. Well, I think she was listening to my respiration and knew when I needed air. Because we were friends and we worked together so much of the time, she began to go toward the surface when I needed air. She seemed to know when to get me there.

I don't know if I believed this about Flipper just because I was a kid and wanted to think that way about the dolphin or if it was something that was true. I'd love to experiment with dolphins, spend time with them now that I'm an adult to find out about things like that.

David Rothel: Did you ever feel that Flipper actually showed affection?

Luke Halpin: Yes, I did. Sometimes at the end of the day when I'd still be in the water with her, she would swim up into my arms and sleep for a minute. Sometimes she would just come over and glide to a stop next to me—just lean up against me and breathe for a while. Then, I think, she was showing that maybe she enjoyed the company of a human, since she was not running wild and free as other dolphins did. Dolphins seem to adapt to people really well.

Sometimes she'd be absolutely frightening. I was underwater a couple of times when she would come swimming at me from out of the blue—out of nowhere—going a hundred miles an hour, swimming right for my face mask. Then she'd come to a dead stop right in front of me. She was just playing; just scaring me (laugh). If she wanted to, at that speed she could go right through me without losing a mile-an-hour.

David Rothel: How long did it take to shoot a half-hour *Flipper* episode?

Luke Halpin: Initially we were shooting one episode a week. Then we went to one and a half; finally we went to two. That was when we started having some quality-control problems. When we began shooting two shows at a time during the week, we began to lose track of which script we were working on, which program a scene was from. We might change T-shirts and shoot a scene from a show we'd started earlier in the week. At times it became somewhat confusing.

David Rothel: When I talked to a director of *The Lone Ranger* television series, he commented that they would go out and shoot the location footage for three episodes and then come back to the studio and shoot all of the interiors for the programs. Did you do that on the *Flipper* series?

Luke Halpin: We did that, only we did it the other way around. Usually, we'd shoot all of the topside stuff in Miami or wherever—the Keys or the Glades, anywhere in the state that we had to shoot—and then we would go to the islands [Bahamas], because it would be easier to match what happened on the surface to the underwater shots than it was to match underwater action to the surface scenes. When we were in Nassau, we would shoot the underwater shots for a number of episodes. We would stay there for a few weeks—however long we needed.

David Rothel: What was a typical day like on the set shooting the *Flipper* series?

Luke Halpin: We would arrive on the set about 6:30 in the morning. It would usually be a 7:30 or 8:00 o'clock shooting, so we'd get there an hour or so early to get into the mood and find out what we would be shooting and to make sure that everybody was up-to-date on the scenes. We'd sit down and talk it out, get it ready with the director. While the crew was getting ready, we would get into makeup and wardrobe, finding out if we had to be wet or dry for the first shot. Then we would start shooting the scenes called for that day.

"Sometimes at the end of the day when I'd still be in the water with her, she would swim up into my arms and sleep for a minute." Photo courtesy of Miami Seaquarium.

David Rothel: Does an actor who spends two thirds of his time in the water have to use makeup?

Luke Halpin: Very often we would use makeup because it would balance us up. I might have more tan than Tommy, or Brian would have more than both of us kids. So often when we were on camera together, the makeup people would have to balance our complexions. When we weren't on camera together, it generally didn't really matter because we were all pretty suntanned from living in Florida.

David Rothel: Shooting a television series means working at a breakneck tempo.

Luke Halpin: Yes, you have to keep going. You've got to have a pace on a television series. But to get what we needed with the dolphin, we took more time, because the dolphin was really the star of the show. When it came to anything the animal was doing, we would wait her out, shoot something else when she wasn't in the mood. When it came to the animal, we were very careful. Occasionally we would get a director who wasn't used to working with an animal and wouldn't have the patience needed, which was a problem for the actors, of course, and a problem for the people working with the animal—a problem for the animal, too.

Anyway, we would stop for lunch at about one o'clock, taking a half hour or hour, depending on how tight the schedule was. Then we'd go back to work, shooting scenes the rest of the afternoon. Sometimes we would go back to a setup we had started early in the morning because the late afternoon light generally matched the early morning light. We jumped around out of script continuity all the time. We would stop the day when we started losing the light.

David Rothel: It sounds like a very long day.

Luke Halpin: It was only difficult during the winter when we were cold and the water was cold and we had to be wet all day. It wasn't much fun doing a dialogue scene when you had to stand just out of the water, soaking wet. You'd have to keep jumping in and out of the water to stay wet for the scene or somebody would have to come by and dump a bucket of water on you.

But there were the funny things, too, that happened on the set. Brian Kelly had trouble at first getting used to running the motor boat. One day Tommy and I were in a scene where we were standing in shallow water near the beach as Dad was supposed to come roaring to the rescue with the motor boat. He was supposed to roar up the beach and come to a stop. We'd say our lines, and then take off. Brian got going too fast in the boat and came roaring in toward the beach, went right past us and drove the boat straight up the beach. We shouted our lines to him as he went by (laugh). They'd save some of those bloopers we'd do and show them to us at the end-of-the-year party. It would embarrass us a little bit, but it was all in fun.

There was also the time when Flipper had learned a new trick—to splash her jaws up and down and squirt water. Ivan Tors, the producer, came on the location one day and immediately walked down to the dock to greet Flipper. As Ivan approached her, Flipper proceeded to fill his shoes with water. Everyone loved it; we roared. Ivan's a great man; he enjoyed it, too, in fact. He likes to see the animals do funny things.

David Rothel: Quite often a kid growing up has a particular person, an adult, in his life who has a considerable impact upon him and perhaps alters the direction of his life in one way or another—at the very least has a strong influence. Do you have anybody in your background who falls into that category?

Luke Halpin: Yes. That would be Ricou Browning. When I met Ricou he was the writer of *Flipper* and was going to be the underwater director of the first *Flipper* movie. Ricou was the one who showed me how to dive, taught me about boats, how to work with the dolphins and put me with people who helped me to learn about these things that I'd always been interested in. At that time, too, I found out that these were the men who had done the *Sea Hunt* television series with Lloyd Bridges. *Sea Hunt* had always been one of my biggest favorites.

Anyway, Ricou and the other divers and the people who worked on this original *Flipper* movie were the Mike Nelsons [the character Lloyd Bridges played in *Sea Hunt*] and they really became my heroes. During the shooting Ricou was always there to help me. If I'd get scared or upset about something while I was in the water, he'd come over and check me out to make sure I was all right. He had a great way of driving me on and keeping me interested and getting the most out of what we were doing. He is really good with people. He made me want to do everything that I'm doing even now — the sailing, the motor boating, the diving. I still love to go diving.

David Rothel: Tell me a little bit about your life now. What are you doing?

Luke Halpin: Well, I'm a licensed captain and occasionally I get a yacht delivery. I often go racing around here locally in midget ocean racers. We sometimes race all night and all day around here and across to the islands. It's for trophies and partying. I'm also in the yacht-painting business with a partner. I do my share of fishing and diving. I own my own boat now and I use it just the way the kids on *Flipper* used their boat. And that's what I'm doing now.

David Rothel: But if someone came along and said, "Luke Halpin, we'd like to star you in this feature," you wouldn't be adverse to going back to acting.

Luke Halpin: Oh, I would love acting some more. I still maintain contact with an agent, but there's not that many offers unless you're living in Los Angeles. I've lived there, but it's a very difficult place for me to live because it stops me from doing a lot of the things I want to do, which is mostly my own boating in my own world. If I lived there, I would have to spend too much time affording to live there. I can survive here in Miami a lot better. Los Angeles has probably got twenty-eight thousand actors living in the city. I don't know how many of them are aged thirty as I am, but I'm sure there are plenty of them, and most of them are plenty good. So what it boils down to, of course, is that there probably wouldn't be that many jobs per year to make it worth my while to be there. Here in Florida I can work as a crew member, too. I worked on *Black Sunday* as a crew member for about six or eight weeks when that film was shot here. I work production for commercials sometimes, and occasionally I act in them. I also do sales films for people. So I still do some acting, only I participate more in production, which I don't think I could do in Los Angeles at all. I don't think I'd ever be allowed to do that.

David Rothel: So many kid actors end up with screwed-up lives in one way or another. You seem, however, to have weathered those years very nicely.

Luke Halpin: Well, my family has been really great to me. They could tell when I was unhappy about not working. They just said, "Keep on working; work at something else. Work as the diver on the film company, or whatever." So I kept on going. My folks live on the Gulf of Mexico now, right on the water. We all love each other. I go over there and visit. I sometimes spend weeks there, right on the water. I've got my boat; I go fishing.

David Rothel: Do you get recognized as Sandy very much now?

Luke Halpin: Yes, occasionally I do. People often recognize the name when I'm making a long-distance call or reversing the charges. And I always get recognized at the post office and at courthouses (laugh). I have a familiar face that they think they've seen on the wall.

"Sometimes she would just come over and glide to a stop next to me — just lean up against me and breathe for a while." Photo courtesy of Miami Seaquarium.

3

Man's Best Friends

Yo Ho, Rinty!

On September 13, 1918, in Fleury, France, in a trench only recently abandoned by Kaiser Wilhelm's German infantry, six pups were born to a near-starving German shepherd. Lee Duncan, a twenty-nine-year-old noncommissioned Air Corps pilot who in civilian life was a sporting goods salesman and dog enthusiast, happened to be on a patrol in Fleury this fateful day in 1918. His mission was to inspect a recently captured airport.

While poking among the rubble, he heard somewhere in the distance the sound of whining—pitiful, mournful whining. Investigating, he found that one of the buildings had apparently been a makeshift kennel which had housed more than a dozen German war dogs. As far as Duncan could see, they were all dead—yet the whining continued. He then noticed a trench about ten feet from the building. There, in a hole clawed in the side of a dugout, was a shepherd and six puppies, all trembling pitifully in the damp and cold.

Duncan quickly got towels and dried the chilled babies and their mother. Warm blankets were wrapped securely around the canine family and they were taken back to the American base and to safety. When the pups were old enough to be weaned from their mother, Duncan's buddies quickly laid claim to the pups—all except one male and one female, which Lee Duncan adopted for himself and named Rin Tin Tin and Nanette.

Rin Tin Tin and Nanette were so named by Duncan after the small, knitted lucky charms which were a legend in France during the First World War. The legend concerned two French lovers, Nanette and Rin Tin Tin, who took refuge in a railway station with forty other people during a German bombing attack. The station was demolished and everyone within was killed—everyone, that is, but the two lovers. They emerged unscathed. So goes the legend.

Unfortunately, the legend did not hold true for the two dogs, because it was reported that the dog, Nanette, died of pneumonia when only a few months old, just three days after reaching the United States. Duncan later raised another female German shepherd which he also christened Nanette and which appeared with Rin Tin Tin in many personal appearances.

After the war, Duncan showed Rin Tin Tin in several dog shows. After a reviewer for a dog breeder's journal criticized Rinty's clumsiness during a dog show, Duncan resolved to train the dog to be a champion. With great patience and affection Duncan worked long hours with the intelligent canine. To teach the dog to sit, Duncan placed him in a sitting position and instructed him to "Sit . . . sit . . . sit."

Rin Tin Tin, Lee Duncan and Nanette in 1930 when Rinty was at the peak of his film career.

Holding a finger gently on the dog's head to keep him from moving, Duncan slowly circled around the dog. Repetition followed, with praise for the dog when he obeyed. Slowly Duncan's circle around the dog widened until he could walk out of the dog's sight. Duncan considered the dog trained to sit when he would sit for three minutes without following the trainer.

Getting Rinty to fetch objects upon command presented another challenge to the trainer. Duncan found that he could teach Rinty and later dogs to fetch more quickly if he worked with them in a private hallway where there was less chance of intruders destroying the concentration of the dog. For fetching training Duncan always used a soft object like a shoe, never a stick, and he never would throw it very far, preferring to work the dog in a relatively confined area such as you would have on a stage or movie set. With Duncan's patient training, the dog was soon not only a graceful animal, but was able and ready to perform a multitude of tricks suitable for the vaudeville stage and silent films.

Rin Tin Tin made his film debut in the adventure picture, *Where the North Begins,* in 1923 for Warner Brothers. The *New York Times* critic felt that in the action scenes the dog lacked some of the zeal of another silent-screen star, Strongheart. As the critic commented, ". . . this dog [Rin Tin Tin] engages in a pantomimic struggle which is not always impressive, at least not nearly as realistic as the work of Strongheart. But in one sequence when he is shown a piece of the villain's trousers he is made to appear in a most vicious mood." Later in the review, the critic did acknowledge that the dog "is a remarkable animal, with splendid eyes and ears. . . ."

Lee Duncan (center) is seen here cuing Rin Tin Tin for a scene in one of the dog's many silent pictures.

The Lone Defender was another 1930 vehicle for the many talents of Rin Tin Tin. The "stirring all-talking serial" proved to be very popular with film audiences.

The critics that count with film companies—the paying public—loved the dog from his first silent bark. *Where the North Begins* launched a fabulous nine-year motion picture career for the French-born German shepherd. At times fan mail for Rinty ran as high as a million letters a year and never less than 10,000 a week. Many, many years later in 1978, upon the death of Jack Warner, *Variety's* obituary for the film mogul carried this comment about the fledgling days of the company, ". . . their entire operation would have capsized except for the saving efforts of a dog. Rin Tin Tin jumped out of *Where the North Begins* to become the Warners' one unimpeachable box-office star."

By 1927 Rinty could do no wrong in his film appearances. In *Tracked By the Police* (which also starred Jason Robards, Senior), one critic enthused, "Rin Tin Tin not only does heroic stunts, but he is made to act as if he reasoned out things. It seemed quite natural for this police dog to tug on a bolt until he succeeded in opening the door, and one is not surprised when Rin Tin Tin escapes through the back of a grandfather clock, but his exploits in determining the levers that close the locks [of a dam] seems like asking almost too much of any animal."

In *Hills of Kentucky* (1927) Rinty's age became the concern of at least one critic: "Considering his age, Rin Tin Tin displays wonderful activity in his new film. . . . If this animal was born in the French trenches during the war he is about 9 years old, roughly the equivalent of a man of 63. There are not many men of that age who could go through what Rin Tin Tin does in this screen adventure. He is like a d'Artagnan of dogs. . . ."

Hills of Kentucky bears a special place in the Rin Tin Tin story since it marked the film debut of Rinty's son, Rin Tin Tin, Jr. In a few years the puppy would carry on the legend of his illustrious sire.

The coming of sound pictures in the late 1920s did not affect Rin Tin Tin's career in the least—Rinty may have been born in France and been of German ancestry, but a bark is a bark in any language. John Gilbert must have envied Rin Tin Tin—or loathed him!

In 1930 Rinty starred in *The Man Hunter* with human actor John Loder. The picture was soundly drubbed by critics, except for the contributions of the talented German shepherd. For example, after railing about the picture in general, the *Times* critic tossed a box of dog biscuits to the canine star: "Rin Tin Tin, it should be mentioned, now that he has achieved what may be known as the barking pictures, gives what is perhaps the most intelligent performance, for he minces no words, makes no gestures and appears graceful at all times. He is a remarkable animal, for when the beachcomber points at something in the distance and speaks to Rinty, presumably in doggerel, Rinty dashes off, to return a few scenes later with a detachment of infantry."

Rin Tin Tin's last film was a serial for Mascot Pictures called *The Lightning Warrior* (1931). On August 10, 1932, United Press ran the following news item:

> Rin Tin Tin, greatest of animal motion-picture actors pursued a ghostly villain in a canine happy-hunting grounds today. More than eighty years old as comparative human age is measured, his passing was announced this morning by his owner and friend, Lee Duncan.

Upon the death of the original Rinty, his son, Rin Tin Tin, Jr., carried on the famous name in motion pictures for several years — starting with the feature, *The Big Pay-Off,* and continuing with serials such as *The Wolf Dog* (1933), *The Law of the Wild* (1934) and *The Adventures of Rex and Rinty* (1935). Later features included *Tough Guy* (1936) with young Jackie Cooper and *Skull and Crown* (1938) with Regis Toomey and Jack Mulhall.

To backtrack a little bit, starting in 1930 Rin Tin Tin was a pioneer in weekly radio-adventure programming. His fifteen-minute Saturday program was sponsored, appropriately, by Ken-L Ration on the NBC Blue Network. Each week the "Wonder Dog," as he was often billed, chased and captured radio badmen with clockwork regularity. Rinty's and, later, Rinty, Jr.'s bark could be heard weekly until 1934 — the last year on CBS — when he ran out of radio villains and the program left the air.

Rin Tin Tin, III, young Bobby Blake and Donald Woods are pictured here in two scenes from the 1947 PRC release, *The Return of Rin Tin Tin*.

By 1938 it looked as if the Rin Tin Tin cycle of popularity had about run its course. The recent films had been mainly for small independent companies and no new films were forthcoming. The radio series had ended several years before. It seemed to Lee Duncan like a good time to slow the pace of his life and to take time to pursue some of the other interests he had. So for the next few years he occupied himself by raising quarter horses, Hereford cattle, and, of course, German shepherds.

In early 1947 Duncan considered making a motion picture with a new Rinty descendant, Rin Tin Tin, III, but was hesitant because there had not been a Rin Tin Tin picture in many years. Duncan was afraid that the American public might have forgotten the name Rin Tin Tin.

He arranged for a survey to be made. The results were amazing. Of all the people interviewed, over 70 percent knew the name of the dog, and of this large group over 95 percent knew what the dog was famous for and indicated that they'd like to see the dog in another film.

Thus, *The Return of Rin Tin Tin* was produced and opened in movie theatres around the country in the fall of 1947. The color film, released by the small PRC studio (just as it was coming under the new corporate title, Eagle Lion Pictures), was a high-budget picture for the tiny independent company and was aimed squarely at the kid and family trade. As such it did very well at the box office and even received some kind words from the critics. Along with Rin Tin Tin, III, young Bobby Blake (years later TV's *Baretta*) and Donald Woods starred in the sentimental story of a young mentally scarred war refugee who finds love and happiness through the ministrations of a kindly priest and a friendly German shepherd. The picture was popular with its intended audience and made money, but no sequel was ever made to the film.

For the next few years little was seen or heard of Rin Tin Tin. It seemed that at long last the famous shepherd was to be permanently retired from show business. Then when television came bursting onto the American scene during the early 1950s, there was suddenly a demand for children's adventure programming—especially during the early evening hours when whole families were tuned to the living-room tube.

Producer Herbert Leonard and the Columbia Pictures' TV subsidiary, Screen Gems, remembered the long-ago popularity of the Rin Tin Tin films with family audiences in movie theatres. Leonard contacted Lee Duncan, now getting up in years and retired, regarding the possibility of Rin Tin Tin being brought to the television screens of America. Not surprisingly, Duncan liked the idea and agreed to cooperate with Leonard and Screen Gems.

A series concept was gradually developed by Leonard and his writers. The program would be placed in the old West of the 1880s. The setting would be in and around a cavalry station called Fort Apache. The stories would contain plenty of action of the B-Western variety, involving the cavalry troops, rampaging Indians and gunslinging Western bad guys. The regular characters would include a young boy named Rusty (Lee Aaker); an adult hero, Lt. Rip Masters (James Brown); comic relief in the form of tough, dumb, but affectionate Sgt. Biff O'Hara (Joe Sawyer); and O'Hara's frequent foil and "general duty" character in the series, Corporal Boone (Rand Brooks).

In the first episode it is explained that the "Wonder Dog" and his young master, Rusty, were found by a U.S. cavalry troop after an Indian raid on a wagon train. They are returned to the fort until a decision can be made regarding their relocation. When a visiting colonel is saved from an Indian attack by the boy's quick thinking and the bravery of the boy and his dog, the cavalry troop decides to reward the boy by making him an honorary soldier and Rinty the troop's mascot—thus allowing them an excuse to stay at the fort for future episodes.

The Adventures of Rin Tin Tin went on the ABC Network Friday, October 15, 1954, at 7:30 p.m. and stayed in that time slot until August 28, 1959. The half-hour weekly series was sponsored by the National Biscuit Company and was, needless to say, a big hit. (Coincidentally, the other TV hit dog series, *Lassie,* went on the air a month previous to Rin Tin Tin's premiere.) Over the years that the program was in production, 164 black-and-white episodes were filmed.

The opening logo for the Rinty television series of the 1950s.

In January 1955 a radio edition of the television series went on the Mutual Network sponsored by Milk Bone. The weekly thirty-minute program replaced the classic radio series, *The Shadow.* Each episode opened with a bugle call and Rusty's yell, "Yo ho, Rinty!" and ended with Rin Tin Tin receiving the ultimate accolade from Rusty: "Okay, Rinty, you've earned your Milk Bone." The radio program was one of the last children's adventure programs on the air. It only lasted one season.

The Rin Tin Tin television series, after its first-run, prime-time years on the air, went into syndication throughout the country for many additional years. Finally, during the 1960s, the series faded away and out of the minds of the general public. Once again Rin Tin Tin retired with his now elderly master.

Rusty (Lee Aaker), Rinty and Lt. Rip Masters (James Brown) in a publicity photo from the television series.

During the summer of 1978, I had the opportunity to discuss the Rin Tin Tin television years with Rand Brooks, the actor who played Corporal Boone on the series.

Rand Brooks: I was about fourth wheel to the dog in the series. We had a lot of fun; we had five years together. Lee Duncan had the original Rin Tin Tin, of course, and he owned the rights to the character. They started the television series with his dog, but Lee had aged some by that time and had some difficulty keeping up with the television series grind. Soon they found another dog to do the series. It was one owned and trained by Frank Barnes, a Carolinian and a wonderful, wonderful trainer. In fact, he trained me to train and I later worked some animals in pictures, just sort of as a sideline and for fun. I think that Frank was the greatest German shepherd trainer that *ever* came along. I can't go back to the names of all the dogs he trained, but there were Gray Shadow and Flame. In fact, the Rin Tin Tin of the television series was Flame's son. He was called Golden Boy, Junior. Frank with his Southern accent, used to call him "Jay-Are," short for Junior.

David Rothel: Flame was the dog that was also used for the *Rusty* series at Columbia Pictures during the 1940s.

Rand Brooks: That's correct. As I said, Frank Barnes was the greatest German shepherd trainer who *ever* lived. I went to his funeral just about a month ago; he was eighty-four, almost eighty-five.

David Rothel: In some of the early publicity for the Rin Tin Tin television series — for instance in a *TV Guide* article — they had Lee Duncan there showing how the dog was cued to do various tricks.

Rand Brooks: Well, he owned the rights and he owned Rin Tin Tin — Rin Tin Tin one, two, three and so forth. He was around; he was on the set most of the time. He was a very nice man. But Frank Barnes did the real training and owned the dog, "Jay-Are," that was used for Rinty in the series. Frank took real pride in J-R and kept him immaculate. If some kid would come up and want to pet the dog, Frank would say in his Southern accent, "Yo ha-ands clean?" (Laugh).

The dog was just unbelievable. He only had to be shown once what you wanted and he did it. Frank trusted me to keep the dog and when he'd leave town, I'd have the pleasure of having Rinty stay at my home where I had other dogs and a kennel. I took Rinty, J-R, over to my vet one day. I was showing the dog off for him a little bit. The vet said, "I saw a dog the other day that was told by a man to go and open a drawer and get his leash. The dog did it and brought it right to him. I never saw anything like it." So the vet leaves the room for a few minutes. I went over to one of the vet's big, steel file drawers, opened it, and put the leash in there, and waited for the vet to come back. When he did, I said, "J-R, go over there and open that drawer and get your leash." The dog went over to the file cabinet and pulled the steel drawer out, picked up his leash and brought it to me. I can't tell you what the vet said, but he almost fell through the floor.

David Rothel: I talked with Kirby Grant a while back about the dog series he did—

Rand Brooks: I worked with Kirby, a lovely man. He worked with that white dog, ah—

David Rothel: Chinook, in the Mountie series.

Rand Brooks: I knew the person who trained that dog; that dog wasn't safe. I was out in a rowboat by myself with that dog once, and I know how to handle dogs, but I was very careful.

Rand Brooks, Corporal Boone on *The Adventures of Rin Tin Tin* television series.

David Rothel: Kirby said that dog bit just about everyone on the set except him.

Rand Brooks: Well, he never bit me, but I was watching for it.

David Rothel: That's why I mentioned Kirby's dog series. I wondered if you ever had any trouble with the Rin Tin Tin dog you used for the television series?

Rand Brooks: That dog got stepped on, everything! He had a quiet, friendly disposition that was absolutely unbelievable. He was never a problem of any sort. I got a female out of the only litter that he sired. He couldn't have any more; he made a jump and hurt himself and they didn't feel that it was advisable to breed him again, but I got a female out of that one litter. A few years later I took her on many personal appearances. She was pretty well trained; you could work her at any distance that she could see your hand signals. Frank Barnes worked J-R and his other dogs by a voice signal and a hand signal. That was so his voice didn't come over the soundtrack.

David Rothel: Were there a number of dogs that were used for Rinty in the series?

Rand Brooks: J-R did everything but the fights. He could have done those, but they can be dangerous. So the fights were all done by a dog called Hey You. There was also another double dog, a marvelous dog called Bearheart. I bred Bearheart to my daughter of J-R and got a pup out of it which I trained and starred in a picture which was made a while ago. It will probably be coming out soon, a picture called *Bearheart of the Great Northwest,* a story of the Northwest about 1890 with quite a lot of action. There is a dog and wolf fight, a dog and bear fight, and lots of beautiful scenery.

David Rothel: Since you've done some dog training yourself, do you know some of the other well-known trainers?

Rand Brooks: At Frank's funeral the other day, Frank Inn [Benji's owner and trainer] was there and Rudd Weatherwax [Lassie's owner and trainer]; it was kind of like old home week, but sad. Of course, Rudd was the greatest man with collies that ever was, and he still is. He just goes on and on. I've known Frank Inn since he lived in a stable near a barn where I kept my horse. He came up the hard way, but now he's a great success. He worked for Weatherwax, you know. Yes, this talking about animals is very dear to my heart.

In addition to the television series, we toured and appeared at the Madison Square Garden, Boston Garden, and many other rodeos and fairs. The way that dog handled himself, I tell you, he was just a gentleman. J-R, of course, passed away some years ago.

David Rothel: Obviously, the dog got along well with Jim Brown and the rest of the cast.

Rand Brooks: Everybody! Of course, everybody loves Jim; anybody could get along with him. The dog was very good with the boy, too.

David Rothel: Do you know what Lee Aaker is doing now?

Rand Brooks: Yes, he's in the contracting business; he's a very good carpenter. He's very happy. I saw his mother recently. I had a reunion party once for the Rin Tin Tin troupe. We had everybody there from wardrobe to camera operators to directors. We had a ball getting back together.

David Rothel: What is Rand Brooks doing these days?

Rand Brooks: Rand Brooks is in the ambulance business. I now have fifteen ambulances, five of them are paramedic. We have the contract for the fire department in Glendale, California, and we back up in Pasadena and Burbank. Last year we ran 18,000 calls. So I'm happy doing what I'm doing. I don't have to worry about the phone ringing with a job as I did when I was acting. The phone is ringing all the time now. People ask me why I ever got into that awful ambulance business. I always say it's tough to make better pictures than Metro and Fox, tough to make better planes than Lockheed and Douglas, but any damned fool can improve the ambulance business. I kid that we're the best in L.A. County, but we're half as good as we should be—we're getting there, though. I'm very happy with it.

After the television series had run its course in syndication, it was shelved with no thought of eventual revitalization. The years passed, during which time Lee Duncan, Rinty's longtime owner and trainer, died. The 1970s arrived, and along with them, a first-time blossoming of nostalgia for some of the early television programs. A fellow by the name of Stan Moger with SFM Media, a television syndication company, sensed the mood of the times and shrewdly brought the old *Mickey Mouse Club* series back into national syndication. It was an immediate hit all over the country. Flushed with this success, Moger's SFM Media searched for another series that might duplicate the Mouse's success. He found it with *The Adventures of Rin Tin Tin*.

In 1976 the series went back on the syndication trail in over sixty cities across the country. The old Lt. Rip Masters, James Brown, was hired to do new color openings and closings for the programs, and the black-and-white episodes were tinted sepia to give them a color tone for color-conscious youngsters of the current generation. For the newly produced wraparounds (the openings and closings) a dog called Rin Tin Tin, VII was used. The producers claimed direct descendancy for the dog, but the late 1970s were a time for skepticism at many levels—the dog was, at the very least, a handsome German shepherd, albeit not highly trained.

For actor James Brown it was a strange experience going back to a series he had originally starred in over twenty years before. At the 1979 St. Louis Western Film Fair (at which Jim was a guest) I got a chance to talk with him about the filming of the original Rin Tin Tin series as well as its more recent revival.

David Rothel: How did you happen to get the role of Rip Masters in the television series?

James Brown: Herbert B. Leonard, the producer, looked at about a hundred guys, I was told, and couldn't decide on an actor to play the role. Then Douglas Hayes, who was the story editor, mentioned my name to him. Bert said, "Oh, my gosh, why didn't I think of him?" You see, Bert Leonard's favorite movie was *Air Force* in which I played a pursuit pilot named Lt. Tex Rader. So he called me in and said, "Would you mind reading with the boy that we've decided on?" I said, "Not at all." They wanted to see how we reacted to each other. Well, we didn't even finish the scene before he said, "You're it!" So evidently the chemistry showed.

David Rothel: And that boy was Lee Aaker. Lee Duncan owned Rin Tin Tin, of course, but I understand that he was not too terribly involved with the television series. Rand Brooks told me that trainer Frank Barnes did most of the work with the dogs.

James Brown: Yes, he did all of it. You see, Lee had retired and he hadn't kept the dog in training. Frank Barnes took over the training and handling of the dogs as Rand indicated. Lee was always there, but Frank did all the training. We had the one main dog called J-R. He did all of the close stuff and it was just playtime to him.

Then we had two double dogs: one to run with horses and one to do the fights—the long shots on the fights. That dog was a relative of J-R and his name was Hey You. Hey You had one eye that was sort of discolored; a chicken had pecked his eye as a puppy. Pretty dog, but he didn't want to fight; you'd have to goad him into it. This was Hey You. J-R was the friendliest dog you ever saw with humans and with the other animals on the series. I remember once when J-R was supposed to go get a lariat off the horn of a saddle and bring it over to me. Frank told J-R to get the rope. The dog got the rope in his mouth about the time the old horse with the saddle turned his head around and looked at the dog. J-R, friendly thing that he was, kept leaning over and leaning over trying to lick the horse. Frank said, "Get the rope!" Well, J-R just couldn't resist. He walked over and gave the horse a big slurp, and the horse bolted around and kicked him. It didn't hurt him too bad, but he limped around for a couple of weeks and we had to shoot scenes around him until he was feeling better. After that, there was no more stuff with horses for J-R; we used the double dogs.

James Brown, Lt. Rip Masters on *The Adventures of Rin Tin Tin* television series.

The dog worked from both voice commands and from hand signals. He would respond to both. Generally, to play it safe, Frank would just do the hand signals. He'd generally only have to do it once. He'd lead J-R over to what was to be done in the scene — just like with that rope thing. He'd say, "Here, get the rope," and he'd put his hand on it. The dog would pick the rope up. Then he'd say, "All right, take it over to Jim." So he brought it over to me. Then when we filmed it, Frank would just wave his hand in a signal and the dog would do it. They'd walk through it once or twice at the most before they would roll the camera.

We would go out to rodeos and fairs and I'd emcee the show. I'd say, "Rinty, what happened when you got your foot caught in that bear trap?" And he'd start limping around. I'd say, "Was it that foot or the other one?" Then he'd get on the other foot and start limping around.

There was one thing he did only on personal appearances that we never got to show in the series. Frank and I were sitting in a hotel room one night fooling with Rinty. Frank said, "Rinty, get your tail." Rinty started around in a circle trying to get his tail. Frank said, "All right, head off the other way." Rinty turned around and went back the other way. When Rinty got his tail in his mouth, Frank said, "Now take it over there to Jim." So there he was, cute as he could be, walking sideways like a crab, bringing his tail over to me. It was so delightful that we put it in the act and used it as the climax of the personal-appearance show. It used to bring down the house.

David Rothel: Did you play a great many fairs and rodeos during the years you were doing the series?

James Brown: Oh, yes, including the Madison Square Garden Rodeo. We were the star act the first year and two years later they brought us back as the added attraction. We were generally contracted for twenty-two minutes. I sang the marching song from the series and we'd have guys in cavalry uniforms on horseback who would do maneuvers as I sang the song. Then we'd do a little skit where an Indian is sneaking up on the boy, Rusty, who is sitting at a campfire. The boy spies the Indian and yells, "Yo ho, Rinty!" and the dog comes running out and jumps the Indian and protects the boy. That was the nucleus of our show.

David Rothel: A few years ago the series was revived and brought out in sepia tone with you doing brand new openings and closings to the episodes. It was something unusual that I don't think has been done before or since. What brought that about?

James Brown: While I was living in St. Petersburg, Florida, for two years, I got to thinking of a way we might try bringing the series back—just to test its potential—because everybody kept saying to me, "When are you going to bring the Rin Tin Tin series back?" The biggest problem was that it was shot in black and white. Well, anyway, I got permission from the studio to try my idea with thirteen episodes. We went to the PBS station there and got them to fix up a set that sort of looked like my old office at the fort. I put on my Rip Masters' cavalry uniform and we went on the air live and in color. I pretended that I was talking to kids who seemed to be off camera. I said, "Hi, kids, remember when Rinty and I did so and so? Well, this is the way it went." Then we would fade into the black and white Rin Tin Tin episode from years back. I would come back at the middle and end of the program for more comments.

I told Bert Leonard about doing the programs this way and the next thing I knew the guy that put the old *Mickey Mouse Club* back on the air got together with

James Brown, Rin Tin Tin, VII and a group of children prepare to film a wraparound scene for the 1976 revival of the Rin Tin Tin series.

us and revived the series for syndication. We shot new openings and closings in color in Kanab, Utah. We doctored up the fort that was there and shot the scenes. But they spent too much money on them. It was only two-and-a-half minutes per program — the intro at the beginning and the closing at the end.

David Rothel: They were certainly elaborately done.

James Brown: That's why there were only the twenty-six completed. I kept telling them, "You're putting too much money into them." Also, the dog we were using wasn't trained and we spent most of our time waiting on him. It would have been a snap with our original dog. Those brief scenes cost like the devil, and when they showed them—I know in Los Angeles—the first time it was on at eight in the morning. Well, there's nobody home but toddlers, and all they know is "doggy, doggy." You've got to have kids watching who understand the stories. The toddlers wouldn't know an Indian from a Schimdian. Then in L.A. they changed it to three in the afternoon, but the kids were still not home from school. I told the syndicators, "You get this on at 6:30 to 7:00 p.m. in the evening and I'll guarantee you an audience." But they never did.

David Rothel: What's Jim Brown doing these days?

James Brown: Well, I'm still trying to stay in the racket. I did a *Dallas* TV episode just before Christmas, then a small thing on the *Rebel* mini-series. I had an interview at 5:30 p.m. the day before yesterday at Universal for an *Incredible Hulk* program. I'm pretty sure I've got it. We'll start next Wednesday on that.

But, you know, I've always loved working with animals. When they changed the format on *Lassie* a few years ago, I was down to the final two for the ranger role. I did a two-parter and a single show for them as, more or less, my test for the part. Then they tested a few others. It boiled down to me and Robert Bray, who eventually got the role. Everybody seemed to think that I should do it, but one of the sponsors thought that the closeness of my identification with the Rin Tin Tin series would distract. People might see me and think they were watching *The Adventures of Rin Tin Tin*. Frankly, I didn't want to do the series; I only wanted to do it for the part. I'm a German shepherd man, really (laugh).

David Rothel: Rand Brooks told me Lee Aaker is a carpenter now. Can you add anything to that?

James Brown: Yes, he's a carpenter now in Redondo Beach. He collects antiques. When we started, he was ten years old and the dog was ten months old. I used to kid his mother about making him sleep in a short bed so that he wouldn't grow out of his part. He was a great kid.

David Rothel: Was the Rin Tin Tin company a happy group to work with?

James Brown: Oh, yes. I felt like Rusty was my boy and he told people that I was his hero, so it made it a good feeling. There were no prima donnas in the cast. We shot the programs in two-and-a-half days on the average, so there wasn't time for that sort of thing.

The Rin Tin Tin of the television series watches over Fort Apache. Rinty won PATSY awards in 1958 and 1959 for his outstanding performance in the television series.

David Rothel: Where did you shoot the locations for the series?

James Brown: Our fort was in Simi Valley at Corrigan's Ranch. It was built by John Ford for the old picture, *Fort Apache*. It was about to fall down when our series went into production, so we went in and rebuilt it. I understand there's nothing standing at all now. Bob Hope eventually bought the ranch from Corrigan. I knew *every* rock on that ranch. That was the hottest place in the summer and the coldest place in the winter! I went into the river there during the winter for a scene we were filming. I was supposed to stay face down in the water as my hat floated ahead of me down the river. They weren't supposed to know whether I was dead or alive, so the director said, "Stay face down." I hit that cold water and, boy oh boy, I gasped. It was *really* cold!

Another time when it was about 110 degrees hot out there, we did some winter scenes where I had to wear the heavy winter uniform, coat and cape. The wardrobe was so heavy it took two men and a small boy to put it on me. I tell you, I thought I was going to die from the heat. But that was Corrigan's Ranch. I spent a lot of time there with Rinty and the rest of the gang.

* * *

As with the nostalgic rebirth of the old *Mickey Mouse Club,* the success of the reborn *Adventures of Rin Tin Tin* in the late 1970s proved to be short-lived. Within a year or so the series was mostly back on the shelf.

Ah, but just you wait, Rinty. The years will pass again and someday in the distant future a young boy will again shout, "Yo ho, Rinty," from a television or motion-picture screen and the cycle will start all over again.

Lassie

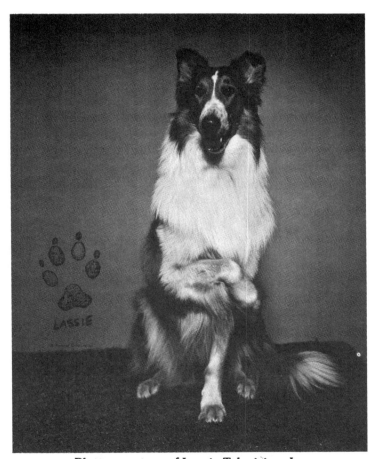

Photo courtesy of Lassie Television, Inc.

Through the camera's eye we see the collie quietly roaming a rolling meadow as the soundtrack trails the gentle strains of a "Greensleeves-like" melody. Presently a young boy's voice calls, "Lassie, Lassie!" The dog turns at once to heed the summons, romping toward the viewer, gracefully leaping across a rustic wooden fence into living rooms across America. For once again it is Sunday evening at seven and time for a half hour of gentle television adventure with Lassie, brought to you by the Campbell kids and their soup.

And so it was each week—with some slight variations on the program opening—for almost twenty first-run years on the *Lassie* television program. Perhaps adventure is too strong a word to describe what happened on the program. Bonita Granville Wrather, associate producer of the *Lassie* programs and wife of Jack Wrather, the owner of the television series, prefers another word to describe the *Lassie* program image. She sees it as "the image of loyalty, courage, compassion, but most of all love." And there are millions who agree with Mrs. Wrather that love best describes what transpires when the *Lassie* program and its audience get together for a half hour—a half hour with Jeff and Lassie, Timmy and Lassie, U.S. Forest Ranger Corey Stuart and Lassie, or any of the other humans and animals who have shared episodes with our collie friend over the years.

But the story of Lassie begins many years before the popular television series or even the MGM movies of the 1940s and early 1950s. We must go back to a 1938 *Saturday Evening Post* short story by Eric Knight called "Lassie Come Home." The success of the short story resulted in the publication of an expanded version, a novella really, in 1939. It proved to be more popular than anyone could have imagined, eventually selling more than a million copies and being translated into twenty-four languages.

Eric Knight, a Yorkshireman by birth, could not have imagined his eventual writing success when he came to the United States with his mother and stepfather in 1912. Eric was fifteen years old at the time. With several years of schooling still required of him, young Eric was soon enrolled at the Cambridge Latin School, where it was discovered that he possessed a certain facility with words. He learned that he could string them together into compositions that impressed the few persons that he allowed to read his written thoughts.

Several years later when World War I was aflame, Eric gladly served his adopted country in the cause, feeling in the process that he was helping to protect his homeland. The post-war years found him honing his writing skills as a newspaperman for the *Philadelphia Ledger,* film criticism being his particular forte. Eventually short stories and novels began to flow from his pen: *The Flying Yorkshireman, This Above All,* the *Sam Small* stories and, of course, *Lassie Come Home.*

With the outbreak of World War II, Captain Eric Knight was again called to service, this time serving with the famous film director, Colonel Frank Capra, on the production of his morale-boosting *Why We Fight* series of war documentaries. The dynamic Capra found a close friend in the transplanted Englishman. In his autobiography Capra describes his first meeting with Knight:

> . . . a red-moustached American captain with a British accent; a Yorkshireman whose unruly shock of dark red hair seemed as full of mischief as his sharp, ferret-like eyes. . . . For me it was love at first sight with Eric Knight. He had all the talents that could be compressed into a single writer: wit, compassion, sensitiveness, an intriguing style, and a great, great love for human beings. He had Keats' "Mighty idea of beauty in all things." But this above all—Eric was a rollicking boon companion. . . .

Holed up in Washington, D.C. in the Carlton Hotel, room 308—a seven-by-twelve-foot crowded cubicle—the indomitable Capra and his companions, including Eric Knight, fought the bureaucracy and red tape of the Capital to produce what have been described as the most inspirational films of the war. The Motion Picture Academy voted *Prelude to War* (the first in the series) an Oscar for Best Documentary of 1942, and the New York film critics presented the series with their Best Documentary Award in 1944. Capra, in accepting the many awards for the series, acknowledged the five key men who worked with him on the *Why We Fight* series—writer/friend Eric Knight was among the five.

But Eric Knight was to be a casualty of the war. As Capra wrote:

> The evening of January 14, 1943, Eric Knight was leaving for Cairo to open a new Armed Forces Radio Station. Eric was charged up. He talked . . . of a better world after the war, and of how films could make it so. I carried his duffel bag from room 308 to the lobby. Lyman Munson (head of the information services) invited us to the bar for one-for-the-road.
>
> At the airfield I wanted to embrace Eric; to tell him that if he did for radio what he had done for our films, all the world's downtrodden would clap hands. I didn't.
>
> Munson and I were in twin beds in New York's Gotham Hotel. The phone rang and rang. Munson groped for it. "Hello!" he growled. He leaped out of bed. "It's Jack Stanley, Frank . . . Eric's plane is down in the Caribbean. Shot down, they think. By a U-boat that mistook it for the plane taking Roosevelt to Casablanca—no survivors."

Jere Knight, Eric's widow, remembers the period of time in 1938 when "Lassie Come Home" was being written. "At the end of each day, when Eric was writing it, he'd always read what he'd written to his daughter Betty and me. And we'd sit there with tears rolling down our faces over the sad parts. . . ."

The Lassie dog in the story was modeled after Jere and Eric's dog Toots, who was "the most warm, the most loyal, the most loving, devoted dog," Jere remembers. When Eric was stationed in Washington during World War II, Toots, like the Lassie of the story, would sit at the front gate of the Knight farm in Bucks County, Pennsylvania, waiting for his return—a loyal vigil that was never to be rewarded.

Though Eric Knight's life was tragically foreshortened by the war, he did live to see his story become a tremendous success both in the United States and England, and to see the MGM film version prior to its public release while he was on active duty during the war. He wrote to his wife, Jere, "The dog is the most magnificent collie I've ever seen in conformation, color and brilliant sense. Oh, gladly do I call him a movie star. I coveted him more than I ever did la Fontaine, la Lamour and all the other pretty stars. (They couldn't get a bitch for the part that looked right, so he's a female impersonator—and thank God he's got a long coat that covers his manhood.) Anyhow, I've been promised a son of his for the farm." Indeed, Knight received little enough for his popular canine inspiration. MGM bought the rights to *Lassie Come Home* for the sum of eight-thousand dollars, which included all theatrical rights in perpetuity. Neither Knight nor his heirs ever saw another penny from the *Lassie* movies.

The man who promised Knight a son of the film Lassie was a fellow by the name of Rudd Weatherwax; discoverer, trainer, protector, friend to and commander-in-chief of the dog that was to become the canine personification of Knight's fictional Lassie.

Rudd Weatherwax over the years has also been the trainer of some 1,500 other animals; some for motion pictures and television, and others for people who have merely wanted to have normal, happy, healthy yet obedient pets in their homes. Weatherwax made it to the top of his profession primarily on the strength of his huge success with the several generations of Lassie dogs he bred and trained.

Lassie
Photo courtesy of Lassie Television, Inc.

Rudd writes in the beginning of his book, *The Lassie Method,* "My interest in dogs began in my early childhood. We lived on a ranch in New Mexico where my father used collies to work the 3,500 Angora goats in his herd." Weatherwax credits his father with having a natural way with animals that he passed along to his sons. As a youngster Rudd amazed his family when he house-trained a pet lamb and taught it to open and close a latched gate. He also trained a white rat to chase household mice out of the house.

In the year 1917 the elder Weatherwax sold the ranch, left the dogs behind and moved his family to Los Angeles. A week after the New Mexicans-turned-Californians were settled into their new home, a fox terrier showed up at the door. Rudd took him in, named him Wiggles and proceeded to train the animal.

"In those days movie studios frequently went into the streets and simply collared passersby when they needed people for extras," Weatherwax goes on to explain in his book. "I hung around the studios, somehow hoping to be picked. And one day, when I was fourteen, it happened." A studio needed someone to play a messenger delivering a telegram. Weatherwax brought Wiggles along and when the scene was filmed, Wiggles held the telegram in his mouth. The ingenuity was enough to land the enterprising youth several other bits with Wiggles in the two years that followed. Professional dog trainer Henry East spotted Weatherwax and gave him a job. Between then (1923) and 1940 Weatherwax trained the dog named Asta who played in the *Thin Man* series with Myrna Loy and William Powell; Corky, who worked with Jackie Cooper in *Peck's Bad Boy,* with Wallace Beery and Cooper in *The Champ,* and in 150 other films; Daisy, who worked in the *Blondie* series at Columbia Pictures; and dogs for later pictures such as *Hondo, Old Yeller* and *Dog of Flanders.* But back to Lassie.

"In 1940 my brother and I opened our own kennel and school. Shortly after we opened, a man brought us an eight-month-old collie named Pal. The animal was driving the man to distraction, barking incessantly and chasing cars. I worked with the animal, found him to be intelligent, quick to learn, friendly and alert. When I called the man to pick up Pal, he didn't want him any longer and asked if I would take the collie in lieu of the seventy-dollar training bill. I said, 'yes.'"

In 1941 MGM is said to have auditioned over one thousand dogs to play the title role in *Lassie Come Home.* Pal, along with all but one of the others, was rejected. The studio wanted a female for the part; Pal was male. Pal had a white blaze on his muzzle and white blazes were held in something less than high regard by collie fanciers during that era. Also, Pal had no papers and the producers insisted on a pedigreed dog. Nevertheless, Pal did get the job as double to the animal which was subsequently set for the part. And then, as they say, "fate stepped in" as the picture went into production. Director Fred Wilcox later recalled the incident:

> The San Joaquin River in northern California flooded and gave us a great opportunity for some spectacular footage. As a last resort we signed with Weatherwax for one scene, using Pal to swim the flooded river. Our feeling was, what the hell, all wet collies look alike. We figured we could match long shots of Pal with close-ups of the dog we had picked [to play Lassie].
>
> Pal swam the river, climbed out on the bank with his tail between his legs and dropped down directly in front of the camera. He put his head between his outstretched paws and slowly closed his eyes. Weatherwax had that dog so well trained that he didn't even shake himself when he came out of the river. It would have ruined the scene, because the dog was supposed to be so exhausted he could barely breathe. Pal jumped into that river, but it was Lassie who climbed out.

And Weatherwax and his collie were in!

MGM's *Lassie Come Home* opened at the prestigious Radio City Music Hall in early October of 1943 and was an instantaneous hit with critics and film audiences. Bosley Crowther, writing for the *New York Times*, called it a story "with such poignance and simple beauty that only the hardest heart can fail to be moved."

Closely following the plot of Knight's short story, MGM's *Lassie Come Home* tells the story of a beautiful collie (Lassie) who belongs to a Yorkshire boy named Joe Carraclough (Roddy McDowall). Because of the family's poverty, the boy's father is compelled to sell the dog. Lassie's new owner, the Duke of Rudling (Nigel Bruce, whose daughter is played by Elizabeth Taylor), takes the animal hundreds of miles away to his home in Scotland. The dog, still possessed by her devotion for the young boy, escapes and begins the long trek home to Yorkshire. On the way she encounters many dangers of nature and man (storms, dog catchers, etc.) and spends brief respites with various kindly humans who tend to her needs and then allow her to continue on her journey. Finally, bedraggled and exhausted, she returns to Yorkshire in time to meet her young master at the schoolhouse at the end of day, a regular afternoon custom established at the beginning of the story. A moving, teary reunion occurs followed by a final story resolution making it possible for the boy to keep the dog.

Lassie and Roddy McDowall are seen here shortly after the boy has been told that the dog must be sold. (*Lassie Come Home*, 1943)

The story situations, already heavy with emotion, needed careful handling when brought to life on the screen if they were to avoid syrupy sentimentality, a constant threat in such a dog-and-boy story. Fortunately, the film skirted those dangers and the emotions expressed on the screen by the actors and Lassie rang true—perhaps causing a heightened emotional impact upon the audience, for theatres around the world were damp with tears for weeks after the showing of *Lassie Come Home*. My own childhood remembrance is of nearly two hours of intermittent weeping exceeded only by that of my mother seated beside me.

Lassie's young master in the film was an English youth named Roddy McDowall who had already established his credentials as a film actor of note in *How Green Was My Valley* (1941) and *My Friend Flicka* (1943), not to mention a host of other films (mostly made in England) that went back to his eighth birthday.

It was early in 1978 that I got to talk with the now accomplished adult actor about *Lassie Come Home* and other animal films he had made as a youngster. Roddy had just completed a performance on stage in *Otherwise Engaged* at the Parker Playhouse in Fort Lauderdale, Florida. After a quick shower, he met me in the greenroom of the theatre. He was casually elegant in a sand-colored jumpsuit. Although he is now in his early fifties—yes, that's right!—he could easily pass for thirty-five.

David Rothel: Does *Lassie Come Home* have a special place in your memory?

Roddy McDowall: Yes, it's one of the three films I am most emotionally attached to that I made as a child. The other two are *How Green Was My Valley* and *The White Cliffs of Dover*. I was very fond of making them. I was extremely happy making *Lassie Come Home*. I loved the dog; it was extraordinary, an absolutely extraordinary animal. It was a very happy movie to make and a very good movie. The actors in it were so good: Donald Crisp, Dame May Whitty, Nigel Bruce, Edmund Gwenn, Elizabeth—it was just a beautifully made film.

David Rothel: You must have observed the handling of Lassie by Rudd Weatherwax. Do you have any comment about his training of the dog?

Roddy McDowall: His training of the dog was phenomenal because the dog was absolutely amazing, stunning—absolutely stunning. He was very good with his animals, and very good as to how the animals related to the people with whom they had to work. I have only the highest admiration not only for Weatherwax, but for all the animal trainers I've worked with in lots of films—right down to the *Planet of the Apes* movies, you know, where there were animals as well as humans as animals. I've found animal trainers very efficient and extremely elegant about the way they do what they do.

David Rothel: Were you allowed to play with Lassie off camera?

Roddy McDowall: Yes, in fact Weatherwax let the dog stay overnight at my house before we started the film, which was an extraordinary and very sensible thing to do. A dog and a child when they work together have to connect [interrelate] otherwise it simply won't work. There have been a lot of Lassies, of course. I'm talking about the original dog. [In *Lassie Come Home* there was only one dog, Pal, who lived to be nineteen years of age. When MGM began to shoot the sequels, Weatherwax trained dogs for special functions. He had a stunt dog, a fight dog, a jump dog, a water dog, and several stand-ins. Pal was the principal dog for six years; then Pal's son, the original lead dog in the television series, worked thirteen years and died at eighteen years of age. That dog was succeeded by Pal's grandson who died prematurely of cancer at seven. Fourth and fifth generation descendants

Roddie McDowall today.

completed the television series. The 1978 Lassie feature, *The Magic of Lassie*, starred a sixth-generation descendant of the original Pal.]

David Rothel: There's that beautiful scene at the end of the movie where you come out of the schoolhouse to discover Lassie, all bedraggled, under a tree waiting for you. You rush to her, hug her, and she lovingly licks your face—

Roddy McDowall: They put ice cream on my face to get her to do that; they did!

David Rothel: You anticipated my question—you were just a young boy at the time that picture was shot.

Roddy McDowall: Well, I wasn't *that* young; I was fourteen years old. I was small and looked younger than I was. The film—the montage-like memory of it is that it was such an incredibly happy movie to work on. It was just a very special atmosphere and I can't pin that down; it was intangibles, and I'll always remember it as being a particularly happy experience. Not glamorous or anything like that. I'm not talking about like in a fantasy either; I'm talking about just a lovely experience.

Lassie and young Roddie McDowall during a happier moment of *Lassie Come Home*.

David Rothel: At that time did you want to have a dog like Lassie that you could take home with you?

Roddy McDowall: No, because there was only one Lassie for me. In fact, I never wanted a collie after that time because that dog was so phenomenal. If they'd given me Lassie, I'm sure I would have taken him, but the point is that the dog was just very special. I don't think I felt that way about any of the other animals I worked with. Some of the horses I worked with I liked, but there never was the same connection. I really adored Lassie.

And Roddy was just one of millions who adored Lassie. MGM, howling with glee over the success of *Lassie Come Home,* quickly went into production on a sequel to be called (What else?) *Son of Lassie* (1945). Contract player Peter Lawford was assigned the role of the now grown-up Roddy McDowall character, Joe Carraclough, from the original film. Donald Crisp was retained as the father, Nigel Bruce as the Duke of Rudling, and June Lockhart was assigned the role originally essayed by Elizabeth Taylor in the first film. (The casting of June Lockhart was especially prophetic since she later played the mother role in the Timmy and Lassie television series over a decade later.)

Peter Lawford and Lassie are seen here in a publicity still from *Son of Lassie.*

Son of Lassie was popular with the public, but was not at all in the same artistic league with the original film. One critic described the picture as "lengthy, contrived and only occasionally suspenseful." The story concerns the now-adult Joe (Lawford) who is an RAF flyer in World War II. Laddie (Lassie's son in the picture), much like his mother, follows Joe wherever he goes—this time into the service of his country. Eventually their plane is shot down over Norway, they bail out and are separated. The story then deals with their attempt to find each other in the Nazi-occupied country and to escape to England and safety. They make it, of course.

Peter Lawford and Lassie are searching for a way out of Nazi-held Norway in this scene from *Son of Lassie*. The "exterior" studio setting is surprisingly obvious considering the usual production values of the MGM studio.

By 1946 MGM was proclaiming that it had under contract "more stars than there are in the heavens." Lassie was one of them and got the star treatment wherever she went. She was the first dog to equal and then exceed the popularity of Rin Tin Tin. The PATSY Awards had not yet been created or Lassie would surely have been a winner. Many fans thought the lovable collie should have won a best-acting Oscar for her performance in *Lassie Come Home.*

Over the next few years, until early 1951, MGM continued the highly popular Lassie series of films. In 1946 the entry was *Courage of Lassie* (first announced as *Blue Sierra*) which starred the youthful Elizabeth Taylor; Oz's wizard, Frank Morgan; and a new MGM leading man, Tom Drake. In this episode Lassie (called Bill in the picture), having faced frontline battle against our World War II enemies, returns from the war maladjusted—an outlaw dog and potential killer. His pre-war owner, teen-aged Elizabeth Taylor, provides gentle, caring rehabilitative training and soon the collie is his old loving self.

Elizabeth Taylor and Lassie enjoy lunch together in this early scene from *Courage of Lassie*.

Elizabeth Taylor and Frank Morgan examine a very changed Lassie who has returned from the war zone. (*Courage of Lassie*, 1946)

In 1948 MGM unveiled *Hills of Home,* the next Technicolor Lassie feature. As with all of the MGM Lassie features, except for the first, the title was really meaningless and the picture was promoted as a Lassie feature, plain and simple. In each of the films MGM provided a strong supporting cast of familiar MGM contract players for the undisputed star and drawing card at the box office—Lassie. In *Hills of Home* the supporting cast included Edmund Gwenn and Donald Crisp (both from the original *Lassie Come Home,* but playing different roles); Tom Drake, again the leading man; and Janet Leigh in the ingenue role.

The *Hills of Home* story is set in the highlands of Scotland. In the story situation Lassie, owned by a dedicated, elderly country doctor (Gwenn), has a deathly fear of water because of mistreatment by a previous owner. Between human patients Gwenn works to cure Lassie of her fear. When the aging doctor has an accident, Lassie overcomes her fear to rush through a blinding storm and swim a torrential stream to bring help for her dying master.

Tom Drake and Edmund Gwenn discuss Lassie's fear of water in this scene from *Hills of Home*.

Lassie is about to go for help to save her injured master, Edmund Gwenn, in this scene from *Hills of Home*.

The Sun Comes Up (1949) (whatever that title was supposed to mean!) finds Lassie encouraging a friendship between a mother (Jeanette MacDonald) who is mourning the death of her son, and an orphan boy (Claude Jarman, Jr.) who is seeking a mother's love. In the sylvan mountain retreat setting for the story the grieving mother and orphan discover each other and, with Lassie's help, old emotional wounds are healed and love prevails. While the story was basically well-handled, the situations were frequently fraught with tearful swamps into which all but the most cynical of viewers would be engulfed. It was what critics used to call a four-handkerchief picture. For the trivia seeker, *The Sun Comes Up* marked Jeanette MacDonald's last screen appearance.

Challenge to Lassie (1949), based upon Eleanor Atkinson's *Greyfriars Bobby* story, was a most fitting vehicle for the talents of the King of the MGM kennels. (Walt Disney was to retell the story in a more true-to-the-original version in 1961.) Once again the setting was Scotland and Edmund Gwenn and Donald Crisp were around to lend support to the famous collie.

In the story Lassie is a sheepdog for Crisp. After some ruthless thugs kill the old shepherd, Lassie grieves at the graveside of his dead master. An innkeeper

(Gwenn) is touched by the animal's devotion to his deceased master and looks after the dog. Presently Lassie runs afoul of the law and is ordered put to death because he is considered a vagrant and because animals are not allowed in the graveyard. Gwenn pleads Lassie's case in court to establish legal ownership and, thus, saves the dog. In the process the whole village is touched by the love and devotion of the dog.

Although the budget for *Challenge to Lassie* was slighter than for earlier Lassie films and the title was again nondescript, the picture is generally acknowledged to be the best MGM Lassie film except for the original *Lassie Come Home*.

The last MGM Lassie feature was *The Painted Hills* (1951). It seems apparent with this final film that MGM had lost faith and/or interest in the Lassie series (perhaps because of the encroachments of television which eventually doomed the "smaller" pictures at the box office). For whatever reasons, the picture was a lower-level B product out of the high-class MGM factory. (MGM, in fact, considered all the Lassie pictures B products. One must realize, however that an MGM B picture was technically and often artistically head and shoulders above B pictures from most other studios.) The running time of only sixty-eight minutes and the less-than-stellar supporting cast revealed MGM's intentions to use *The Painted Hills* as supporting fare on double-feature bookings.

The film, despite its modest expectations, is really a very good, sentimental, adventure film suitable for family audiences—as, of course, were all the Lassie films. The story, based upon *Shep of the Painted Hills* (hence the film title) by Alexander Hull, concerns a dog who avenges the murder of his master, a gold miner who is done in by one of his greedy partners. Lassie plays Shep, Paul Kelly is his unfortunate master and Bruce Cowling is the murderer. Kelly's other partners in the mining venture are Ann Doran, supplying the requisite feminine support and young Gary Gray the *derigueur* boy for Lassie.

Following the death of her son, Jeanette MacDonald tries to get away from everything that reminds her of the boy, but her housekeeper Esther Sommers pleads with her to take Lassie, the boy's dog with her. (*The Sun Comes Up*, 1949)

Innkeeper Edmund Gwenn pleads Lassie's case in court in this scene from *Challenge to Lassie*.

Lassie is captured by constables at the grave site of his dead master. (*Challenge to Lassie*, 1949)

Lassie and Gary Gray are pictured here in a scene from *The Painted Hills*, the last MGM Lassie feature film.

And so, after seven features which had earned millions for MGM and approximately $264,000 for herself and her trainer, Lassie was "at liberty." MGM retained its logo lion, but dropped its option on the collie. Weatherwax, in lieu of some $40,000 still due on the books, offered to settle for all rights to the Lassie material owned by MGM. The short-sighted studio agreed. "It looked like a pretty stupid deal at the time," Weatherwax admits now, "and for a while it seemed to prove out that way. Only thing was, I loved Lassie."

The Lassie Television Years

Photo courtesy of Lassie Television, Inc.

Two uneventful years passed after the conclusion of the MGM-Lassie pact. Rudd Weatherwax began to fear that his Lassie was all past with no future. Then one day in late 1953 television producer Robert Maxwell met with Rudd to discuss the possibility of a television series for the unemployed collie. Rudd, eager to work in films again with Lassie, was easy to persuade. Soon a television pilot film was created, written and produced by Maxwell. In order to finance the Lassie venture, Maxwell, a man with an idea and a confirmed belief in the television potential of the canine, sold his rights to the profitable *Superman* television series to finance the Lassie production.

The Campbell Soup Company took one look at the pilot film when it was finished and immediately agreed to sponsor the half-hour weekly series. It was to be one of the longest sponsor/program associations in show-business history, running from 1954 through the early 1970s.

The first *Lassie* program went on the air on September 12, 1954, over the CBS television network. It starred Tommy Rettig as eleven-year-old Jeff Miller, Jan Clayton as his widowed mother Ellen Miller, George Cleveland as Jeff's grandfather George Miller (Gramps) and Donald Keller as Jeff's friend Sylvester "Porky" Brockway. In the series they all lived in a rural farming area called Calverton.

The first *Lassie* cast: Tommy Rettig, Lassie, George Cleveland, Jan Clayton, Donald Keller and his dog Pokey. Photo courtesy of Lassie Television, Inc.

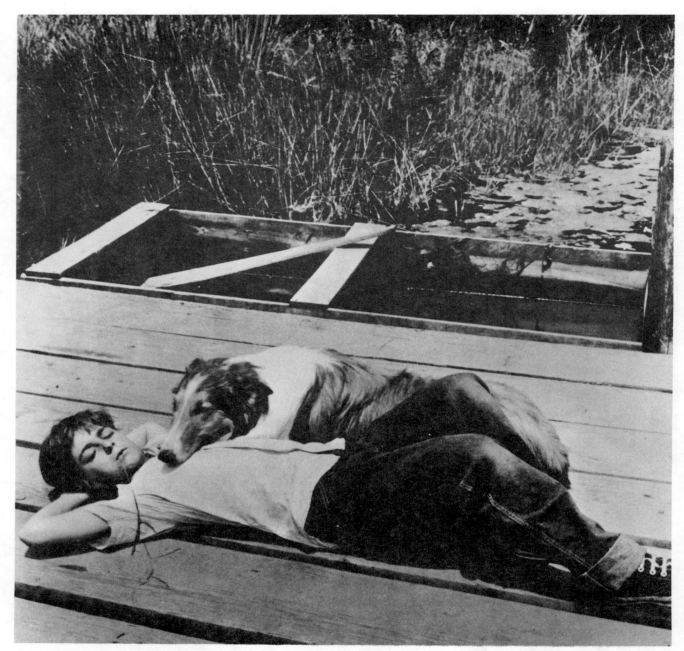

Jeff (Tommy Rettig) and Lassie are seen here during a restful moment in one of the early *Lassie* episodes. Photo courtesy of Lassie Television, Inc.

In the first episode the regular characters were established for viewers and Lassie's relationship with Jeff was introduced. The story explained that farm boy Jeff Miller inherited the dog from a neighbor who has just died. As the situation develops, Lassie is still mourning for his lost master, so Jeff has the task of winning the dog's love. Jeff finally succeeds when, in the climax to the episode, the two of them together capture the neighbor's hired hand who has run off with some money that was hidden by the deceased neighbor just before he died.

Tommy Rettig, seen here in a 1979 photo, is now in his late thirties and has two sons in their late teens. He has fond memories of the *Lassie* series. "I really enjoyed doing the show," he commented a while back. "The amazing fact about the series was the trained obedience of Lassie, being able to play dead and things like that." Rettig, now divorced and with both sons in college, plans to return to his acting career.

At least one critic carped that the series had better strive for more action and less sentiment in future episodes, since the only action in the initial story was the windup capture of the thief. Wisely, producer Maxwell and his staff ignored such suggestions. They were aiming for the early Sunday evening family audience. They wanted to tell gentle, family type stories about a farm boy, his dog and his friends and relatives. Even though television was still (relatively speaking) in its infancy, there were already cries from concerned parent groups around the country that there was too much violence on the home tube—a cry which continues unabated to this day. Maxwell was determined that *Lassie* would never cause such parental concern; that *Lassie* stories would depict a world of love and adventure as shared by a boy and his dog.

Maxwell's philosophy toward his series succeeded. The program's ratings were good from the beginning, the Campbell Soup Company was happy with the series and soon awards started tumbling in. For 1954 alone they included: an Emmy Award for Best Children's Program, the American Mother's Committee Award, the U.S. Army Recruiting Service Award, the Gold Star Award from Milky Way for Best Children's Performer, the General Federation of Women's Clubs TV Award, the *Billboard* Awards for Best Network Adventure Filmed Series and Best New Network Adventure Film Series, the National Association for Better Radio and Television Award and the Parents and Teachers' Association Award (both locally and nationally). In 1955 *Lassie* again received an Emmy Award for Best Children's Program and also won the prestigious Peabody Award—just to name two of the bigger awards for the year.

In 1956 *Lassie* was purchased by Jack Wrather from Robert Maxwell Productions for $3,500,000. Weatherwax's continued services, of course, went along with the deal.

Over the eighteen years—from 1954 through 1972—the series was in production, the characters and plot situations changed several times with only the collie remaining throughout—although there were several generations of Lassies that played the part. The "Jeff's Collie" (as it is called in syndication) format ran for three years with a total of one hundred three episodes filmed. By 1957 Tommy Rettig was getting a little gangly for the boy's role (although he never grew any taller than about five feet five inches), Jan Clayton wanted to change her acting image ("I was tired of wearing the same old housedress.") and George Cleveland wanted to retire (he died two days before his part in the series ended).

In September 1957 a new set of characters was unveiled for viewers. In the transition episode it is explained that Gramps has died and the Millers are having trouble trying to keep up the farm. During this time of family turmoil, Lassie finds a runaway boy from an orphanage—seven-year-old Timmy (Jon Provost). Ellen Miller decides to sell the farm to a childless couple named Phil and Ruth Martin (Jon Shepodd and Cloris Leachman). They immediately fall in love with Timmy and decide to adopt him. Because Jeff's collie can't be taken to the city where he and his mother are moving, Lassie, in a tearful farewell, is given to Timmy. Thus, the stage is once again set for more stories about a young boy and his dog. Veteran actor George Chandler was brought into the series as Timmy's uncle, providing the series once again with a Gramps-like character.

It appeared to the public that the transition from one *Lassie* family to another was logical and without incident, and that they would live happily ever after. Such, however, was not the case on the *Lassie* set. Cloris Leachman, up to that time

Lassie is seen here with her second television family: (left to right) Jon Shepodd, Jon Provost and Cloris Leachman. Photo courtesy of Lassie Television, Inc.

primarily a New York actress, found herself temperamentally unsuited to "playing house," as she described her role. She and George Chandler, who was smarting under criticism that he wasn't as appealing as the late George Cleveland, quickly took a dislike to each other and squabbled constantly on and off the set. Sheppod, who was relatively new to show business, tried to stay out of the line of fire between Leachman and Chandler. It was reported at one point that Cloris Leachman couldn't understand why the dog got all those close-ups. Seven-year-old Jon Provost stayed close to Lassie where it was always safe for a little boy.

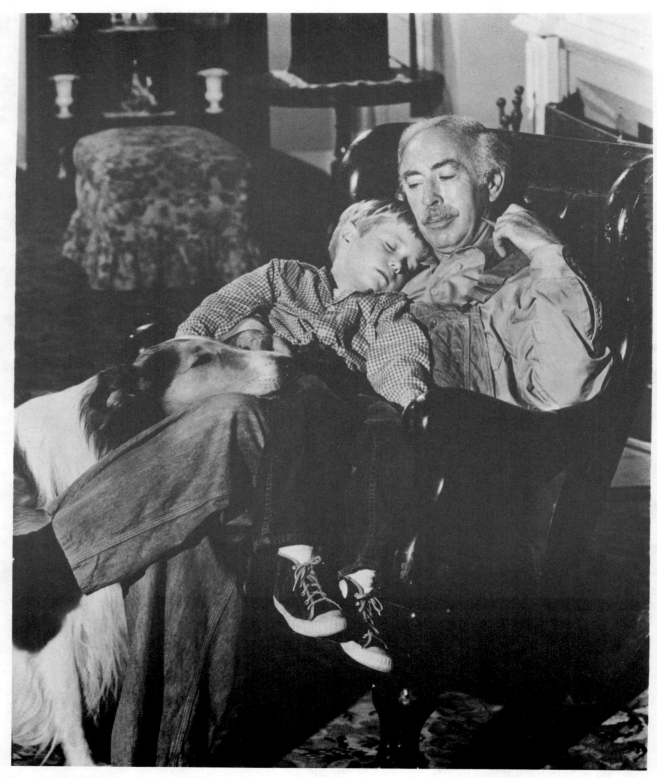

Lassie and Timmy rest in the lap of veteran actor George Chandler, who portrayed Timmy's uncle in the series. Photo courtesy of Lassie Television, Inc.

At the end of one television season, Timmy, over the summer, suddenly acquired a new set of loving parents—June Lockhart and Hugh Reilly. Chandler's role was gradually de-emphasized and finally eliminated altogether. The lovable old comic actor, Andy Clyde, was brought into the series as Cully, "Timmy's friend." For the next few years—until 1964 when Jon Provost was outgrowing his Timmy role—the *Lassie* set was once again a happy home for a boy and his collie dog.

The stories, with slight modifications, were basically the same as in earlier years with the Tommy Rettig cast: Jeff/Timmy saves Lassie; Lassie saves Jeff/Timmy; or Jeff/Timmy and Lassie save someone else—either a human or an animal. The story formula worked for ten years and, following the old show-business axiom, the *Lassie* producers didn't tinker with success.

Timmy's second television family: June Lockhart and Hugh Reilly look on as George Chandler reads to Timmy and his friend Todd Ferrell (called Boomer in the series). Photo courtesy of Lassie Television, Inc.

Lassie follows Timmy off to school in this scene from the *Lassie* series. Photo courtesy of Lassie Television, Inc.

Lassie and Timmy (Jon Provost). Photo courtesy of Lassie Television, Inc.

By 1964, though, the slower-paced, more family oriented times of the 1950s had given way to a generation of youthful rebellion. The flower children, drugs, Viet Nam and a plethora of other pollutants entered and began to change our lives. The Lassie producers sensed that the gentle, homespun boy-and-his-dog stories needed to expand from the now almost quaint, small family farm milieu to a flexible, more expansive setting which would allow for a greater variety of story situations. Jack Wrather commented about his *Lassie* property: "Children today are more sophisticated. You have to involve them in situations—Timmy can't afford just to sit around and fish any more. Lassie? She remains the same. I mean, basically—with the possible exception of Robin Hood or Mickey Mouse—she is the most appealing character invented."

In what was then thought to be a drastic, almost un-American format change, Lassie acquired a new master who was not a young boy, but rather an adult—a forest ranger. The American myth, bordering on sacredness, of "a boy and his dog" was challenged with the new *Lassie* format. Wrather and his producers were not sure what the reaction of the public would be.

Lassie and her new master, U.S. Forest Ranger Corey Stuart. Photo courtesy of Lassie Television, Inc.

This is the Lassie and Corey "autographed" photo that was sent to fans during the years the two of them appeared together in the series. Photo courtesy of Lassie Television, Inc.

They need not have worried. The television audiences quickly took to U.S. Forest Ranger Corey Stuart (Robert Bray). Starting in 1965 the adventures of Lassie were shot in color in some of the most scenic areas of the United States.

As with the Jeff-to-Timmy format change, the Timmy-to-Corey Stuart transition was handled logically within the weekly story line. Timmy's father, heeding a call for American farmers overseas, talks the family into selling the farm and moving to Australia. Because of the quarantine laws, Lassie is left in the care of the family's elderly neighbor, Cully. Soon after the family leaves, Cully has a heart attack which leaves him unable to adequately care for the dog. He gives Lassie to forest ranger Corey Stuart who needs just such a dog to assist him in his work.

During the seasons Lassie traveled with Ranger Corey, the series was beautifully filmed on locations all over the United States—on an Alaskan glacier, floating down the Mississippi and among the imposing rock formations of Monument Valley—just to name a few of the settings. The series became a veritable travelogue during those seasons.

Corey and Lassie remained together for four television seasons at the now long-established Sunday at seven o'clock time slot on the CBS television network. In the fall of 1968 another series format transition took place. Corey Stuart was seriously hurt in a forest fire and Lassie was put in the charge of two young rangers, Scott Turner (Jed Allan) and Bob Erickson (Jack DeMave). Exit Ranger Corey Stuart from the *Lassie* series.

From 1968 through 1970 Lassie became essentially a free agent in the stories, roaming from place to place, assisting humans and animals in distress. For some of the stories she associated with Rangers Turner and Erickson whose roles were bland enough to be interchangeable. It mattered little, though, because Lassie always remained the focal point of story attention whoever the humans in the cast happened to be.

For the last two years the series was in production, it was syndicated to individual television stations across the country in its regular Sunday night time slot. The Wrather Corporation was following the pattern of the successful off-network first-run syndication of such popular programs as *The Lawrence Welk Show* and *Hee Haw*.

During the last two seasons of *Lassie* the free-roaming animal stayed for a while with the Holden family on their ranch in northern California. For these episodes the series took on a new relevance with up-to-date family situations and conflicts. The young people of the Holden family, though close-knit, were more representative of the teen-age youth of the early 1970s—in some ways light years away from Jeff and Lassie during the mid 1950s.

Larry Wilcox, who years later went on to the *CHIPS* series, played a late teenager in the Holden family episodes of *Lassie*. Larry commented on his *Lassie* series' experiences:

> I was only four years old when the *Lassie* series first appeared on television. I laughed and cried through a lot of the collie's adventures. Like millions of others, I loved Lassie and I secretly wished that, well, I might have a collie just like her someday. That was just a kid's dream, though. Then I got a chance to be a real part of Lassie's life on the TV series. For me it was a dream come true.

Lassie is seen here with her new U.S. Forest Ranger friends, Jack DeMave and Jed Allan. Lassie won the coveted PATSY award more times than any other animal in show business — nine times between 1958 and 1971. Photo courtesy of Lassie Television, Inc.

Lassie and the "Holden family" cast: (clockwise) Larry Wilcox, Ron Hayes (later replaced by Larry Pennell), Skip Burton, Joshua Albee and Lassie. Photo courtesy of Lassie Television, Inc.

With the completion of the 1972-73 season, the live-action *Lassie* television series ended. But when the fall of 1973 came around, Lassie was back—this time in animated cartoon form as a Saturday morning feature on the ABC television network. The series was called *Lassie's Rescue Rangers,* and ran on the network until August of 1975. Once again the stories placed Lassie at a forest ranger station—this time in the Rocky Mountains. In the animated series, Lassie's masters are the Turner family. The mission of the collie's Rescue Rangers is to save animals and humans in distress and to protect the environment of the mountain range.

Though out of production from the mid-1970s, the tremendous backlog of *Lassie* episodes remains a popular syndicated feature in television markets throughout the world. Whether it is the "Jeff's Collie" package of programs, the "Timmy and Lassie" episodes, or the adventures with the forest rangers and the Holden family, *Lassie* can be found at some time of the day or night on just about any television set in the world. Another indication of Lassie's enduring qualities came in December 1975 when *Esquire* magazine named Lassie as one of the "Great American Things." She shared the honor with such other "Great American Things" as: Fred Astaire, John Wayne, Marilyn Monroe, Jackie Robinson and Walter Cronkite.

The animated Lassie for *Lassie's Rescue Rangers*. Photo courtesy of Lassie Television, Inc.

All was quiet on the Lassie front for almost two years. Then in the spring of 1977 word leaked out that perhaps a new Lassie feature film—the first since 1951—was in the works. In July it was formally announced that Jimmy Stewart had been signed to star in the as yet untitled Lassie theatrical feature for producers Bonita Granville Wrather (Jack's wife) and William Beaudine, Jr. Jack Wrather was to be the executive producer and Don Chaffey was to direct. Richard and Robert Sherman (who composed the score for *Mary Poppins*) had written the story with Jean Holloway as well as some songs for the picture. Rudd Weatherwax was scheduled to again provide the dog, which was a descendant of the original Lassie. Cameras were scheduled to roll September 19 in Sonoma County, California.

Gradually, other names were added to the cast of the film (which was in production under the working title of *Lassie, My Lassie*): Mickey Rooney, Stephanie Zimbalist (daughter of actor Efrem), Pernell Roberts, Mike Mazurki and Alice Faye (making her first screen appearance since 1962 in *State Fair*). During location shooting, further word was released about the collie who would essay the title role in the film. A news release stated that:

> She [sic] is a two-and-a-half-year-old sixth-generation descendant of the original who came to screen stardom along with Elizabeth Taylor in *Lassie Come Home* in 1943. That amazing collie worked in six succeeding Lassie films before she retired and gave way to her progeny. Four generations that followed were starred in the

Lassie television series. . . . Rudd, a gentle and affable man, treats Lassie with tender, loving care, and brought along for her company Lassie's stepbrother and grandmother, the latter an eleven-year-old partly deaf and utterly handsome animal who worked in television for the last five years and whose portrait appears on Recipe Dog Food cans.

The collies did not exactly rough it on location for the new film. They had a special air-conditioned and heated van which was well-provisioned with dog food, supplied with shampoo and dryers for their coats and special towels embroidered with Lassie's name. Lassie also had her own groomer, a young blond woman named Kathy Webb, and two handlers, Rudd's son Robert and Sam Williamson. All in all, not exactly a dog's life for the great-great-great grandson of the original Lassie.

Prior to its premiere in the summer of 1978, the film was retitled *The Magic of Lassie*—the new title no more memorable than the MGM titles of old, but like those films, conveying the most important information: this is a Lassie film!

The great-great-great grandson of the original Lassie and the star of the 1978 Lassie feature film, *The Magic of Lassie*. Photo courtesy of Lassie Productions, Inc.

Owner-trainer Rudd Weatherwax and Lassie. Photo courtesy of Lassie Television, Inc.

Mickey Rooney and Lassie. Photo courtesy of Lassie Productions, Inc.

In New York *The Magic of Lassie* opened at the Radio City Music Hall, just as *Lassie Come Home* had in 1943, and like its predecessor, did tremendous business. The first four days at the Music Hall *The Magic of Lassie* took in $196,000, a box office record for the theatre.

The plot of *The Magic of Lassie* was to a great extent an updating and Americanization of the original *Lassie Come Home* with music added. Crusty, but lovable, old Jimmy Stewart, with the help of Lassie, is raising his two orphaned grandchildren on his vineyard in northern California. The villain of the piece is rich, land-covetous neighbor, Pernell Roberts. When he finds that he can't talk Gramps into selling his prize-winning vineyard, he vindictively arranges papers which indicate that the family's beloved Lassie is a long-lost collie that really belongs to him. Roberts brusquely claims ownership and takes the dog away to his mansion in Colorado.

Lassie, after repeated attempts to escape her evil new master, finally succeeds in dumping him unceremoniously into his own swimming pool and escaping. On the long trek back to California, Lassie encounters many helpful humans—fight manager Mickey Rooney and his pug Mike Mazurki, and warmhearted waitress Alice Faye among others. The determined canine climbs mountains, fords treacherous streams, escapes a burning building (rescuing a tiny, frightened kitten in the process), all in unswerving determination to return to Gramps and the kids in northern California.

Finally, limping and bedraggled (as was the collie in the original story), Lassie arrives home just as the family is preparing to eat a Thanksgiving dinner for which, until this point, there was little to be thankful. The reunion is tender and tear-producing—both on screen and in the theatre audience. By this time Gramps has evidence that the neighbor's ownership papers are false. Lassie, thus, can remain with him and the kids forevermore.

During a break in the shooting of *The Magic of Lassie*, Alice Faye poses for a picture with Lassie. Photo courtesy of Lassie Productions, Inc.

During the Radio City Music Hall engagement of *The Magic of Lassie,* the stage show starred the screen star, Lassie, with her owner and trainer Rudd Weatherwax. They did four shows a day on stage to packed houses. It was reported in *Time* that Lassie and Rudd shared a $380-a-day suite in the Plaza Hotel. Protection for the two of them was provided by Pinkerton detectives. *Time* also revealed that Lassie got into one bit of trouble while on her New York sojourn. A policeman in Central Park ordered Bob Weatherwax, Rudd's son, to put the collie on a leash. "This dog never wears a leash," protested Weatherwax. "This is Lassie!" The cop responded "Right, and I'm the King of Siam. Now get a leash or I'll have to arrest you."

The Magic of Lassie reportedly cost just under four million dollars to produce, and according to Jack Wrather [in the bizarre business of film marketing], the film would have to gross approximately twelve million to break even—a tough nut to crack with a G-rated family picture in the late 1970s.

ABC television purchased the TV rights to the feature prior to its theatrical release and entered into an agreement for a two-hour Lassie special for the fall of 1978, with provision for a possible series or additional specials if the rating results proved satisfactory. Faced with stiff competition on the other networks, the two-hour two-part Lassie special—again with a lost-dog-returning-home plot—did not garner impressive ratings and a future series or specials remain uncertain.

There is little doubt, though, that Lassie will come home again on theatre and television screens. The beautiful collie is, without a doubt, the most beloved animal of all time. Her adventures, from the original short story through the latest television episode, represent over forty years of unequalled popularity for a single animal.

Over the years, of course, there have been those individuals who have called the Lassie stories contrived, unrestrained sentimentality—treacle of the most blatant order. They cry that even the animal relationships have been denatured: Lassie saving a baby chick from an oncoming train; Lassie protecting a woodland mother owl and her babies from a hungry mountain lion; Lassie, the psychologist, healing the hurt and loss a young boy feels at the death of his dog by making a gift of one of her own puppies; Lassie, the free-roaming world traveler of later television years who befriends humans and fellow animals as she continues her self-directed odyssey across the land, immaculately well-groomed despite the lack of human care and feeding. Ah yes, so true, so true, we must grudgingly acknowledge to the naysayers. But for all of us who have ever loved a dog, however, there is the knowledge that a human/canine relationship can be a magical, personal bond—an understanding and love, if you will—that transcends rational explanation. And this is what the Lassie stories aspired to through the MGM films, Jeff, Timmy, Corey and all the others who came in contact with Lassie over the years. And if the animal-to-animal relationships were not always true-to-life in the Lassie stories, they were at the very least models for human behavior—parables of sorts—that are not lost on young viewers still seeking appropriate understandings of interpersonal relationships. And for the impressionable youngster of years ago and now, Lassie offers, to quote Mrs. Wrather again, "Loyalty, courage, compassion, but most of all love."

Rudd Weatherwax sums it up proudly, "Pretty good for a dog that chased cars and wasn't wanted, eh?"

Photo courtesy of Lassie Television, Inc.

Benji

Photo courtesy of Mulberry Square Productions.

In July 1972 a small, ambitious production company in Dallas ran for itself what was then a rather cocky full-page advertisement in *Daily Variety*. The ad predicted that in a few years the reader probably wouldn't remember where he had first heard of Mulberry Square Productions, "a sincere little outfit making some pretty big waves with some unusually nice philosophies." Then with all the bravado of a Citizen Kane proclaiming his manifesto to the multitudes, Mulberry Square Productions made a declaration of intentions:

> Mulberry Square is a production place people can believe in because we promise to care about everything we do—to get totally involved in every production and give it our undivided attention from start to finish.
>
> That's probably why we achieved our first goal a short year and a half after opening our doors by becoming one of the most talked-about, most highly respected television commercial producers in the country.
>
> Our next goal is to get solidly into entertainment with some philosophies apparently shared only by a very few. To us, entertainment means to entertain. And when that's done well enough, things like box office, audience shares and demographics take care of themselves without the need of four-letter words, nude bodies and gross violence.
>
> It has been said that it's a rare person today who possesses both a broad and effective creative instinct and a solid professional knowledge of tape and filmmaking. Joe Camp, our president and chief producer-director, is such a person. Even more, he's a perfectionist. In fact, all Mulberry Square people are perfectionists. We figure if you keep reaching for it, the worst you're going to do is get close.

It is very easy, of course, to make proclamations; it is quite another thing to carry them out. The pleasant surprise is that Mulberry Square has been amazingly faithful to its words.

Disregarding the so-called experts of Hollywood who said it was folly for a motion picture company based outside Hollywood and New York to embark upon a major film, and who further said it was pure insanity for such a company to set its sights exclusively on the family market because nobody had ever been able to compete successfully with Disney, little Mulberry Square announced its first motion picture, *Benji*, the story of a loveable, vagabond mutt. Joe Camp wanted the freedom to write, produce and direct his dog story without the vicissitudes that plague most Hollywood-produced films—in short, he wanted to be his own man, and he knew that would only be possible if he remained in Texas. So Camp rounded up some well-heeled Dallas businessmen to stake him to the capital he needed to launch his project.

When it came time to cast the star, Camp started contacting dog trainers for the type of talented dog he envisioned. Eventually, Camp met with trainer Frank Inn and a huggable little ragamuffin he owned that had just retired from a long-running television series. When Camp saw the dog, he said, "He's the one." Inn countered, "You don't want him. He's thirteen or fourteen years old." Not to be denied, Camp got Inn to bring Higgins (the dog's show-biz moniker) out of retirement to play Benji.

Higgins had been rescued by Inn back in the 1960s at the Burbank Animal Shelter. Inn describes the dog as a mongrel blend of cocker, poodle and schnauzer—a cross between Burbank and Hollywood. For seven years he and Frank Inn toiled happily in Hooterville with the *Petticoat Junction* yokels. Then Joe Camp entered their lives.

Producer, director and writer Joe Camp and the star of his first major motion picture, *Benji*. Photo courtesy of **Mulberry Square Productions**.

"It makes for interesting challenges when you have to come up with new ways to do things like follow a dog running thirty-five miles per hour with the camera four feet away at *his* eye level."
Photo courtesy of **Mulberry Square Productions**.

"Joe told me what he wanted to do," Inn recalls, "and I told him it was impossible. Then we went to work." The "impossible" film that Joe Camp outlined to Inn consisted of the following, as relayed by Camp: "*Benji* is a story-in-film about a dog, but not like any that has gone before it. Nor is it a story about people and dogs, or even a story about dogs as told by people. *Benji* is a story revealed entirely from the dog's viewpoint. It is a subjective film seeking the same identification and emotional involvement that the Disney people get from their animated characters, yet *Benji* is not animated; he is real. He can't talk and we can't hear him think . . . yet by living the story with him, we always know. In effect, *Benji* is the first live-action attempt to reach out into an audience and get the same kind of emotional involvement and response that the Disney people have always been able to get with their animation."

Joe Camp freely admits that the idea for *Benji* came to him while watching Walt Disney's animated feature *Lady and the Tramp*. As Camp observed to Bruce Cook for *The National Observer*, " 'Wouldn't it be possible,' I asked myself, 'to achieve the same kind of involvement with *live* animals?' I got up early the next morning with this idea at the back of my head, and the treatment just fell out of me, a complete outline of the film. And with very few changes the outline is the movie we shot."

The problems created in producing this type of picture were almost as unique as the end result. For example, all standard camera-support equipment, like tripods and dollies, are designed to be used for filming from a "people-point-of-view." So Mulberry Square had to design support equipment to allow them to spend twelve weeks with the camera lens about four inches off the ground. "It makes for interesting challenges," Camp says, "when you have to come up with new ways to do things like follow a dog running thirty-five miles per hour with the camera four feet away at *his* eye level."

The simple plot line of *Benji* revolves around the kidnapping of a boy and girl who are special friends of a footloose pooch named Benji. The dog discovers that the boy and girl are being held in an old deserted house where he makes his home. Benji tries valiantly to communicate his knowledge of the hideaway to various humans in the town, finally with success.

The camera was specially mounted at dog-eye level for the *Benji* films. Photo courtesy of **Mulberry Square Productions.**

Child performers Cynthia Smith and Allan Fiuzat are seen here with Patsy Garrett and Higgins, the dog star of *Benji*. Photo courtesy of Mulberry Square Productions.

When *Benji* went into general theatrical release in early 1974, the critical and box-office response bore out Joe Camp's faith in his G-rated dog story. Though the picture itself was highly praised, most of the critical raves were reserved for the star of the film:

Variety—"In this case it isn't a dog performing, but a dog acting, just as humans act."

News Sentinel, Knoxville—"Is there an Academy Award for best dog actor?"

Baltimore News American—"It sounds rash to say it, but the dog *can act!* OK, go see for yourself."

The National Observer—"The film features one of the most accomplished canine actors in America. He can, it seems, do just about anything on command and even (I swear!) show emotion."

Benji is seen here with his owner-trainer Frank Inn. Photo courtesy of Mulberry Square Productions.

In an ad which ran in many national magazines at the time, Benji was pictured in a rascally, fun-loving pose with the caption: "Robert Redford, move over. America has a new most-huggable hero."

An interesting facet of the *Benji* success was the demographic breakdown of approval for the film. In a card survey taken in fifteen different cities across the country, 79 percent of the teenagers and adults surveyed rated *Benji* as "fantastic"; 97 percent said "fantastic" or "good"; 97 percent said they would recommend it to their friends; and 72 percent said they would like to see it again. Benji was a star with the release of his first feature film, Mulberry Square Productions was highly solvent and the Dallas backers had an unexpected gusher of a very different kind.

Frank Inn, the celebrated animal trainer who taught Benji how to act, is not generally thought of as a performer himself. Yet the truth is that he has to give a strong, believable acting performance behind the camera in order for Benji to perform in such a convincing manner before the camera. Inn explains, "Animals relate to your attitudes. Benji senses the mood that I'm in, then he develops that same mood. He can be happy or sad or angry, depending on whether I'm acting happy, sad or angry. Benji is even happy to look sad because he knows he has pleased me."

Inn, during his long career, has trained hundreds of animals for television and motion pictures. He originally had no intention of being an animal trainer, but a tragic automobile accident left him confined for a time in a wheelchair. A friend gave him a little dog named Jeep. And Inn remembers, "I spent all of my time communicating with that little mutt, teaching him to do things."

When Inn recovered from the accident and returned to his job as janitor at MGM studios, he discovered a noted trainer having trouble with a dog during the filming of a scene in a movie. "That's a famous dog you have," Inn told the man, "and you can't get him to perform. I got a little old mutt dog that can do that trick better than he can." Taken aback, the frustrated trainer countered, "You'll have to show me to make me believe it." So Frank Inn did.

The trainer, Henry East, hired Inn on the spot as an assistant to work with Asta in the original *Thin Man* series of pictures with William Powell and Myrna Loy. Inn later spent a term as assistant to Rennie Renfro, training Daisy and the pups for the *Blondie* films. Then he rounded out his apprenticeship serving for thirteen years with Rudd Weatherwax, the owner/trainer of Lassie.

During his career, Frank Inn has collected more than forty PATSY Awards, given to the top animal performers of the year by the American Humane Association. Frank's animal stars include Cleo on *The People's Choice*, Pyewacket in *Bell, Book and Candle*, Tramp in *My Three Sons*, Arnold the pig in *Green Acres*, Waldo in *Nanny and the Professor*, the whole animal menagerie on *Beverly Hillbillies*, and, of course, Benji in *Petticoat Junction*.

Inn, who still has about six hundred animals on his place in California, says, "Some people have remarked to me that it must take a lot of patience to train animals. But it never takes patience to do what you like to do. For me, it's a wonderful feeling just knowing that I've made a living doing what I love to do and that what I've done has made so many people happy."

Frank Inn is now in his sixties, a rotund, walrus-mustached, Pillsbury doughboy of a man. When he started work on the *Benji* film, he began to wear a black-and-white yachting cap. The cap has apparently attached itself permanently to the man, since it never seems to leave his head. "The cap symbolizes all the years I was a nobody," Inn says. "Now, I don't take off my cap for nobody."

Along with the public and critical acclaim for Benji, awards began rolling in for the little ragamuffin. At the American Humane Association's annual PATSY Awards ceremony, Benji was inducted into their Hall of Fame, an honor only previously bestowed upon Lassie. The American Guild of Variety Artists named the dog "Animal Act of the Year for 1976" and awarded him a Georgie.

"What an incredible surprise," Joe Camp beamed when he heard about the award. "Our star has received accolades and honors from all over the world, but when it comes from within the industry, voted by your peers, it makes it all that more rewarding." Frank Inn agreed: "Benji and I are so pleased over this honor." "Winning the Georgie Award was most unexpected. And to be ranked with the likes of Johnny Carson, John Denver and Eydie Gorme makes it that much more meaningful. I just hope it doesn't go to Benji's head."

Roly-poly trainer Frank Inn puts Benji through his paces for the camera as Joe Camp looks on. Photo courtesy of Mulberry Square Productions.

With the multimillion-dollar success of *Benji*, Joe Camp and his Mulberry Square Productions quickly started plans for a film sequel to be called *For the Love of Benji*. Again Camp served as writer, producer and director of the feature—a tale portraying Benji's struggle during an accidental excursion through the islands and ruins of ancient Greece. "Why Greece?" Camp anticipates the question.

"It's a gorgeous and charming land yet it can feel very uncomfortable when you realize that you not only can't speak the language, you can't even read the alphabet. There's nothing familiar to hang onto. The story needed this combination of visual charm and discomfort."

Dog lover, Doris Day, poses with PATSY Award Hall of Fame inductee, Benji. Photo courtesy of Mulberry Square Productions.

The story finds Benji (now played by an offspring of the original Benji) in Athens, embroiled in international espionage. He accidently becomes involved with government agents, crooks, policeientist who has the formula to turn one barrel of oil into twelve. The plot may be guilty of being a bit contrived and the loose ends are tied up a little too neatly during the last five minutes, but one must remember that *For the Love of Benji* is a star vehicle. The audience is there to watch Benji act—and act he does, being on camera almost the entire eighty-five-minute running time. As the *Variety* reviewer commented: "It's possible there's another dog somewhere with a more expressive face than the present Benji's, one that can show guilt, frustration and bewilderment more effectively. But it's unlikely."

Benji emotes for the camera during the location filming of *For the Love of Benji* in Athens, Greece. Photos courtesy of Mulberry Square Productions.

By 1978 *Benji* and *For the Love of Benji* had made over sixty-five-million dollars at worldwide box offices—all of this on a total initial investment of well under five million dollars. Benji was now in the super-star ranks of animal or human film stars. In addition to his film roles, Benji starred in an occasional television special—*The Phenomenon of Benji* and *Benji's Very Own Christmas Story* among them. In July 1978 *TV Guide* reported that in the annual Performer Q Survey, a study prepared by Marketing Evaluations, Inc. that measures the popularity of personalities in show business, Benji was listed right up there alongside of such favorites as John Wayne, Bob Hope and Carol Burnett.

As 1980 approached, a third *Benji* feature film was under way, again produced and directed by Joe Camp and co-written by Camp and Rod Browning. Pre-production planning called for the film to be a six-million-dollar "adult comedy" entitled *Oh Heavenly Dog,* co-starring Chevy Chase as a quickly murdered detective and Omar Sharif as the villain of the piece.

As *Variety* reported the new film:

> Chase will limn the role of a private detective who is killed but witnesses his murderer. The sleuth winds up in heaven and asks to go back to earth to clear a woman who is falsely accused of the crime. [The] only body available is that of a dog, leaving Benji to play the reincarnated detective aided by the voice of Chase.

With the success of the two *Benji* features, the television specials and a new Benji motion picture in the works, Frank Inn was signed by Mulberry Square Productions to a lifetime contract. The yachting cap became even more firmly ensconced on Inn's head.

Joe Camp spent a lot of time during his growing-up years going to movies that would reach out, involve and exhaust his emotions. "I always used to sit there wishing I was the one creating the things that made me feel that way," he recalls. Today he is.

"I'm a great believer in inspiration and hope," Camp says, "because without either all is lost, and with both, anything is possible." He feels that filmmakers who take audiences through an hour and a half of misery only to end by saying that there is no hope are doing their audiences an injustice. "I say that anyone who has the talent to affect the emotions of large numbers of people should temper that capability with responsibility. In other words, why make somebody feel that life isn't worth living, when maybe you can make them feel that it is.

"Too many people in the motion picture industry today put the dollar sign first," Camp says. "Walt Disney never did this. He was first and foremost interested in putting a super piece of entertainment before the public, to involve an audience in his stories and to send them out feeling good. His philosophy was that if you do that well enough, the dollars will take care of themselves. That's my philosophy, too."

Joe Camp and his little star. Photo courtesy of Mulberry Square Productions.

Asta

William Powell, Myrna Loy and Asta in a scene from *The Thin Man Goes Home* (MGM, 1945).

From 1934 through 1947 one of the most popular, charming and sophisticated comedy-mystery film series was produced by MGM—the *Thin Man* series starring William Powell and Myrna Loy in the roles of "the happiest, merriest married couple" (as they were sometimes billed), Nick and Nora Charles. Offering strong support to William Powell and Myrna Loy was a frisky little wire-haired terrier named Asta.

The basic plot of the *Thin Man* films called for a mysterious murder to occur during the first few minutes of the story, somewhere in the immediate vicinity of the urbane Nick and Nora Charles—he an astute retired criminologist/detective; she his inquisitive, sharp-witted helpmate. Presently the police would arrive and proceed to totally bungle the investigation. After eighty or ninety minutes of witty repartee and, perhaps, another murder or two, a suspenseful denouement would take place in which the clever team and their canine would point out the guilty party to the dumfounded police and explain how they had figured out the clues which led directly to the murderer—generally the least likely participant in the whole affair.

Millions of moviegoers found the *Thin Man* adventures a happy way to spend an evening at the movies. Undoubtedly, many in the audience longed to lead the cosmopolitan and exciting life of the rich, charming Charles couple.

Asta's task in the series was to be cute, amusing and to occasionally help Nick and Nora in their attempts to uncover clues leading to the murderer. Asta's popularity with fans of the *Thin Man* series was not really based on how much the dog was involved in the plot convolutions of the murder mystery. The dog was generally presented as a delightful little pooch that seemed to exemplify the Charles' *joie de vivre*. Over the years there were several dogs that were assigned the role of Asta. They all looked about the same, so audiences generally assumed the same dog was used throughout. At least three trainers worked with the various Astas that were used in the series. They included Henry East, Rudd Weatherwax and Frank Inn.

For the record, the six William Powell and Myrna Loy MGM *Thin Man* features were as follows:

The Thin Man (1934)
After the Thin Man (1936)
Another Thin Man (1939)
Shadow of the Thin Man (1941)
The Thin Man Goes Home (1945)
Song of the Thin Man (1947)

Starting in 1941, a radio series spun off from the films. It was called *The Adventures of the Thin Man* and was an almost exact audio replication of the successful film series. The producers worked so hard to achieve the breezy, sophisticated ambience of the films that most listeners mistakenly thought that William Powell and Myrna Loy were portraying the radio Nick and Nora. Asta was included in the radio series, albeit his presence was not as noticeable as in the film series.

The Adventures of the Thin Man ran from July 2, 1941, through September 1, 1950, with few breaks in its weekly half-hour continuity. Claudia Morgan portrayed Nora throughout the run; Les Damon was the first radio Nick Charles, followed by David Gothard, Les Tremayne and Joseph Curtin.

From the end of the radio series in 1950 until 1957, MGM left its *Thin Man* property on the shelf. Finally, on September 20, 1957, a television series called *The Thin Man* premiered on NBC-TV. It starred Peter Lawford and Phyllis Kirk as Nick and Nora; a perky, talented wire-haired terrier named Asta played Asta, winning

PATSY awards in both 1959 and 1960. Seventy-two half-hour comedy-mystery episodes were filmed before the series expired in 1959. The critics' assessment of the television version was that it seemed a pale imitation of the Powell-Loy film features.

Some fourteen years passed without a new *Thin Man* adventure appearing before the public. Finally, in 1975 a ninety-minute television special entitled *Nick and Nora* was produced starring Craig Stevens (late of *Peter Gunn*) and Jo Ann Pflug as the engaging Charles couple. Sure enough, Asta was there, too. If the Lawford-Kirk television series looked pale beside the movie series, the 1975 television special could only be called anemic. Any thought the MGM brass might have had regarding the possibility of the television special becoming a new *Thin Man* series was quickly forgotten.

There's a clue hidden there somewhere! William Powell, Myrna Loy and Asta are pictured here in a scene from *After the Thin Man* (MGM, 1936).

Jo Ann Pflug, Craig Stevens and Asta pose for this family portrait from the 1975 *Nick and Nora* television special.

It was a chilly November evening in 1977 as I wound my way through the backstage hallways of the Country Dinner Playhouse in St. Petersburg, Florida, looking for Myrna Loy. At seventy-two years-of-age she was playing the dinner-theatre circuit—to packed houses, I might add. She had just finished an evening's performance in Alan Ayckbourn's frothy comedy, *Relatively Speaking*, and was expecting to meet with me in her dressing room.

There were a lot of things I wanted to talk to Myrna Loy about, but the *Thin Man* series was uppermost on my mind. It had been a long time since the *Thin Man* films for Miss Loy—the last one having been produced in 1947. She seemed tired after her performance, but she was game for a few questions about another time and another place when she was the engaging and slightly zany Nora Charles and delightfully solved complicated murders with her debonair husband, Nicky.

David Rothel: Was the *Thin Man* planned as a series or did the success of each feature lead to the next one?

Myrna Loy: No, it was not planned as a series. W. S. Van Dyke was the director, a man who hasn't had enough attention, I think. He was a wonderful, wonderful director. He had directed me in two films, so he asked if I might play the role of Nora Charles. Actually it was a B picture; it was quite a low budget, but it was such a fantastic success. Of course, it had a wonderful script. It was based on a story by Dashiell Hammett and the script was written by Albert Hackett and Frances Goodrich. They're probably most famous for their play, *The Diary of Anne Frank*.

David Rothel: The *Thin Man* series was certainly marked by its sophistication and wit, and seemed to be saying, "Well, you see, marriage can be fun." You and William Powell seemed to be having such great fun in all of those films. Was it as much fun to work on them as it appears when we watch them?

Myrna Loy: Oh, yes, they were marvelous to make. As it turned out, of course, we did only six films over a period of ten years or so.

David Rothel: William Powell was such a fine actor.

Myrna Loy: He's still with us, fortunately. He lives in Palm Springs and he doesn't allow any publicity about himself at all, so everyone thinks he's dead. I have to keep telling people that he's still alive; that he's still very handsome with his white hair and white mustache. He's a man with enormous grace. He's a great friend of mine; we've been friends for many years. I don't get to see him very much, but we correspond from time to time and I talk to him on the telephone.

David Rothel: He's one of the few actors who actually retired, just stopped working.

Myrna Loy: He stopped because he had had a very long career going back to silent pictures. He was a big star before I ever got started.

David Rothel: Tell me about the famous dog Asta from the series.

Myrna Loy: We couldn't be friendly with Asta because he was a trained dog and he had to respond to his master, who was a wonderful man and was very good to his animals.

David Rothel: Who was the trainer?

Myrna Loy: Weatherwax. You couldn't interfere with that control he had to keep with the dog, so we never could play with Asta. He did everything for a little squeaky mouse. I'd squeak the mouse and put it in my pocket and then Asta would do whatever he was supposed to do because he thought he was going to get the mouse. He never got the mouse; he'd get a cracker or something. He was a wonderful dog.

David Rothel: They used several dogs during the run of the film series, didn't they?

Myrna Loy: Oh, yes, because he was getting along in age (laugh). His name was Skippy and he was a beautiful animal. The others were very cute, too. No one ever knew that there were different dogs, I'm sure. They never advertised that the dogs were different.

Miss Loy and I talked about other memorable times from her career. Then my questions ended; it was late and she had a matinee the next afternoon. As I packed my tape recorder, she prepared to go back to her motel. I helped her into an unpretentious cloth coat made of nubby light-blue material and of indeterminate age (a very unNora-like cloak, I thought). Together we walked through the hushed darkness of the now vacant dinner theatre out into the night. A Toyota car was waiting to whisk her back to the motel.

She seemed very happy to still be working at her craft in a dinner-theatre comedy in St. Petersburg, Florida; she certainly wasn't doing it because she needed the money. Who was I to question her reasons? But Asta would have been very out of place in this late-night scene.

Take a card, any card! Myrna Loy, William Powell and Asta in a light moment from *Song of the Thin Man* (MGM, 1947).

Bullet

Roy Rogers and his German shepherd Bullet.

One of the most popular dogs on television during the 1950s was Roy Rogers' German shepherd, Bullet. The dog had started with Roy during the last year of the King of the Cowboys' films for Republic Pictures, making his debut in *Spoilers of the Plains* in 1951. When Roy ended the feature-film series and moved into television in 1952, Bullet got featured billing just below Roy's mount, Trigger. The dog did all the standard canine stunts expected in an adventure series where bandits must be thwarted; children romped with, affectionately; and chases made alongside Roy's palomino, Trigger.

Roy commented to an audience in 1977, "We made all of the TV pictures with the one dog, Bullet [one hundred half-hour, black-and-white episodes of *The Roy Rogers Show* between 1952 and 1957]. As you probably know, though, it's necessary to use attack dogs for some action scenes, and you can't very well use a specially trained attack dog as the loveable dog that has to play with the kids in other scenes. It doesn't work very well. You're liable to give the dog the wrong cue and he'll chew someone's leg off.

"We sent to Germany at the beginning of our TV series and bought an attack dog to be used only for special action scenes where Bullet, who was a most gentle animal, would not work so well. One day we were shooting a program where Freddie Graham, who played a lot of heavies in our pictures, had to run by the camera, jump on his horse and start to ride away as Bullet—in this case the new German double—leaps after him.

Prior to shooting the scene, Freddie Graham had his left leg padded with thick leather up to the knee, because the dog was supposed to get him by the calf of the leg as he tried to make his getaway. As the scene began, Earl Johnson, who was the trainer, turned the dog loose. When the dog took off after Freddie, he jumped too high and got him in the thigh above the knee. Freddie tried to keep moving, but that dog was just hanging on.

"Poor old Earl Johnson suddenly realized that the dog didn't understand English. He had just come from Germany and he was trained in German. In desperation Earl shouted, 'Achtung! Achtung!' I guess it meant 'Stop!' or 'No!' or 'Get him off me; he's chewing me up!' We had to take Freddie to the hospital to get his leg fixed; get a tetanus shot and a few other things. That was one of the unexpected incidents that happened with the dogs on the set."

When the television series ended, Bullet lived out his years on Roy's ranch. When the dog died, Roy had him mounted. Today Bullet can be seen standing next to the similarly mounted Trigger and Buttermilk, Dale's horse, in the Roy Rogers and Dale Evans Museum in Victorville, California. Stop by and see them all some day.

Chinook "The Wonder Dog" and Kirby Grant

Today Kirby Grant is remembered mainly for his characterization of Sky King in the long-running television series of that name. Prior to his stint as captain of the Song Bird and owner of the Flying Crown Ranch, Kirby had a rather checkered show-business career. He appeared first on the scene as a singer-bandleader in Chicago (once unknowingly being booked for a private party thrown by mobster Al Capone for which Kirby and his band members each received a one-hundred-dollar bonus—an unheard-of sum for a one-nighter in those days of the early 1930s).

After gaining radio prominence in Chicago on NBC, Kirby was shipped out to the Los Angeles NBC station. Pretty soon he was voice-overing the singing parts for non-singing actor-stars in movie musicals. Eventually he appeared in person in small-budget musicals for Universal and other film companies.

After time out for service duty during World War II, Kirby returned to Universal Pictures as a contract player only to find that there was not much interest in him as a musical-comedy star since fewer and fewer "small" musicals were being produced. Events were occurring, however, that would lead Kirby far afield from the type of film work he had been performing up to this time.

One of Universal's cowboy stars, Rod Cameron, had achieved some degree of recognition about this time and had been elevated to better roles, thus leaving a void to be filled in the cowboy stable of actors. One day Universal Western-film producer Wallace Fox spotted Kirby in the studio commissary at lunch time and quickly envisioned the countenance of a cowboy hero in the handsome features of this Butte, Montana, lad. Kirby informed Wally Fox that the only thing he knew about a horse was one end from the other and, furthermore, had no desire to increase his knowledge of the four-legged beasts. Despite Kirby's pleas to let him continue in musicals and light comedies, Fox (and, later, the other studio chiefs) was adamant—finally threatening a suspension if Kirby did not see the writing in the trail dust. Reluctantly, a new cowboy star was born, albeit the Westerns that resulted from this birth were never to be very memorable.

Universal was well-known for its frequent front-office shake-ups that usually caused fallout from the upper echelons all the way down to the lowliest contract players. During one of these periodic mogul-produced quakes, Kirby Grant felt the Universal ax along with just about everyone else at the studio.

Kirby Grant is seen here as Sky King in a recent photo. Kirby still makes many personal appearances each year as Sky King.

Lindsley Parsons, a producer over at Monogram Pictures, was about to produce a B musical and quickly signed the now "at liberty" actor to star in the picture. About this same time (the late 1940s) Parsons acquired the rights to the popular James Oliver Curwood stories of a North woods Mountie and his dog. Upon observing Kirby's work in the musical, Parsons began to see what a natural this former cowboy star Kirby Grant might be as the clean-cut hero in his new series. Parsons talked with Kirby's agent and a deal was made for Kirby to star in the series. His co-star: a pure white dog named Chinook.

The series ultimately consisted of ten features produced between 1949 and 1954. The films were moderately popular and well made considering their limited budgets and the times. The fact that the series lasted until 1954 attests to the relative popularity of the films, since most B features had been dropped before this because of the powerful onslaught of television during the early 1950s.

Supporting casts in the films featured some of the better-known second-rank actors and character people that were active in films at the time. The leading ladies in several of the pictures would eventually go on to bigger and better roles. The following is a list of the ten features in the Chinook series with leading ladies and supporting cast members of special note indicated:

Trail of the Yukon (Monogram, 1949) Dan Seymour, Jay Silverheels, Iris Adrian and Stanley Andrews.

The Wolf Hunters (Monogram, 1949) Jan Clayton.

Snow Dog (Monogram, 1950) Elena Verdugo, Rick Vallin and Milburn Stone.

Call of the Klondike (Monogram, 1950) Anne Gwynne, Lynne Roberts and Tom Neal.

Yukon Manhunt (Monogram, 1951)

Northwest Territory (Monogram, 1951) Gloria Saunders, Tristram Coffin.

Yukon Gold (Monogram, 1952) Martha Hyer, Harry Lauter.

Fangs of the Arctic (Allied Artists, 1953)

Northern Patrol (Allied Artists, 1953) Dale Van Sickel, Gloria Talbot and Emmett Lynn.

Yukon Vengeance (Allied Artists, 1954) Monte Hale, Mary Ellen Kay.

Kirby and I had met briefly in 1976 when we were both guests at a nostalgia convention (OrlandoCon). When the Chinook chapter of this book loomed near, I thought it time to sit down with Kirby for a chat about the so-called "Wonder Dog" he had co-starred with in the late '40s and early 1950s. A fellow writer and friend, Rob Word, was able to provide Kirby's unlisted Winter Springs, Florida, telephone number. He answered the phone himself and quickly agreed to an interview regarding his former canine cohort.

A few days later Kirby welcomed me at his fashionable condominium, proffered a lemonade and then settled back in his easy chair to reminisce about this Mountie role and the big white dog that was always by his side in those days.

Kirby Grant: Chinook! (laugh) I have to laugh. Do you know what the word Chinook means? It's an Indian word meaning warm wind (laugh). Chinook was not exactly a warm wind; he was *very* temperamental. I don't know for sure what breed he was; I don't know whether he was a police dog or what. He had the conformation of a police dog.

David Rothel: I saw *The Wolf Hunters,* one of the films in the series, the other night. My veterinarian, who's a close friend, watched it with me and said that Chinook appeared to be a shepherd in absolutely beautiful condition, but that he didn't have good conformation for a shepherd according to today's standards.

154 Man's Best Friends

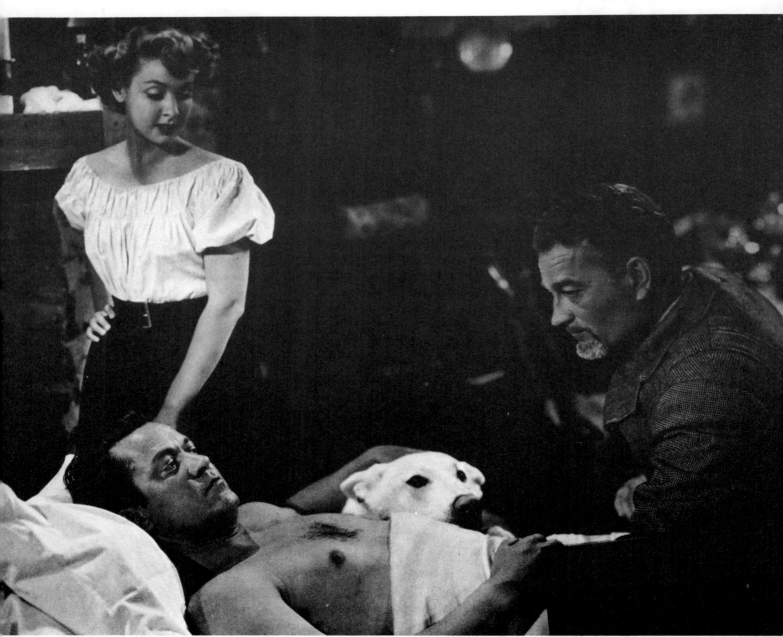

Milburn Stone is practicing on Kirby for his Doc Adams role of years later on *Gunsmoke*. That's Elena Verdugo looking seductive in the background as Chinook looks after his master.

Chinook and Kirby Grant are seen here on location for *Yukon Gold* at Cedar Lake, California.

Kirby Grant: He was pure white, but he wasn't albino; his eyes were dark. His real name was Harvey. At that time [late 1940s] Frank Fay had recently made a smash hit on Broadway with the play called *Harvey*, a story about an imaginary big white rabbit. I think Joe E. Brown was going around the country doing the show, too. Dorothy Crieder, who owned the dog, named him Harvey, and it was pretty incongruous.

As I indicated, there wasn't anything gentle about the dog Chinook; a gentle warm wind was not Chinook. He was very temperamental. He bit almost everybody on the set at one time or another with the exception of myself. He really did; he bit just about everybody. Surprisingly though, he and I got along very fine—and we, of course, worked very closely together all the time. He was not vicious; he was just very temperamental.

David Rothel: Was it generally when he got tired that he acted this way?

Kirby Grant: Yes, I think so. He just got out of sorts like people do. People don't go around biting each other, though, but that was the only equipment Harvey had to work with. He did a good job, too (chuckle). I don't mean that he viciously attacked anyone. It was usually a snarl and a snap, and that was it, you know. He wouldn't go for the jugular or anything like that; at least I never saw him do that. But the potential was always there because he was a big, powerful dog.

David Rothel: Was he a trained dog? I mean, a really *trained* dog for movie work.

Kirby Grant: No, not in that sense of the word, not like Lassie and some of the other dogs the Weatherwax people had trained. Harvey sometimes would just refuse to work. A scene would go along with take after take and, finally, he would just walk away and lie down. And there was nothing you could do. We had people there to handle him; Dorothy was there, but she couldn't do anything with him either. He really was a star in *every* sense of the word!

David Rothel: Was there a trainer on the set?

Kirby Grant: Yes, we had several. There was a little, short fellow with a mustache named Sam Williamson who wouldn't have weighed seventy pounds soaking wet. I thought surely that dog was going to eat him up at times. Then we had another guy by the name of Duke York. Duke was a stunt man and also played heavies. Inevitably there would be a fight between the dog and the heavy, and poor Duke would have to put the things [padding] on his arms to protect himself and get in there and fight that dog. Harvey loved that because he would grab Duke where there was no padding. And he knew where to reach for him!

David Rothel: In preparing to shoot a scene with the dog—let's say one of those man/dog fight scenes you mentioned before—would they run through all of the action in rehearsal with the director?

Kirby Grant: There was no such thing as rehearsal on a thing like that. The director just had to set the camera up where he had a lot of room to go through a one-hundred-eighty-degree turn if he had to. The camera would just try to stay with them, stay with the action. The trainer, usually Duke in our case, would start the action. He would give a cue like "come on" or whatever. The dog would run, jump and grab. It would generally start out to be play, but as it lasted the dog would get so excited he would snarl and snap and it really was something! Poor old Duke used to show up the next day after one of these fight scenes with puncture holes and black-and-blue marks.

Kirby and Chinook enter the cabin cautiously as leading lady Martha Hyer looks on apprehensively.

Chinook/Duke York fight. Scene from *Yukon Gold*.

David Rothel: In *The Wolf Hunters* Chinook has a love interest. He goes off at night and meets a female dog which looks just like him. Did they have two or three of these white shepherds that they used as backups for Chinook?

Kirby Grant: No. We had no double, really, and that was a bad thing. They should have had a double for the animal just like other star animals have. The problem was that the dog was unique; there weren't too many like him around. I recall the dog that they used for the other dog in that particular film where Chinook had the love interest. The dog was a female and didn't have the look that Harvey had. Harvey was a beautiful animal, very alert looking and a big animal.

David Rothel: And there wasn't an ounce of fat on his body. He was just as lean and tough as he could be.

Kirby Grant: Well, we would run it off him (laugh).

David Rothel: Tell me more about Chinook on the set, things that happened while you were shooting.

Kirby Grant: Some of the things I don't think I could tell (laugh). In one picture we had a scene where I was wounded in a canoe and had collapsed over the paddle. Chinook was supposed to lick me, you know, whine and lick me. I was just floating along in the canoe. The cue was, "Kiss me, Chinook, kiss me; Harvey, kiss me." The danged dog was stubborn and wouldn't do it. Finally it got to the point where I got very exasperated. I said, "Harvey, you so and so and so (only I used much stronger language than that), kiss me! You so and so!" I kept saying the bad words under my breath. I didn't realize that they were recording this; I thought it was just a silent shot with the dog and me and that they would dub the sound in later of him whining and the slurps when he would lick my face. They recorded all of it and I was a little embarrassed, I must say, when we heard it later while watching the daily rushes.

During the shooting of the first picture I did in the series, when I'd walk out at the end of a scene with the dog, I would say, "Come on, boy." Well, the way the film was edited, "Come on, boy" was said one scene after another. It was almost as bad as that expression the heavies say when they are going to get out of a scene: "Let's get out of here!" Instead of doing it, they say it. I got kidded about my "come on, boy" line. They said we should have called the picture *Come on, Boy.*

David Rothel: Did they call the dog Harvey on the set?

Kirby Grant: Oh yes (laugh). That poor animal was certainly confused with two names, Harvey and Chinook.

David Rothel: That wonderful name Chinook sounds so right for the dog. It's rather disconcerting to know his real name was Harvey.

Kirby Grant: A few people sometimes shortened Chinook to Shnook (laugh). But, you know, it's pretty tough on an animal—the camera, lights, and everybody hurrying because of the budget. I can readily understand why the dog got upset. We used to get terribly tired. I know I would get awfully tired. Very often with budget pictures like these you tell about what happens rather than showing it on the screen. It saves time and money to do that. So consequently I had a great many lines to learn. After a hard day of shooting, I would go back to the Paramount lodge there at Big Bear, get cleaned up and have my dinner. Then I would study all evening long, go to sleep and get up early and go back to work. The rest of the crew would be out having a good time because they didn't have all those lines to learn.

David Rothel: It looked to me as if most of *The Wolf Hunters* was shot on location except for the interiors of cabins and things of that sort.

Kirby Grant, Chinook and Suzanne Dalbert pose for this publicity picture for the first film in the series, *Trail of the Yukon*.

Kirby Grant today.

Kirby Grant: Yes, that's true. We did very little shooting in the studio. Most of it was done outdoors. Incidentally, we filmed up at Cedar Lake above Big Bear Lake. As a matter of fact, the dam there was built for *The Trail of the Lonesome Pine* back around 1936. You may remember that picture with Fred MacMurray, Henry Fonda, Sylvia Sidney, Fuzzy Knight and that whole gang. There were cabins up at Cedar Lake, too, that we used for some of the interiors for the Chinook series. They were left from that original picture that was made there.

I enjoyed the Chinook series because it was outdoors. It was pretty difficult at times because Cedar Lake is at about seven-thousand-feet altitude. In the spring—particularly when there were still snowdrifts around—a chase could get pretty exhausting when you had to run a hundred yards across country, across the rocks and things, sometimes in the snow. That could pull your cork pretty good! (Laugh.) We had come from pretty close to sea level [in Los Angeles] up to seven thousand feet, and it wasn't easy.

David Rothel: I know at the end of *The Wolf Hunters* there is a *long* chase. You and Chinook are chasing the bad guy across hill and dale. It goes on for about ten minutes. You just keep on running. I was thinking as I watched it that they must have given you plenty of time to rest between setups because it would have been absolutely exhausting if you had done it in one take after another.

Kirby Grant: It was done in short takes, of course, like all of those things are.

David Rothel: Was the Chinook series a rip-off of *Sergeant Preston of the Yukon,* which was on radio at that time, but had not yet made it to television or motion pictures?

Kirby Grant: No, no. Dick Simmons and I used to kid around about that. Of course, Dick played the part of Sergeant Preston on television. It just happened that the format and the locale, in particular, were the same—the snow country, the big trees, timber, mountains and all of that. My pictures were based—loosely, I might add—on the James Oliver Curwood stories. As you know, he was a very famous writer of that type of story. He was not quite on a par with Zane Grey, but very well known, just the same, for his stories of the North woods.

David Rothel: How long did you take to shoot the average film in the Chinook series?

Kirby Grant: Usually ten to fifteen days.

David Rothel: How much of a budget did Monogram and later Allied Artists put into films of this sort?

Kirby Grant: Well, I really don't know what the budgets were. I only know what my salary was. I had a deal for so many pictures a year. The budgets, though, were fairly reasonable for those years. When you look at the costs now, even the cost of a television commercial costs more than we spent on those films.

David Rothel: The series ran from 1949 until early 1954, and there were ten films in the series. Are there any particular ones from the series that stand out in your mind?

Kirby Grant: No, not really. They were all pretty much alike. I remember the people and some of the incidents, some of the humorous things that happened along the way.

David Rothel: Did you ever mind being upstaged by a dog in the series—playing second fiddle, as it were?

Kirby Grant: No, no. I should say not.

David Rothel: You're not very temperamental, I feel.

Kirby Grant: No, not really. It never bothered me at all. Most people are intrigued by animals. Kids, particularly, seem to have an affinity for animals. Lassie, of course, is the greatest example of this in the world. You know when you say "played second fiddle," I can't help but think of the Lassie pictures with such fine actors as Donald Crisp, Edmund Gwenn, Roddy McDowall and, of course, Elizabeth Taylor. They all got their start playing second fiddle to a dog (laugh), a dog or a horse. *National Velvet,* look what it did. It brought Elizabeth Taylor to the fore immediately. It was a magnificent story. I think that any time you have animals and kids in a picture you're home free.

David Rothel: Having them in the picture with you makes you look better, too.

Kirby Grant: Why sure! If they do upstage you, it's not consciously—like a lot of actors do (laugh).

David Rothel: Do you have any idea whatever became of Chinook after the series?

Kirby Grant: I haven't the slightest. Of course, that's been quite a few years ago now.

David Rothel: He's passed on to dog heaven, I'm sure.

Kirby Grant: He's up there in the big studio in the sky (chuckle).

David Rothel: I do know, however, that he went into the *Corky and White Shadow* serial they did on the *Mickey Mouse Club* from 1955 through 1959. He played White Shadow. Others in the cast of the serial included Darlene Gillespie, Buddy Ebsen and Lloyd Corrigan. I lost track of him after the *Mickey Mouse Club* series.

Kirby Grant: I didn't know anything about that. Did they put ears on him, mouse ears?

David Rothel: I don't think so (laugh).

This title lobby card from *Snow Dog* is a perfect model for action/adventure publicity.

Cleo

Cleo, a droopy-eared, dour-countenanced basset hound achieved a considerable measure of television popularity during the 1950s as the co-star of a half-hour comedy series called *The People's Choice*. Jackie Cooper and Patricia Breslin were the nominal stars of the one hundred four episodes filmed for NBC between 1955 and 1958.

Cooper played Sock (Socrates) Miller, a young, idealistic city councilman who constantly ran afoul of Mayor Peoples, the father of Sock's sweetheart, Mandy Peoples—hence the political and personal play on words resulting in the series title. Cleo was Sock's pet basset hound, a woebegone observer and commentator on the weekly predicaments of her master.

Cleo was generally referred to as a "talking" dog, which was not exactly accurate. Cleo never really spoke to anyone in the cast; her comments were meant to be asides representing the hound's thoughts on the comical or perplexing events at hand or exclamations of exasperation to the viewing audience. Thus, the cast members never acknowledged hearing the dog and no attempt was made to "wire" the dog for mouth movements. Close-ups of the basset were combined with the voice of actress Mary Jane Croft to achieve the desired effect. Cleo never had to do tricks or to perform in the usual sense; she only had to stay awake long enough for the camera to catch her basset-hound expression and for Miss Croft to voice-over the appropriate, slightly cynical riposte.

The People's Choice was a lightweight romantic-comedy series that was successful enough to last three seasons on NBC and win a PATSY award for Cleo and her owner-trainer Frank Inn. When the series ceased production, Cleo retired to Frank Inn's ranch in California where her thoughts remained her own. *TV Guide* reported in late 1978 that when dogs especially close to Frank Inn go to the "Big Doghouse in the Sky," Inn cremates them and keeps their ashes. Some may find it comforting to know that Cleo's ashes rest in a tiny bronze urn in Frank Inn's dining room.

A despondent-looking Cleo is pictured here with tomboyish Carla Merey in a scene from one of the episodes of *The People's Choice*.

Jackie Cooper and Patricia Breslin are seen here in a romantic moment from *The People's Choice*, Cleo would have had plenty to say about this scene!

Daisy
and
the Bumstead Family

Chic Young, one of the most successful cartoonists of all time, created "Blondie" back in 1930 for the King Features Syndicate. The strip and its characters developed through a period of evolution—Blondie was originally a flapper, jazz-baby type; Dagwood, her boyfriend, was a rich man's bumbling son—until 1933 when Young married the two-dimensional couple. Dagwood's snooty, Nob Hill-type parents disowned the boy when the marriage occurred, leaving the young couple broke, but in love. From then on, Chic Young built his strip around the middle-class house-in-the-suburbs, young-married-couple-struggling-to-get-along format—a situation not unlike that faced by many American families during those Depression years. Eventually two children were added: Baby Dumpling (later called Alexander) and a daughter named Cookie. The most memorable addition to the family was probably their pet dog Daisy, a precocious little mutt that demonstrated considerable character and impishness even in the comic-strip pages where she originated.

In 1938 "Blondie" was made into a film series starring Penny Singleton and Arthur Lake in the lead roles. Baby Dumpling and Daisy were on board from the beginning of the twenty-eight episode film series; Cookie came along in 1942.

Daisy was highly visible in the *Blondie* films, there being several features in which she was the center of attention. For example, Daisy has some memorable scenes in *Blondie on a Budget* (1940) in which she happens to imbibe a rather strong drink and ends up hilariously tipsy. In *Life with Blondie* (1945) Daisy is selected pinup pooch by the Navy, gets dognapped by some underworld gangsters and is held for ransom.

Daisy had at least two stock bits that audiences loved and that were used often in the *Blondie* films: one was her ability to do a doubletake (writer David Zinman compared Daisy's doubletake favorably to the famous ones of comedian Franklin Pangborn). The other Daisy distinction was an incredible raising of her ears to show surprise or incredulity. For this stunt Daisy and her trainers relied on some "invisible" wires to help with the illusion. Rennie Renfro, Rudd Weatherwax and Frank Inn trained Daisy at one time or another over the years the film series was in production.

A *Blondie* radio series quickly grew out of the film series, taking to the air in 1939. The opening to the radio series soon became a national catch line: "Uhh-uhh-uhh—don't touch that dial! Listen to . . . Blonnnndie!" The radio series contained all the characters from the comic strip and film series, including the ever-loveable Daisy. Arthur Lake and Penny Singleton duplicated their film roles in the radio series which lasted until 1950. Lake stayed through the entire run of the program; Penny Singleton left the radio series during the mid-1940s and was replaced by Patricia Van Cleve (Lake's real-life wife) and, later, by Ann Rutherford.

The Columbia Pictures' film series ended in 1950 also, and it wasn't until 1957 that the property was reactivated for television as a half-hour situation-comedy series. Arthur Lake returned as Dagwood, though a little on the elderly side to be playing the young father (Lake was fifty-two at the time); Pamela Britton played the irrepressible Blondie. A Daisy descendant was on hand, too, of course. The series was not a success and only lasted a season on NBC.

In 1968 *Blondie* was once more revived as a television series, this time with former *Sugarfoot* Western star Will Hutchins playing Dagwood and Patricia Harty as Blondie. Again the series failed as a television entry, lasting only five months on the CBS air. By this time the proliferation of "Father is a Dummy" situation-comedy series had saturated the home screens and *Blondie* was, unfortunately, just another rehash off the same old plate. Not even the prankish scene stealing of the newest Daisy could spark the fun and foolishness of the original *Blondie* film series.

Blondie (Penny Singleton), Baby Dumpling (Larry Simms), Daisy and Dagwood (Arthur Lake) are seen here during a troubled moment in one of the early *Blondie* films.

Daisy and Blondie have just jumped to safety — probably from a rampaging mouse!

The last *Blondie* television cast: Will Hutchins and Patricia Harty are pictured here with Peter Robins (with Daisy) and Pamelyn Ferdin.

Rusty

Flame, one of the top dog performers of the 1940s and early '50s, played Rusty in the popular Columbia Pictures' series.

During the mid-1940s a talented German shepherd by the name of Flame began to be noticed by movie audiences because of its appearances in a variety of films. The longest-running series in which the dog appeared was the *Rusty* films made by Columbia Pictures between 1945 and 1949. During those same years, however, Flame played a dog named Shep in two films made by Screen Guild—*My Dog Shep* in 1947 and *Shep Comes Home* in 1948. Flame was also featured in *Northwest Stampede* (Eagle Lion) and *Night Wind* (20th Century-Fox) in 1948. One of Flame's most important roles came in 1951 in *You Never Can Tell* (Universal). In the picture Dick Powell played the dog's alter ego in a reincarnation situation in which the murdered Flame reappeared on earth as Powell to seek out his murderer. The whimsical tale was an especially fine showcase for Flame's talents.

Rusty (Flame) and Danny (Ted Donaldson), the two stars of the *Rusty* film series.

But let's return to Flame's main film series, the *Rusty* films, in which the German shepherd was co-starred with young actor, Ted Donaldson. There were eight Rusty films produced in the low-budget series. The films were undistinguished but, nevertheless, very pleasant, sentimental dog-and-boy stories that were very appealing to juvenile audiences. They could be compared conceptually with the later "Timmy and Lassie" television series, although Donaldson's character was several years older than Timmy. There was never very much action in the *Rusty* films, and nothing very earthshaking happened, but they made for a pleasant hour or so at the movies during the late 1940s. The eight Rusty films were:

The Adventures of Rusty (1945, in which Ace "The Wonder Dog" played Rusty)
The Return of Rusty (1946)
For the Love of Rusty (1947)
Son of Rusty (1947)
My Dog Rusty (1948)
Rusty Leads the Way (1948)
Rusty Saves a Life (1949)
Rusty's Birthday (1949).

Ted Donaldson played Rusty's master, Danny Mitchell, throughout the series. Danny's father was first played by Conrad Nagel. In succeeding episodes John Litel and Tom Powers essayed the role—causing some father-figure confusion among steady followers of the series. Ann Doran was Danny's mother throughout, except for the first film in which Margaret Lindsay played Danny's stepmother (Don't try to figure it out; they obviously hadn't planned the series very far in advance.)

Ted Donaldson is now in his late forties. He is not married and has no children. He lives in Los Angeles; has a "private income"; acts a little, but has not done so professionally for years. From time to time he has taken occasional jobs—"in casting departments and, sometimes, bookstores—so forth, but I try to reserve time for my writing which is mainly writing for the theatre and poetry." Ted told me all of this when I talked with him about his *Rusty* films.

David Rothel: Was the *Rusty* series based on a novel or was it an original screenplay?

Ted Donaldson: I think it was an original screenplay. It seems to me the series was originated with me in mind because I was under contract to Columbia at the time. They wanted something for me to be in on a regular basis. Even though I was only under contract to Columbia for two years, I, nevertheless, made all of the *Rusty* films.

David Rothel: Do you feel the series was inspired by the success of Lassie?

Ted Donaldson: Oh, I'm sure it must have been. However, the *Rusty*'s were never on the scale of the Lassie movies. While the Lassie movies might not have been considered A pictures by MGM, at Columbia they would have been A movies. I make this distinction between the Lassie and Rusty pictures: Lassie movies were first-run, main features; the *Rusty*'s never were. The *Rusty*'s were always second features on a double-feature bill.

David Rothel: In the first film, *The Adventures of Rusty,* Ace "The Wonder Dog," as he was billed, played Rusty.

Ted Donaldson: It has been about thirty-five years since I made that first film, but it seems to me that I didn't get along too well with Ace. As I remember it, he snapped at me the first time I ever met him. After Ace came Flame, who did all the other films. Flame was simply marvelous. Flame was just a beautiful animal, both physically and in his nature; he was just so affectionate, so sweet. I didn't see him for about two years one time and the moment I saw him, he was all over me as if he recognized me as a long-lost friend. He was just a beautiful animal and fabulous to work with. Frank Barnes was the trainer of Flame. He was very gentle, but very firm with the animal. There was obviously great affection and love between him and the dog—that was very, very clear; he was a sweet man. I think Flame was one of his favorite animals. I've never had a dog myself, but in a sense, of course, I did with Flame. During the time we made the series, I really began to feel that he was mine.

David Rothel: Did the dog work from hand or voice signals, or both?

Ted Donaldson: Most, as I remember, were hand signals. Also, it seemed that the dog simply knew what he was supposed to do. Of course, the trainer was always right by the camera whenever anything was being shot.

I can only remember the plots of the first *Rusty* film and the third one; the others are a total blur—they all kind of merge, one into the other. The third *Rusty* was by far the best—*For the Love of Rusty*. It was directed by John Sturges. He had the best script to work with—the kid runs away from home after a misunderstanding with his dad and meets an old man who's camping in the woods. Aubrey Mather, a charming old chap and a fine character actor, played the part of an old traveling veterinarian. Rusty and the vet help to bring Danny and his father together again. It was a nice little script and Sturges, who was very young at the time—late twenties, I would guess—had not directed very much. Here he was making a film that was on a two-week budget and he's taking as much time and devoting as much attention and care to the scenes as he, obviously, later did with his big films. [Films such as *Bad Day at Black Rock, The Old Man and the Sea, The Great Escape* and *Ice Station Zebra*.] Around the twelfth or thirteenth day, maybe earlier than that, calls began to come down from the head office wanting to know why in the hell he was behind schedule on this *Rusty* film. He was two or three days behind schedule because of the care that he was taking. The calls came every day and he'd have to stop and go to the set phone. We'd hear him say, "You gave me this assignment and that means that I'm going to do the best possible job I can do with it. If I come in over [budget], I come in over. If you don't want me to continue with it, pull me off it." It was really remarkable. He brought the film in, finally, in seventeen or eighteen days. The result was, by far and away, the best *Rusty* film in the series and he had great respect and admiration from every member of that cast and crew. He was the talk of the set because he cared enough about the script and about the actors to really work with them, and he resisted the front-office pressure. If you ever get a chance, see *For the Love of Rusty*. It's the best one we ever did.

Danny, running away from home with Rusty, stops to visit with a kindly old itinerant veterinarian (Aubrey Mather) who's camping in the woods. *For the Love of Rusty* (1947).

Yukon King

In the late 1940s kids all over the United States began to fine tune their radios to a popular new ABC network program called *The Challenge of the Yukon*. The program's main characters were Sergeant Preston and his malámute dog, Yukon King. The characters became so popular that the original title of the program got lost to many kids who simply called the show "Sergeant Preston" or "Yukon King." Eventually the producer, George W. Trendle, changed the name of the program to *Sergeant Preston of the Yukon*.

Soon the young listeners were reciting the stock program opening with the announcer. It went in part:

*Yukon King: Barks
Announcer: (over wind sound) It's Yukon King, swiftest and strongest lead dog in the Northwest, blazing the trail for Sergeant Preston of the Northwest Mounted Police, in his relentless pursuit of lawbreakers.
Preston: On King! On, you huskies!
Announcer: Gold? Gold, discovered in the Yukon! A stampede to the Klondike in the wild race for riches! Back to the days of the gold rush, with Quaker Puffed Wheat and Quaker Puffed Rice bringing you the adventures of Sergeant Preston and his wonder dog Yukon King, as they meet the Challenge of the Yukon.
Theme up: "Donna Diana Overture."
*©Lone Ranger Television, Inc.

And we were off on another thrilling adventure in the frozen North country during the days of the gold rush.

Radio actor Paul Sutton played the Mountie for much of the long network radio run—1947 through 1955. Other actors who played the role on radio included Jay Michael and Brace Beemer. Beemer, who was the most famous radio Lone Ranger, played the role of Sergeant Preston during the last year it was on the air, *The Lone Ranger* series having been cancelled in 1954.

The Challenge of the Yukon was the third big, hit program for producer George W. Trendle, the first two being *The Lone Ranger* and *The Green Hornet*. All three programs were produced in and broadcast from WXYZ radio in Detroit, considered the extreme hinterlands by most network broadcasters. Although *The Challenge of the Yukon* never reached the level of popularity of its two predecessors, it was, nevertheless, a very successful show-business property that made the transition from radio to television with little difficulty. Seventy-eight half-hour color

Yukon King

Photo courtesy of Lone Ranger Television, Inc.

Sergeant Preston (Richard Simmons) and Yukon King are ever on the alert for danger in these two scenes from the television version of *Sergeant Preston of the Yukon*. Photos courtesy of Lone Ranger Television, Inc.

Yukon King

television episodes of *Sergeant Preston of the Yukon* were produced between 1955 and 1958 on location at Aspen, Colorado, and Big Bear Lake and Hollywood, California.

Charles D. Livingstone, now retired and a fellow Floridian, was the producer of the radio series for many years and, later, directed several episodes of the *Sergeant Preston of the Yukon* television series. I drove over to Chuck's Longboat Key home to talk with him about the famous Mountie and his malámute.

David Rothel: I listened to *Sergeant Preston of the Yukon* when I was a youngster and I thought it was great, but I never realized then—or at least I don't remember that I realized—that the sounds of Yukon King were made by a man and not a dog. Why was that?

Charles Livingstone: Because he made better sounds of a dog for radio than any dog ever could. That was Ted Johnstone. Ted was terrific! He could do any dog sound so you'd swear it was the real thing!

David Rothel: Did you ever use real dog sounds on the program?

Charles Livingstone: Yes, for background sounds of the team. But for King, it was Ted Johnstone. People used to write in about that wonderful dog (laugh). I don't know if they ever knew about the man playing King.

David Rothel: You went on, years later, to direct some episodes of the television series.

Charles Livingstone: Yes, that was quite an experience. I didn't do too many of those shows, but I did do some. I remember I had quite a time with one show in which there was a team of huskies, King and a little dog which belonged to a little boy in the story. Now if you know anything about directing shows, you know that animals and children are things you don't like to get mixed up with. There I was with a team, King, a little dog and a little boy. I don't know how I ever got through that one. You know, much of the series was shot on studio sets which were designed to look like outdoor sets—exteriors of cabins, trees and fake snow. I remember an early scene in the series called for the entire team of huskies to be lying out in the snow in front of Preston's cabin. All of a sudden, one after another of the dogs started to get sick. We watched them to see what was wrong and discovered that they were eating the white sand, thinking it was snow—the sand that was supposed to look like snow on the studio set. The dogs were eating it, poor things.

David Rothel: Richard Simmons played Sergeant Preston in the television series.

Charles Livingstone: Great guy! He was an excellent actor with a good voice. He was always very helpful, not the least temperamental, very cooperative. He's now retired from acting and lives in Carlsbad, California, where he manages a mobile-home park with his wife.

The athletic Richard Simmons discovered that the television series held more challenges than just those of the Yukon—like driving a team of huskies. "A harnessed team is a quivering mass of supercharged energy," Simmons explained to a reporter on the set of the series. "But they're trained not to move until they receive a verbal command. Consequently, 'All right,' 'Ready,' 'Let's go,' or 'Action' is forbidden language when working around the dogs. If you make a slip, they're off like rockets."

To prevent premature starts, Simmons and handlers devised a code to outsmart the huskies. "When everything is ready for the sleds to move," Simmons continued, "we use the number thirteen. We use this number because in the years these dogs have been trained as a team, they've learned all the numbers through twelve, which were used earlier as ready signals. I never thought I would have to brush up my arithmetic to keep one step ahead of a pack of dogs."

Simmons also had to learn a new language to drive the dogs. "Boodle-dehooey" means "Let's keep moving." When Sergeant Preston wants a faster pace, he yodels "biddle . . . biddle . . . biddle" rapidly. "Mush," the popular conception of the starting signal, is seldom used according to Simmons. Sergeant Preston barks out "Hite, hite, hite," a contraction of "all right."

Yukon King would occasionally show some star temperament on the set. When the pressure of shooting became too great, the giant malámute would simply lie down and refuse to continue until the hubbub of set activity subsided. "He had more sense than a lot of people," commented Dick Simmons. After a long day of filming, King's trainer, Beverly Allen, often relaxed the dog by turning on an old phonograph. Music, apparently, soothed the not-so-savage beast.

Yukon King and his Mountie master always got their man — in all seventy-eight television episodes. Photo courtesy of Lone Ranger Television, Inc.

4

The Gentle Giants

Gentle Giant, a feature film, marked the first starring screen appearance of the bear, Gentle Ben. Young Clint Howard played the bear's master; Dennis Weaver was the boy's father, an Everglades' game warden in the picture. The bear's delightful performances in the movie and *Gentle Ben* television series resulted in dual PATSY awards.

Gentle Ben

In the 1960s Ivan Tors had the magic touch when it came to producing successful animal series for movie and network television screens. *Flipper* started it all, first as two MGM features and then with a three-year run on NBC. *Daktari* was a natural jungle-setting follow-up, again first as a feature called *Clarence the Cross-Eyed Lion* and then as the television series call *Daktari*.

By then it was the late 1960s and Ivan was looking for a new animal series to spring on eager viewers. Using the feature-to-series formula that had worked so well before, he took a little-known novel by Walt Morey about a gentle, easygoing bear and a young boy, and transposed the more northern setting to the Florida Everglades near where the Ivan Tors Studio just happened to be located.

The movie, called *Gentle Giant,* was a gentle affair in more ways than just in the description of the burly bear named Ben. Howard Thompson, reviewing for the *New York Times*, was typical of the picture's critics when he welcomed the bear to New York and acknowledged that in those perilous times of the late '60s "maybe the world needs more tame bears and seven-year-old boys who love them."

Thompson was also able to find pleasure in what was later to become a common critical gripe of many adventure-seeking, puberty-and-beyond humans who watched the movie and/or television series. Thompson found it appealing that, "with a singular lack of guile or real excitement the picture simply sticks close to its little hero, a snaggle-toothed towhead, as he raises his furry pet to full bruinhood." Thompson liked what he called "a tangy-spirited tameness" that permeated the film. "Ben, the bear," he rhapsodized, "is a pretty wonderful old critter. And the child, Clint Howard, couldn't be more unstudied or appealing, even when saying, 'I must be the only kid in the world with a bear for a friend.'"

Gentle Giant wasn't the bear's first show business appearance. Ben was first cast in the Ivan Tors feature film, *Zebra in the Kitchen*, and had been a guest star in episodes of the Tors television series, *Daktari*.

The *Gentle Giant* movie served as an introduction to the Florida Everglades locale and to the characters that would become weekly guests on television just a few months after the release of the feature. The story concerns seven-year-old Mark Wedloe (Clint Howard) who befriends a bear cub whose mother has been shot by drunken hunter and general no-good, Fog Hanson (Ralph Meeker). Fog keeps the cub penned up, but unbeknownst to him, Mark sneaks in each day and becomes fast friends with the rapidly maturing bruin.

Clint Howard and his gentle pal, Ben.

Finally, months later, Fog reveals he's going to kill the now fully grown bear and sell the meat. Panic-stricken, little Mark bear-naps Ben and together they take off into the Florida wilderness. Eventually Mark's distraught parents (played in the movie by Vera Miles and Dennis Weaver) find the boy and his bear, realize the love that exists between the unlikely pair, and, after some unpleasant business with the bully Fog Hanson, they buy the bear. The fact that Mark's father has taken the position of game warden in the Florida Everglades helps to make the whole situation seem perfectly natural.

This basic family-living-in-the-Everglades-with-bear situation was the springboard for the weekly television episodes that began on CBS on September 10, 1967, and lasted until August 31, of 1969—fifty-six half-hour episodes in all. If you saw one, you knew just about what to expect each week. Critic Cleveland Amory, a longtime animal lover and vocal supporter of humane treatment for all animals, *wanted* to like the series, but even he (writing in *TV Guide*) said that the people responsible for the series "must be criticized—not for their humane shortcomings (they have virtually none) but for their *human* ones. Even admitting that these programs are produced for children, there is no excuse for the prevalence of scripts that would bore a baby."

Ivan Tors was no fool, of course, and was just following a formula that had led him to success, fame and wealth. After all, *Flipper* and *Daktari* also suffered from anemic scripts and mild action, but they were fantastically popular with the small fry and, to a slightly lesser degree, with the old folks. Young parents, although very likely longing for more exciting fare for themselves, would happily tolerate the innocuous weekly episodes of *Gentle Ben* because their kids loved them so.

The series had two basic things going for it: an appealing human cast and the fascination of having a 650-pound bear placed in juxtaposition with the human cast—especially with the little tyke, Clint Howard.

Ben really didn't do a great deal on the program—compared to other animal stars who would constantly perform tricks—or at least do cute things. Ben was just there with the boy, lumbering along and being pleasant. As Ricou Browning, the director of some of the episodes recounted, "Gentle Ben was a big puppy dog, just a tame puppy dog. He wasn't well-trained; he was just tame. It was difficult filming him because he wasn't well-trained. We had other bears, some trained better than him, that we used as doubles and backups, and also for stunts and tricks. One was larger and another was smaller, but when you had the animals away from people, isolated, you couldn't really tell the difference. Gentle Ben's main capacity in the show was to work with the boy and to be friendly and nice."

While many of Ben's television episodes were rather mild in the action department, Ben's real-life experiences prior to the series would have made a rip-roaring adventure. Ben and his brother Smokey were orphaned when they were cubs in White Lake, Wisconsin, and were about half grown when they were brought to the original Africa, USA, the wild animal "affection training" ranch in Soledad Canyon near Los Angeles. (This ranch was destroyed in floods during January and February of 1969.) Young Ben was tethered in an open pen outside the dining hall. He took to affection the same way he took to sweets fed to him by ranch employees and film workers as they returned to jobs from lunch.

Ben's regular diet, by the way, consisted of five loaves of bread, some bunches of carrots, two and a half pounds of a packaged "chow," half a dozen apples and oranges, Bucatone (a fatty acid for his coat), Vionate powder, and supplementary vitamins and minerals. All of this, of course, was in addition to whatever he could mooch from passing humans who would delight in "feeding the bear." Cokes, Life Savers, donuts—just about anything edible would please ole Ben.

Ben, with his love-and-kisses disposition, seemed to lead a charmed life. Three times in a little more than three years he escaped potential disaster. In December 1965, a dam broke above Africa, USA, sending a torrent of water down the canyon. Before rescuers could get to Ben, his cage was washed away. It was hoped that the cage would be broken against boulders, freeing Ben to swim to safety—his one chance for survival. An all-points alarm went out urging anyone who saw a tame bear loose to please give Ben a soft drink and call the ranch. Ben was not heard from for three days. Then a trainer found him sitting wet and hungry on the spot where his cage had been.

Father Rance Howard, Clint, Beth Brickell and Dennis Weaver on the set for *Gentle Ben*.

In July 1966, a work car on the Southern Pacific track bordering the ranch broke loose and jumped the track, demolishing several cages, including Ben's. Happily, Ben's cage was vacant. The previous day he had been sent by animal-transport to the Ivan Tors Studios in Florida to become acclimated before beginning work in *Gentle Giant*. And, finally, while storm and flood conditions were devastating the wild-animal ranch in Soledad Canyon in 1969, Ben was safe at Homosassa Springs, Florida, by then his permanent home.

Ben's little friend, Clint Howard, was a lad of only seven years when they met up for *Gentle Giant*. Clint was born in Burbank, California, on April 20, 1959. Older Brother, Ronnie, was already acting on television at the time of Clint's birth. As a matter of fact, Ronnie was playing a character by the name of Clinton at the time. Jean and Rance Howard, their parents decided they liked the character's name so well that they tagged their newborn with it.

Clint's first show-business appearance was at two years of age when he played a role with his brother on the *Andy Griffith Show,* a television series in which brother Ronnie co-starred as Opie. Next came a small role in the MGM feature, *The Courtship of Eddie's Father* (later to be a popular television series). Again, big brother Ronnie was the main youngster in the movie (Brandon Cruz later played the role in the television series). By the time Clint was an old man of four years of age, he had signed for a continuing role in *The Bailey's of Balboa* television series, a short-lived CBS series of the 1964-65 season. Clint played the tiny fisherman who constantly bests the skipper, played by crotchety old Paul Ford.

One of young Clint's most memorable performances was in a *Star Trek* episode where he played an alien adult named Balok, who in our culture appeared to be a child, but was in reality the eerie adult commander of a gigantic space vehicle. Then the call came from Ivan Tors for *Gentle Giant*.

Tiny Clint immediately took to his 650-pound co-star, Ben the bear. "He's as gentle as my cat Mitts," Clint exclaimed. "It doesn't matter how big he is; I'm not afraid of him and he's not afraid of me."

Director Ricou Browning remembered the two of them together on the set of the television series: "A number of times Ben accidently stepped on Clint's foot; you know, a 650-pound bear stepping on your foot can hurt a little. Tears would come into Clint's eyes, but he was a rugged little boy; he managed well. Clint was one of the finest child actors I ever worked with. He isn't as active now acting-wise as he used to be. I think at this point he's in a period where he's interested in other things. His older brother, Ronnie, has been in *Happy Days* and has directed a feature that he and his father wrote. I believe Clint played a role in the picture. His dad, Rance, and I are very close friends. We talk on the phone maybe once a month. His family is the nicest family, nicest people, you'll ever meet. They're really super."

Clint's film father for the *Ben* feature and television series was Emmy award-winning actor Dennis Weaver, who in the early 1960s had entered an awkward phase of his acting career. For several years he had co-starred on the fantastically popular Western television series, *Gunsmoke,* as the gimpy character, Chester, the role for which he won the coveted Emmy. But eventually a fear gripped the young actor that if he didn't leave this highly popular character part, he would be forever typecast in the role and never develop further as an actor.

Finally, after ten years as Chester and much soul-searching, Weaver announced that he was going to leave *Gunsmoke* to strike out into new acting opportunities. Strike out is exactly what happened when Dennis Weaver starred in his own television series, *Kentucky Jones*. After twenty-six mediocre episodes on NBC during the 1964-65 season, the series was shelved. And many people (probably Weaver himself) wondered if his decision to leave *Gunsmoke* had been a wise one.

"I wanted to grow as an actor, to create, to expand, Weaver commented. "Quitting *Gunsmoke* was the biggest decision I had to make in my life. From the standpoint of money and security it could not be beat. But money is a drag if you let it become an end instead of a means. In addition, I just couldn't make one character my whole life's work."

Ben the bear and his young master Mark Wedlow (Clint Howard) on location for the *Gentle Ben* television series.

Dennis Weaver and Ben are seen here roughhousing — but gently — on the *Gentle Ben* set.

Time passed as Weaver guested on many popular series and, occasionally, acted in a movie. In 1967 when Ivan Tors approached him about the *Gentle Giant* feature, Weaver's career was languishing. Although he was aware of the dangers of being obscured on the screen by a child and an animal, Dennis felt the role might help to break the "Chester" image that was still clinging to him. His role of Ranger Tom Wedloe was rather blandly written and seemed unlikely to type him for further roles when the series ended. Also, the role would combine the qualities of a warm fatherly image along with occasional moments of action/adventure that might lead to a variety of future roles.

Anyway, for all those reasons and more, Dennis Weaver became father/Ranger Tom Wedloe in the feature and television series. And despite the competition from Ben and the boy, Weaver showed his stuff as an actor of considerable depth and ability—to such an extent did he match his competition on the program, that several critics praised Weaver as the guiding force in the series' success. Curmudgeon critic Cleveland Amory grew almost euphoric when it came to Mr. Weaver:

> *Gentle Ben* has something going for it that somehow makes it almost immune to them [the program's faults]. This is the remarkable believability brought to the program each week by Dennis Weaver. Mr. Weaver . . . is equally convincing whether patting the backside of his wife or that of his (and his son Mark's) 10-foot [sic] black bear. And he is positively dashing as he makes waves in the most fascinating airboat we've seen since Howard Hughes gave up on his *Spruce Goose*. Furthermore, Mr. Weaver is so good that you feel he is a benign influence on his son, who would be, without Weaver, too cute even for our words.

Vera Miles played the all-but-thankless role of the wife/mother in the feature *Gentle Giant*. This very talented actress wisely saw that she could only come in last in a field of three humans and a bear, so she left the Everglades after the feature. A blue-eyed Texas gal by the name of Beth Brickell gamely rushed in where Vera feared to tread.

A serious student of the theatre (Beth had been accepted and studied at the famous Actor's Studio in New York), she nonetheless put on a happy face when questioned in interviews about her vacuous role in the *Gentle Ben* series. "The stories about a boy and a bear and a game warden are limited," she would acknowledge, but "the mother adds both dimension and diversion. There's no need to be wishy-washy, always washing dishes or baking a cake. I see the role as a chance to present the best things we have in this country. For example, just because this woman is a game warden's wife living in the country doesn't mean she's a frump. She can read the magazines, know fashions, and even run up a few things on a sewing machine. I see it as an all-American family in unusual circumstances and it provides the wife an opportunity to become involved in unlimited situations."

All the comments from the young actress were very appropriate and professional, but the bottom line was that the role never became more than a stock mother/wife role with little dimension. To quote critic Cleveland Amory once again, "[Beth Brickell] has so little to do her part is silly." It should be added, however, that Ms. Brickell did the best she could with what the writers provided. The character just didn't figure importantly enough in the *Gentle Ben* series to stand out. According to one report, Beth saw the series as a springboard to stardom. It was reported that she rankled some of the *Gentle Ben* people when she hired her own press agent.

Dennis Weaver, Clint Howard and Beth Brickell, the human stars of *Gentle Ben*.

Working on the series was quite often a tedious affair. Just trying to get the bear's scenes in the can could be an excruciating, time-consuming ordeal. The Florida heat would often make Ben extremely drowsy and occasionally hard to motivate in a scene. Once as the bear ambled languidly through a scene slightly wrong for about the eighth time in a row, a crewman was heard to grouse, "We'll get this shot by six o'clock if it takes till midnight."

Murry Wood, Clint Howard's sixty-year-old midget stand-in would pass the time playing a game with Ben—allowing the bear to steal cigarettes from his mouth. Monty Cox, Ben's chief trainer, had to look after his ward and try to have him prepared for frequently impatient directors. Once, when a scene called for Ben to not eat his food, Monty stuffed him with twelve loaves of bread, ten apples, ten oranges, ten carrots and a gallon of milk in preparation. But the strategy didn't work. "Every time we started to shoot," Monty recalled, "he'd eat again. So we put cold cream on the food and Chanel No. 5—everything on the set labeled nontoxic. Just to discourage him. But he still ate it. He smelled good for quite a while."

Producer Ivan Tors and his star, Gentle Ben.

Keeping Ben in a happy mood was also one of Monty Cox's chief concerns. When Ben would sink into a moody blue funk, Monty would take him home to his Miami apartment a few miles from the studio. There they would eat, shower and sleep together—providing Ben with companionship, attention and (most of all) affection. As Monty put it, "If he doesn't get affection, he comes to a slitherin' halt. I hop in the shower and Ben hops in beside me. He'll get all wet and soapy and then crawl in bed with me. If he'd sleep on his own side, it'd be OK."

Ben's real name was Bruno. His main stand-in was a bear named Buck. If Ben got out of sorts for a time, Buck would be hustled in to cover until the big fellow was happy again. Monty, Ben's trainer, was always very sensitive about comments that a bear was a dangerous animal that could not be trusted. Monty would not accept this possibility regarding Ben. Director Ricou Browning acknowledges that Ben was a gentle soul, but insists that one must always be alert where bears and other such animals are concerned. "I learned one thing quickly about bears," Ricou noted. "If a bear gets aggravated when you're trying to get him to do something and he hits at you, don't hit back at him. It's the biggest mistake you can ever make. A bear will fight you until he's dead. I mean, he's not going to quit."

Working day in and day out on location with several huge black bears, it was only natural that eventually something untoward was bound to happen. Ricou recalls, "I'll never forget the day one of our Gentle Ben bears got excited over something we were doing and took off to the woods down here in south Miami. We all went after him with lassoes, but nobody could find him—a 650-pound black bear running loose in Miami. What we were mainly afraid of was that somebody would see him, bring out a gun and shoot him. Finally it got dark and we still hadn't found him. We kept cars on major roads surrounding the area during the night and let the police know. We had everybody that we could alert, alerted. The night passed with no incident and the next day we continued to look for the bear and still couldn't find him. On the third day a little girl was riding her bike on one of the bicycle trails they have down there and rode up to our bear. She had her lunch basket with her, so she shared lunch with the bear and then let us know that she'd found our bear. Why the little girl wasn't frightened to death, I don't know."

Producer Ivan Tors was not a bit amazed by the outcome of the modern-day "Goldilocks and the Bear" story. A pioneer in affection training for wild animals, Tors calmly explained, "Humans have only given Ben good experiences so Ben only gives good experiences in return."

Ben is seen here spending a few quiet moments between scenes on the location for one of the *Gentle Ben* episodes.

Ben and Grizzly Adams

The other Ben the bear is really a female named Bozo and is a grizzly, considered by many trainers to be the most ferocious and untameable of all animals. Not so with this grizzly who shared the television screen with animal trainer/actor Dan Haggerty from February 9, 1977, until July 26, 1978, in the series, *The Life and Times of Grizzly Adams.*

Set in the American West of the late 1800s, the NBC series was loosely based on the story of a mountain man by the name of James Capen Adams. During the days of the 1849 gold rush, Adams was known to stroll into the town of San Francisco with two unleashed grizzly bears at his sides—hence his nickname. Apparently a born wilderness wanderer, Adams made his home in the Sierra Nevadas, living on game, fish and berries.

The Grizzly Adams of the television adaptation is the story of a man in exile. Accused of a crime he didn't commit, he seeks refuge in the wilderness and becomes a friend and guardian to all the denizens of the woods, sharing their home with them. Adams learns the ways of the wilderness and decides to forsake civilization and to live his life in harmony with the animals and nature.

The television series was filmed in the great outdoors of Wasatch National Forest near Park City, Utah, and at Payson, Arizona, by Sunn Classics Pictures, an otherwise undistinguished independent production company which earlier in the 1970s produced such low-budget, exploitation "classics" as *Chariot of the Gods, The Outer-Space Connection* and *The Lincoln Conspiracy* and then forced them on a gullible, publicity-saturated (via mass regional and local television ads) public.

Sunn Classics' shining glory was the unpretentious feature, *The Life and Times of Grizzly Adams,* which grossed between twenty-four and sixty-five million dollars—depending on whose press release you believe. Regardless, the sentimental, gentle story of a man's love affair with nature and its animals struck a chord with two large segments of the population—the very young and the elderly. NBC bought the television rights and, much to its surprise, got a very respectable rating with the feature. Based upon the viewers' favorable acceptance of the feature, NBC ordered production on a one-hour series.

Before *Grizzly Adams* came along, Dan Haggerty was an animal trainer/handler who occasionally did bit parts on screen to help control the animals in his charge. Pat Frawley of Sunn Classics spotted the burly, blond-haired trainer while viewing some daily rushes for *When the North Wind Blows*, a feature Sunn Classics

Bozo (known as Ben on the series) and his friend Dan Haggerty.

was shooting in Calgary, Canada. Frawley was immediately taken with the rugged good looks of Haggerty ("He's got great screen presence.") and decided to star him in their upcoming feature, *The Life and Times of Grizzly Adams,* for which Haggerty was paid the munificent sum of five thousand dollars. The rest, as they say, is history.

Bozo, the grizzly bear co-star with Haggerty, was nine years old when the series went into production. The bear is owned by Lloyd Beebe, a well-known "animal impresario" who runs an animal compound in Sequim, Washington. Beebe found Bozo working in a circus but could uncover no previous background on the animal. Based upon her amazing affection for humans—at least some humans—it can be easily deduced that she was raised as a pet from infancy. There is no known previous grizzly that has performed with humans without some sort of restraint—except, perhaps, the original Grizzly Adams' bears and they weren't really performers. Bozo was only put on a leash when she finished a scene before the camera. Her four doubles, however, had to have their movements controlled by charged electrical wires during filming of the series.

Bozo was especially affectionate to her co-star, Dan Haggerty; some on the set claimed the bear was absolutely in love with the former trainer. Bill Davidson, writing in *TV Guide,* reported on Bozo's frolicking with Haggerty: "Who can forget the memorable scene in which Bozo awakened Haggerty by pulling the blanket from his bed, then chased him coquettishly through a meadow, then allowed Haggerty to chase her—equally coquettishly—and finally rolled over on her back in the grass to allow Haggerty to scratch her belly."

Bozo seemed to take all of the attention and activity in stride during the filming of the series, although she did put on over a hundred pounds during the production schedule. This weight increase came about because she was rewarded with marshmallows or other treats every time she performed accurately for the camera. Sometimes she didn't want to quit performing even when the scene was shot to the director's satisfaction. During one scene Bozo was to pick up a stick and walk along beside Haggerty. For one reason or another, the director repeated the scene several times. Each time Bozo got her treat. Finally, when the director had his shot and called, "Cut," Bozo wanted to do it again for her treat. It took very gentle persuasion by the trainer to change Bozo's mind.

Eight trainers worked on *The Life and Times of Grizzly Adams* to keep the more than sixty different animals used in the series in check. There were birds, beavers, bobcats, chipmunks, skunks, a burro—you name it! If it was an animal indigenous to the American West, it was sooner or later seen on the program.

Many of the animals on the series were taught to perform to the sound of a buzzer. As Haggerty explained to reporter Davidson, "With a small animal like a bobcat, you can teach him a certain trick like knocking over a pot, and he learns that when he does it on cue—the sound of a buzzer—he gets rewarded with food." This technique was used often on the series.

Generally, not a whole lot happened in a *Grizzly Adams* episode. Through a survey technique carefully computerized by Sunn Classics, it was determined that viewers of the program only wanted the thread of a storyline carried through the hour with a plentiful supply of waterfalls, pretty vistas, high mountain ridges—all preferably viewed with actors and non-violent animals as part of the scene. Snow was determined to be only appropriate at Christmas; otherwise, summertime ruled supreme.

Young Frank Martinez is seen here in a tender scene with Ben during a *Grizzly Adams* episode.

Haggerty occasionally complained that the program needed "more growth, more pizazz." He suggested that there might even be a love interest introduced that would go beyond Bozo and him. The Sunn Classics' computer would have none of it. The survey print-out indicated that audiences didn't want women in the wilderness; so it was a celibate existence for Grizzly Adams. Haggerty wasn't all that unhappy, though. "I think the response to *Grizzly Adams* shows something very important," he commented. "I think it shows that people like blue skies and animals and simple things that are clean and honest. When you watch *Grizzly Adams*, you don't have to figure out some exotic plot."

Unfortunately, by the time the series had been on NBC for only a year and a half, viewers grew restless and left Grizzly Adams and Ben the bear to their wilderness home and sought the suburban adventures of the *Eight is Enough* family, the new ABC network competition. I wonder what the Sunn Classics computer thought of that?

5
Daktari

It's time to primp for the television camera. Clarence the cross-eyed lion and Judy the chimp prepare for a scene in the *Daktari* television series.

Back in the early 1960s, Ralph Helfer and Ivan Tors became partners in an "affection training" animal compound called Africa, USA, located in Soledad Canyon some sixty miles above Los Angeles. There, in a simulated jungle setting more than three hundred African and Asian wild animals—really, animals from all over the world—lived uncaged and free to roam about almost at will. Africa, USA initiated a totally new concept in wild-animal training that, hopefully, replaced forever the whip-and-chair fear method. An important aspect of Ivan Tors' affection training included human contact with each of the animals every day—touching and petting by the trainers to show affection. "I feel," Tors stated, "it's really a physiological process." Helfer concurred and stated, "If an animal has only fear of you, you can only go so far with him."

One day Helfer introduced Tors to a new addition to Africa, USA, a young lion cub named Freddie who had a most peculiar affliction—he was cross-eyed. Helfer suggested to his partner that they give the cub away. Tors, a lifelong animal lover plus a shrewd show-business entrepreneur, shook his head and said, "No, Ralph, I've never seen a cross-eyed lion and neither has the rest of the world. I made Flipper famous and I'll make Clarence famous." Tors had already decided that Clarence was a funnier name for the cub and, Tors added, "He *is* a funny lion."

In 1965 Clarence was introduced to the world as the star of an MGM-Ivan Tors motion picture entitled, appropriately enough, *Clarence the Cross-eyed Lion*. The lion was an immediate hit with millions of moppets and their parents. As with other Ivan Tors productions, the plot for the picture was simple, the humans in the cast were stereotypes, and the animals cute and up to their furry ears in humorous shenanigans.

The film, shot in Africa, USA, concerned animal research being conducted in East Africa by a so-called Wameru Study Center for Animal Behavior. Marshall Thompson led the human cast, portraying Marsh Tracy, the doctor in charge of the center. Cheryl Miller played his daughter, a teenager with an affinity for wild animals. Other prominent non-human roles were taken by Judy the chimp (who was eventually to become almost as popular as Clarence) and Mary Lou the snake.

Based upon the huge success of the feature film, MGM and Tors developed a television series on the same general format. The study center now became the Wameru Game Preserve and Research Center and the series was retitled *Daktari*, which means "doctor" in Swahili.

Marshall Thompson and Cheryl Miller were retained from the feature film as were the animal stars, Clarence the cross-eyed lion and Judy the chimp. Additional regular cast members in the television series included Hari Rhodes and Yale Summers as zoologists, and Hedley Mattingley as a district game warden.

Daktari, like all of the other Ivan Tors animals series, dealt with humans involved with animals that were normally considered wild. Here, however, they were gentle, non-violent creatures (unless provoked) meandering with humans through rubberband-like story lines that were stretched to an hour's length each week. Considerable credit is due to the animals and the human cast members that audience interest was sufficiently maintained to allow the series to survive three years on the CBS television network. Eighty-nine episodes were filmed between 1966 and 1969.

Clarence and actor Marshall Thompson.

The *Daktari* cast: Marshall Thompson, Judy the chimp, (back) Hari Rhodes, Hedley Mattingly, (kneeling) Cheryl Miller and Yale Summers. Clarence was off somewhere sleeping when the picture was snapped.

Clarence the cross-eyed lion and Judy the chimp were certainly the main kiddie attractions on the series. Tors, in his book, *My Life in the Wild*, described Clarence as "an unusual creature without any instinct of aggression. He was a lover, not a fighter. As he grew up, we lavished affection on him, and eventually he became one of the most beautiful full-maned lions I had ever set eyes on . . . his temperament was even and friendly. He was one of the few lions that tolerated children. Nor did he mind Judy, the chimp, sitting on his back or pulling his tail. . . . He was the Shirley Temple of the lion world."

On the *Daktari* series, Clarence's point of view would be shown in double vision. Tors, who had the lion's eyes checked periodically, maintained that the animal really did see double. One time when Clarence's vision was feared to be worsening, Tors consulted an eminent human-eye specialist. The diagnosis was that the condition was stable and that an operation would not improve the vision. Therefore, Clarence, who seemed content, was left to his double-visioned world.

Judy the chimp was, according to Tors, "a miracle." She would obey some seventy-five hand signals from trainer Frank Lamping. She soon learned filming techniques and realized the necessity for accurately duplicating physical actions when repeating master shots in medium close-ups and from different angles so that they matched in the editing process. Judy quickly learned the signal that indicated the lunch break and would return after lunch to the same scene and position that she had been in when the noon whistle had blown. She was ready to pick up the scene from where she had stopped.

Clarence and Judy were honored with PATSY awards, both for the feature *Clarence the Cross-eyed Lion* and for the popular *Daktari* television series. They became internationally famous when the series was sold to countries all over the world. Clarence and Judy were hits even in Russia where *Daktari* was the first American series to be shown.

Clarence and Judy

Judy the chimp smiles her approval for two new cast members of *Daktari* for the 1968-69 television season. Ross Hagen (standing, left) played a guide for camera safaris, and seven-year-old Erin Moran portrayed an orphan who became part of the Marsh Tracy family. Clarence was still off sleeping somewhere when the picture was taken.

6
Thundering Hoofbeats

Roy Rogers and Trigger, Jr.

A Visit with Glenn Randall, "One of America's Finest Horse Trainers"

I've never met horse trainer Glenn Randall in person; we only talked on the telephone for an hour or so, but I've met his kind several times in my dealings with horse people in recent years. They're a breed all their own—fiercely independent, tolerant (barely) of the ignorance of people unschooled in the ways of the horse, crusty, crafty and of few words when dealing with strangers. And I was a stranger on the other end of the line.

David Rothel: Did you grow up on a ranch?

Glenn Randall: Yes, I came from Nebraska. My people had a ranch there which was later divided up into farms.

David Rothel: How did you happen to get into the business of training horses?

Glenn Randall: Well, I don't know. My mother used to say I talked to horses. I've always loved horses. I've trained them all my life.

David Rothel: Have you trained other animals, too?

Glenn Randall: No. I know how, but I never took it on. I know how to train dogs and elephants, camels, but horses are my love.

David Rothel: I understand that you have a horse stable that supplies horses for films.

Glenn Randall: Yes, we have a motion picture rental stable, the largest in the world. We supply horses and other animals, wagons, what have you.

David Rothel: I know you've trained several well-known horses in films—Trigger, Rex Allen's Koko and Buttermilk, Dale Evans' horse. Are there some others I haven't mentioned?

Glenn Randall: I trained Autry's last horse.

David Rothel: Was it the Champion he used in the television series?

Glen Randall: Yes, it was the last horse he used.

David Rothel: In the old days of motion pictures were you under contract to a studio to supply and train horses?

Glenn Randall: No, no. I worked personally for Roy Rogers and then I free-lanced. I trained horses for whoever wanted to hire me, but Roy was my main source of income. I trained for him, but he would release me to train horses for other people.

David Rothel: Then you were under contract to Roy?

Glenn Randall: No, sir. Just word of mouth.

David Rothel: How did you happen to meet Roy Rogers?

Glenn Randall: I met him through Ace and Art Hudkins who owned a motion picture rental stable. They were from Nebraska, too. Ace was the "Nebraska

Wildcat Fighter." They came out here [California] and they established the rental stable. Then eventually I came out here, too. I'm originally from Nebraska, as I mentioned. So we made the acquaintance and they gave me my first start. Fact of the matter is that they're the men who introduced me to Roy. That was back near the beginning of his picture career.

David Rothel: Did you have anything to do with Roy selecting Trigger for his films?

Glenn Randall: No. Roy rented Trigger from Hudkins or the studio rented the horse, I'm not sure which.

David Rothel: When did you start training Trigger?

Glenn Randall: Well, Roy had started making his pictures quite a while before. I started training Trigger the same year as the attack on Pearl Harbor, whenever that was.

David Rothel: 1941.

Glenn Randall: Right! I induced Roy to buy the horse; I bought him for Roy after he employed me.

David Rothel: You bought the horse for Roy? How did that work? I don't quite follow.

Glenn Randall: Well, they were renting the horse and I said, "Roy, why don't you own him?" He said, "Fine, go buy him."

David Rothel: I see. You were sort of the middle man.

Glenn Randall: Right! Roy furnished the money and I made the negotiations.

David Rothel: I believe Roy told me he paid $2,500 for him.

Glenn Randall: That's exactly right!

David Rothel: That was a good buy, wasn't it?

Glenn Randall: We stole him!

David Rothel: What do you look for in a horse when you're selecting one for training purposes?

Glenn Randall: Well, horses are like people. You look for a sort of even temper, a good facer.

David Rothel: How would you determine that?

Glenn Randall: Well, you don't want a flighty, idiotic horse; you want an even-tempered one with a lot of . . . horse sense.

David Rothel: Is there a particular breed that you like?

Glenn Randall: Breed doesn't make any difference to me; it's the individual horse itself.

David Rothel: Does the sex of the animal make a difference in training?

Glenn Randall: Well, I prefer males for the simple reason that the mares come in season and they have their bad days. Now you can eliminate that by spaying them, but why not have a gelding?

David Rothel: By what age do you need to start training a horse to do tricks?

Glenn Randall: Well, that depends. You can train them simple tricks when they are two years old. For the more strenuous things the horse should be four or five years old.

David Rothel: You wouldn't start training a horse when he's a colt, then?

Glenn Randall: Well, you would. You'd do what we call colt training. Same as you'd put a child in kindergarten. You don't put them in the fifth grade; you start them in kindergarten.

Trigger and Glenn Randall help Roy Rogers get his exercise by skipping rope.

David Rothel: How long does it generally take to train a horse for film work?

Glenn Randall: Well, how long it takes is a very hard question to answer. As fast as they accept the training. How long does it take a child to go up to the ninth grade? Some children a little longer; some children a little shorter; some learn two grades' worth in one year. As with a child, horses can progress as fast as they can accept the knowledge you're teaching.

David Rothel: Did you find Trigger to be a particularly fast learner?

Glenn Randall: He was a very exceptional horse. The title he had of "The Smartest Horse in the Movies" absolutely fit. He was almost like a human; you could talk to him. He could do forty things by word cue. You'd just tell him and he would do it. But a lot of that comes from developing his intelligence through training and living with him.

David Rothel: What do you mean when you say, "living with him"?

Glenn Randall: Everyday at it, repetition. I'm only talking to you tonight. If I talked to you every day, you'd get a hell of a lot more knowledge. If I talked to you once a year, there'd be a lost gap. Right?

David Rothel: So you would work with Trigger day in and day out.

Glenn Randall: Every day. I was with Roy Rogers twenty-four years. I kept Trigger right at my house over the years. I only had to go out the kitchen door to the stable to train him. You see, I lived in North Hollywood and so did Roy. I stabled the horse at my place for many years.

David Rothel: Did you find that as Roy worked from picture to picture that there would be special tricks that would come up?

Glenn Randall: The story writers were always adding something new. Then it was up to me to train Trigger to do whatever the trick was so that it fit the story situation.

David Rothel: What tricks was Trigger especially good at?

Glenn Randall: He was exceptionally good at mouth work. You could send him over to untie a horse or untie a hobble off himself, or he could go retrieve an article—like a retriever dog. He could take a pistol out of your holster. He could take the rope off the saddle. He could hold a rope in his mouth and you could swing one end and children or Roy could jump the rope.

David Rothel: I have a photograph of Roy jumping rope with Trigger holding one end and you holding the other.

Glenn Randall: Yes, sir. I have a copy of it in my den. That's a good example of mouth work by Trigger.

David Rothel: Now, Trigger, Jr., I believe, specialized in several dances and was used primarily on the road tours.

Glenn Randall: Trigger, Jr. was a horse we acquired later. He was an understudy for Trigger and Little Trigger. You see, we had Trigger number one for pictures; we had number two, Little Trigger, for personal appearances. Then we acquired Trigger, Jr. as an understudy for either one of the others. [When I talked with Roy previous to my conversation with Glenn Randall, he never mentioned a Little Trigger.] Both Little Trigger and Trigger, Jr. were educated to do different dances—Spanish march, Spanish trot, hoochie-coochie, so forth. Trigger, Jr. was the last horse we owned and trained.

David Rothel: How do you go about training a horse to do a dance?

Glenn Randall: Well, it's artificial action, it's nothing new. You see it in the circus and other places. It's simply a thing of teaching the horse to pick up his feet in rhythmic steps on cue.

David Rothel: What would be the cue?

Glenn Randall: It could be a whip or the bit and spur. You know, you're getting into things that you'll write about and people won't know what the hell you're talking about. You point the whip at one leg and he kneels; you point it at his rump and he hoochie-coochies; you point it at his chest and he does a Spanish march; you point it at his lips and he throws a kiss.

David Rothel: I see. So he learns that wherever the whip is placed....

Glenn Randall: That depends on how good of a teacher he's got, whether he learns what to do where you point.

David Rothel: Once you had Trigger or Trigger, Jr. trained, Roy, obviously, worked with you so that he knew exactly what to do.

Glenn Randall: Absolutely! Roy is a very good horseman, but he doesn't have time to train his horses. But you could tell Roy what to do and he could do it exactly and get as good results as I could.

David Rothel: When you were filming a horse and you wanted him to do a trick, what did you generally use for the cue, a voice or a hand signal?

Glenn Randall: If there was sound on the film, you didn't dare use your voice unless it could be edited. Generally you had to use hand signals from outside of the camera range.

David Rothel: There is a very famous fight scene in the film *My Friend Flicka*. Can you give me some idea how you would train two horses to fight like that?

Glenn Randall: There are various ways of photographing that, a lot of tricks in the photographing. They could also be two schooled horses or they could be two horses that you've kept apart that are rivals. You are getting into a deep, deep subject—how they film all of this. There are many, many ways, but most of your filming of such things is with horses that are schooled.

David Rothel: Define "schooled," if you will.

Glenn Randall: You tell me what schooling means for a child; they've gone through school. They're schooled for this particular episode.

David Rothel: Was Trigger really trained in some manner not to—how shall I say it?—relieve himself while he was on stage?

Glenn Randall: Definitely! He was definitely housebroke.

David Rothel: How does one even begin to train a horse for that?

Glenn Randall: You know, it would take me all night to explain it to you. Very few people have mastered it with their horses and I'm damned sure not going to tell it to you over the phone and have you print it. Fair enough?

David Rothel: Fair enough. Is most training based on immediate reward and punishment?

Glenn Randall: The training is based—whether it's horses, children, dogs, chimps, elephants—on only one system: it's reward-punishment. But punishment doesn't mean you have to knock an animal down with a two-by-four, and reward doesn't mean you have to run and get a cube of sugar. A kind voice—"Good boy, good boy"—will do just fine.

David Rothel: What would you use for punishment?

Glenn Randall: I might take a little whip and start stinging him on the leg like a fly bites him. When he kneels, I'll pet him—that's reward. You can't beat anything into a horse, dog or child. Reward-punishment was the system of training, with a lot of horse sense in it.

David Rothel: You trained Rex Allen's horse Koko.

Glenn Randall: Yes. Koko was quite an intelligent horse, but he never was trained to the degree that Trigger was. Not that he couldn't have been, but it was never demanded.

David Rothel: You know Mr. Ed, the talking horse of the television series. Did you ever have anything to do with his training?

Glenn Randall: No, not for the television series. I trained the last Mr. Ed that they used for commercials. The first Mr. Ed was trained by a dear friend of mine, Les Hilton, who was a very good horse trainer. He trained the first Mr. Ed to work [talk] on wire.

David Rothel: What do you mean?

Glenn Randall: You know how puppets work? Mr. Ed had a wire through his mouth, then up through his halter and down the side of his neck on the side away from the camera. When you pulled the wire, he opened his mouth.

David Rothel: So the wire was the way they made Mr. Ed appear to talk.

Glenn Randall: There is a better system, though. You train the horse so that when you open your hand, he opens his mouth and leaves it there. When you close your hand, he shuts his mouth. You can dub in a yodeling cowboy if you want.

David Rothel: You said you worked with the last Mr. Ed.

Glen Randall: They had a Mr. Ed that they used for breakfast food commercials or some kind of snacks. I trained him. Les Hilton, the trainer of the original Mr. Ed was dead—so was the original Mr. Ed. About four or five years ago I trained this other horse which they called Mr. Ed, and they did some commercials with him. He was trained to work with hand cues so we could eliminate the wires. If you remember the original Mr. Ed, you remember that you only saw him photographed from his shoulders to his head, unless it was some scene where he did mouth work—where he picked up a bowl or something. That was for the simple reason that a wire was on the off-camera side and the trainer was standing by his backside. When the trainer would pull the wire that ran through his mouth through the halter, the horse would open his mouth. When he released it, the horse would shut his mouth. That was the gimmick.

David Rothel: Did they use that same thing for Francis the Talking Mule?

Glenn Randall: Yes. I had the chance to train Francis three times, but every time they called me, Roy was ready to do a tour, so I couldn't do it.

David Rothel: Did you usually go on tour with Roy?

Glenn Randall: Always. I transported the horses and took care of them.

David Rothel: Would Roy generally take a number of horses with him when he would go out on tour?

Glenn Randall: He would take whatever we needed. Usually one for him, one for Dale, and sometimes an extra horse for Roy.

David Rothel: I certainly want to thank you, Mr. Randall, for taking time to answer my questions.

Glenn Randall: I hope you'll keep the title up there—"One of America's Finest Horse Trainers."

David Rothel: "One of America's Finest Horse Trainers, Glenn Randall." I sure will!

Champion

> In those days the horse was virtually a co-star. The kids all knew that the Lone Ranger's mount was Silver and Roy Rogers rode Trigger. But who could tell you, years later, the name of Jim Arness' horse or Paladin's or what the Cartwrights called theirs? . . . Not for nothing were they called horse operas.
> —Gene Autry

From silent picture star William S. Hart and his pinto horse, Fritz, through singing cowboy star Roy Rogers and his palomino, Trigger, the cowboy film stars—at least those that starred in film series—generally shared close-to-equal billing with their trusty horses. Some of the horses became almost as popular with the fans—especially the youngsters—as the cowboy hero, himself. On personal appearance tours the horses would often get equal billing and their tricks would comprise a large portion of the show, especially if the cowboy was not of the singing variety.

Although disagreement is always fierce among cowboy and horse fans, it would seem that the three most popular horses of the cowboy stars over the years were Gene Autry's Champion, Roy Rogers' Trigger, and Tony, Tom Mix's long-time co-star.

Of the three most famous cowboy movie horses, Champion ("World's Wonder Horse") was the only horse to star in his own television series totally apart from his "role" as Gene Autry's saddle-mate in movies and in *The Gene Autry Show* television series. *The Adventures of Champion* was a twenty-six episode half-hour series that appeared on CBS during the 1955-56 season and then went into syndication. Actually, the television series evolved out of a comic-book series which began in 1950 called "Gene Autry's Champion." The television series was produced by Gene Autry's Flying A Productions and (like the comic-book series) concerned Champion, a wild stallion who befriends twelve-year-old Ricky North (Barry Curtis) and his Uncle Sandy (Jim Bannon) as they struggle to make a go of things on their ranch located somewhere in the great Southwest during the 1880s. For additional animal interest during interior scenes, Ricky also had a German shepherd dog named Rebel. No mention was ever made of Gene Autry in either the comic-book or television series' stories—he just didn't exist as far as these Champion adventures were concerned.

Since Gene Autry's own production company produced the series, special care was taken to make it worthy of the famous horse. When *The Adventures of Champion* series was revived on British television in 1976, John Brooker, writing in the publication *Wrangler's Roost*, commented that the series "still packs a punch." Brooker continued, "Gene Autry's Flying A unit certainly knew how to mix the right

Pictured here is the horse that played Champion in the television series *The Adventures of Champion*. This Champion was trained by Glenn Randall.

ingredients; while I'm watching out for the action stuff and familiar faces, my kids are wrapped up in the adventures of the boy Ricky, the dog and horse.

"Although director Ford Beebe reveals that it was a hard series to work on—the boy was often missing for schooling and the dog and horse loathed each other—it stands the test of time as a very enjoyable series of mini B Westerns."

Although it's hard to get the cowboy stars to admit it, there were quite a few horses that portrayed Champion, Trigger and Tony over the years. Autry, especially, seemed to have a whole herd of sorrel/chestnut horses with blaze faces and four white stockings that he used interchangeably in his films—sometimes even making changes within a given scene. Interestingly, it seems that only the original Champion broke the description—he had only three white stockings. Autry in his autobiography, *Back in the Saddle Again*, comments on the different Champions:

> *The Strawberry Roan* . . . marked the debut of Little Champ, the son of the second screen Champion. I used three different Champions in my movies (although they all had their own understudies). Little Champ's sire had been a Tennessee Walking Horse, a dark chestnut with a flaxen tail and mane, the blazed face and four white socks to the knees. He was marked exactly like the first Champion [sic] and I paid fifteen hundred dollars, the most I spent for a horse."

Later on Autry comments that "the original Champion had four stand-ins at one time when Greta Garbo had one."

When I personally talked with Gene Autry for my book, *The Singing Cowboys*, he told me that he got the original Champion from Oklahoma and that it was a dark sorrel with a blaze face. It died while Autry was in the service during World War II, around 1944, and was buried at Autry's Melody Ranch.

"Evidently he had a heart attack," Gene told me, "because he just suddenly dropped dead there at the ranch. I wasn't in the country at the time and didn't learn of his death until about a month later."

Champion, Jr., as he was called for a time, took over for the original Champion and was used in Autry's post-war films. When the Gene Autry TV series came along in 1950, Gene retired Champion, Jr. and began to use the third Champion. Regarding Little Champ, Gene told me, "Oh, Little Champ *was just a pony*." Even Gene, bless him, seems to have his Champions and Little Champs confused.

The touring Champion and "Little Champ" are seen here in a photo from the souvenir program of the 1949 cross-country tour of *The Gene Autry Show*.

Gene Autry is astride Champion Jr., the second main horse that Gene used in feature films. This horse took over for the original Champion after World War II and was still alive in 1977 when the author talked with Gene.

Gene is singing to his third Champion, the horse used mainly for Gene's television series and *The Adventures of Champion* series.

To make matters even more cloudy, Autry's original film horse was not generally used for personal appearances. Gene stated that for several years his personal-appearance horse was Tony, Jr., Tom Mix's second horse. As Gene told me:

> When Tom Mix quit making films, he went on tour with the circus. A fellow named Johnny Agee, who had been the top horse trainer for Ringling Brothers' Barnum and Bailey Circus for many, many years, had this horse that he had trained—what he called "high schooled"—to do tricks. He called the horse Lindy because he was born on the day Lindbergh flew the Atlantic. He looked exactly like Mix's original Tony. When Tom Mix went on tour with the circus, he made a deal with Johnny. He hired him and leased the horse [Lindy] to ride in the circus. They called the horse Tony, Jr. After Mix retired, Agee came over to me—that was about '36 or '37—and had a talk. He said he'd like to go to work for me taking care of my horses and he'd like for me to use his horse Lindy when I did any stage appearances because the horse was trained for the stage and for rodeos.
>
> So I made a deal and Johnny went to work for me taking care of all my horses. He worked the original Champion, too, as to certain tricks he had to do in pictures. When I went on rodeos, I used Lindy because he looked like Champion, too. He had four stockings and a bald face.

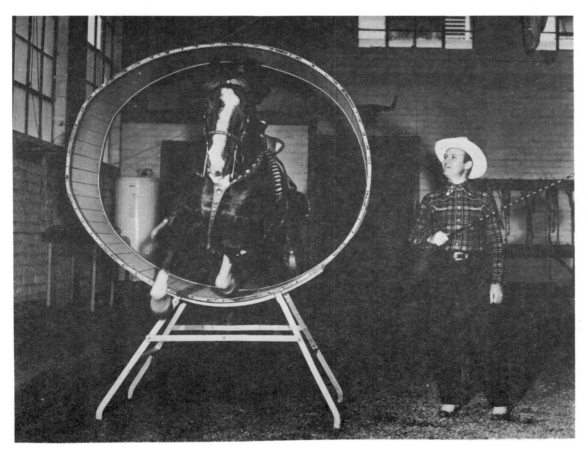

Gene is putting the personal-appearance Champion of the 1940s through his paces in the training arena just off the main building of Gene's old Melody Ranch.

The end of the trail.

H. F. Hintz, writing about the various Champions in his book, *Horses in the Movies*, lends even more confusion to the Champion stories. Hintz writes that the original Champion was Lindy and was a double for Tony, Jr. (All of the evidence that I have and that Autry reports would refute this.) Hintz also states that Champion, Jr. (the post-war horse) was purchased from a Charles Auten in 1946 for $2,500 as a four-year-old. (Autry, of course, claims that he never spent over $1,500 for any of his horses.) Auten, who lived in Ada, Oklahoma, had a horse named Boots that he had shown in area fairs and rodeos. When he heard that Autry was looking for a new Champion, so the story goes, he went to Fort Worth to meet Autry. Auten sold Autry the horse named Boots who was then redubbed Champion, Jr.

My reason for belaboring the confusion regarding Gene Autry's Champion is only to illustrate that in reality most of the famous cowboy-movie horses existed in at least triplicate. At the time the films were made and the horses were very popular, their multiplicity was kept a deep, dark secret. The feeling probably was that the thousands, maybe millions, of broomstick buckaroos who idolized these horses would find it disquieting to discover that there were carbon copies hidden behind the rocks—after all, it was only a while back that these youngsters had found out that Santa Claus didn't exist at all!

Trainer Johnny Agee and the touring Champion.

My Pal Trigger

Roy Rogers' golden palomino, Trigger, probably got the biggest publicity build-up of all the movie horses during his years of filmmaking. Plugged continuously as "The Smartest Horse in the Movies," Trigger was said to be able to perform some sixty tricks. For a publicity stunt when Roy and Trigger first played Madison Square Garden, Trigger was taken into the hotel where Roy was staying. Holding a pencil in his mouth, Trigger signed the register with his "X" and then went up to the room with Roy for a press conference. Trigger could drink milk from a bottle, walk 150 feet on his hind legs and do simple addition and subtraction as well as count to twenty. Perhaps his greatest feat was his ability to display "self-restraint" while indoors—mentioned earlier in my conversation with trainer Glenn Randall. In 1953 Trigger was awarded the PATSY for his fine performances.

Trigger's first known film appearance was as Olivia De Havilland's horse during her ride through Sherwood Forest in *Robin Hood* starring Errol Flynn. He was three years old at the time and belonged to Hudkins Rental Stable in Hollywood. When I talked with Roy for my book, *The Singing Cowboys,* I asked him how he happened to select Trigger as his movie mount:

> When we got ready to pick a horse for me when I was starting my series at Republic, all the stables that leased horses to the studios were called and told to send out their lead horses. If a stable could get one of their lead horses on a picture, then they could get a studio to take their posse horses, buggy horses and the street horses for the picture. So they all brought their horses out—I think there were about six lead horses there that day. I got on a couple of them and rode them down the street and back. Then I got on [the horse that was to become] Trigger and rode him down the street and back. I never looked at the rest of them. I said, "This is it. This is the color I want. He feels like the horse I want, and he's got a good rein on him."
>
> The name [Trigger] came up when we were getting ready to do the first picture. Smiley Burnette and I and some others who were there got to kicking it around. I was fooling around with my guns as we talked. I believe it was actually Smiley who said, "As fast and as quick as the horse is, you ought to call him Trigger. You know, quick-on-the-trigger." I said, "That's a good name." And I just named him Trigger.
>
> Trigger was not only a beautiful horse, but he was a good "using" horse for all those chases and things. You know, Trigger did those chases through the rocks and over the mountains, down steep grades and never had any ankles, hocks, or knees go wrong—nothing! He was just tough as a boot. I could do those running

mounts and dismounts and never have any problem with him at all. He could just outrun any horse on the set—just flatfooted outrun them. But you had to be "with him" whenever you gave him the cue to go left or right or he'd spin right out from under you.

He was half thoroughbred. His sire was a race horse at Caliente and his dam was a cold-blooded palomino. He took the color, white mane and tail from his mother and the stamina, speed and conformation from the thoroughbred side. He took the good parts from both of them. His registered name was Golden Cloud as a palomino.

I always owned four or five extra palomino horses in case anything should happen to Trigger. So in any long-distance shots where they weren't identifiable, we would use one of the other horses to give Trigger a break. But if the shots were close-ups, Trigger had to do them. But he was tough; if you gave him a little breather after each one, he could just go all day. And we took care of him. He was checked thoroughly every six months by a vet. I'm the only cowboy in the business, I think, that started and made all my pictures with one horse.

Roy Rogers is seen here putting Trigger, Jr. through his paces during a personal appearance.

I asked Roy about Trigger, Jr.:

> Well, we used him for personal appearances. He wasn't worth a nickel as a cowboy horse, but he could do a beautiful dance routine, so we used him for personal appearances. But Trigger—he was something else! I retired him in 1957 after the TV series we made. He was twenty-five then and he lived to be thirty-three years old, dying in 1965. A horse's life is over three to one in comparison to a man's. So that made Trigger over a hundred years old in human terms.

Certainly the most controversial thing Roy Rogers ever did was have the remains of Trigger mounted and placed on display at his Roy Rogers and Dale Evans Museum in Victorville, California. Trigger, Jr., Dale's horse Buttermilk, and Bullet the dog have experienced a similar fate. They are all on view for their fans who stop by for a visit. I asked Roy why he had Trigger mounted for display at the museum.

> When Trigger died I had mixed thoughts about what to do. I'd seen what a beautiful job they do mounting animals. If I put him in the ground, I knew what would happen to him. If I put him here in the museum, people could see him from now on. So I had him mounted. He looks beautiful. I'm so happy I did it. He appeared in all my pictures and countless personal appearances. It would have been a crime to bury him.

Make no mistake and assume there is any mercenary motive in Roy's decision regarding Trigger. Roy loved that horse as much as anyone could love an animal. A few months after our conversation, Roy spoke to a film-festival crowd in Houston, Texas; I was in attendance. Roy was asked by several members of the audience to reminisce about Trigger and their work together in films over the years. As Roy was recounting some of his experiences with Trigger, he suddenly paused, tears came to his eyes and he had to turn away for a minute or so to regain his composure. Then he quietly commented, "It was a sad day in the Rogers' household when Trigger died, let me tell you."

Roy Rogers astride Trigger (circa late 1940s).

Tony the Wonder Horse

There are several stories from reliable sources as to how Tom Mix happened to find his famous mount, Tony. One story goes that Tom, a young Western film star on the ascendancy, was riding along Vine Street in Hollywood in his new Stutz when he happened to notice a rather striking-looking horse either (depending on your storyteller) pulling a vegetable cart or following along behind one as his mother pulled the cart. Horse-wise, Tom immediately saw potential in this young sorrel with the white hind socks—the animal was obviously too showy to be pulling a vegetable cart, or tagging along behind one (if you like the other version of the story better).

Anyway, Tom asked the Italian vegetable peddler if he wanted to sell the sorrel. The peddler hesitated, uncertain of this flashily dressed cowboy, but reassurance quickly returned when he saw the roll of greenbacks the cowboy nonchalantly removed from his pocket. One story has it that Tom magnanimously peeled off ten-dollar bills until the vegetable peddler finally acquiesced to the sale. The other version is that the peddler told Tom the horse was his son's and that Tom would have to strike a deal with him. This legend claims that Tom negotiated with the boy and got the horse for $17.50.

Tom reportedly asked the peddler what the horse was called. "He doesn't have a name," was the response. Tom asked what the peddler's name was. "Tony," came the reply. "Good enough," replied Tom. He hitched the new Tony onto the back of his Stutz and drove off with the future wonder horse. There's another version of the story—that Tom simply purchased Tony from a friend. Take your choice of stories.

With many incidents regarding the life of Tom Mix, one, perhaps, should harken to the words of the famous stunt man and second-unit action film director, Yakima Canutt. Yak knew Tom from the early days and liked him, but he also knew where Tom's greatest talent lay. As Yak said:

> His outstanding talent was that he was one of the last great Western storytellers. He spent a number of years traveling with various Wild West Shows and he did, in fact, work at mastering riding, roping, bulldogging, bronc riding and shooting, but his main attraction was always his tall tales. Most of the exploits in these tales exceeded Tom's (or anybody's) capacity to perform. Tom was a showman extraordinaire.

One time when Yak indicated to Tom that he may have been reckless with the truth in recounting various personal exploits, Tom half-angrily retorted, "What do you

Tom Mix and Tony

mean 'reckless'? They wanted to be entertained, so I took a few sequences from my pictures and turned them into reality. . . . Look, Yak, when you're in show business, you've got to meet people and entertain them. As long as a lie don't hurt anyone, there's no harm done."

Anyway, getting back to Tony, there is evidence that the animal was born in Los Angeles. The sire's background is lost from knowledge, but the dam is said to have been a range-bred mare from Arizona. By whichever means Tom found Tony, it happened some time during the early part of the second decade of this century. Tom Mix started with the Selig Polyscope Company in 1914, making mostly two- and three-reel Western shorts. His first film horse, Old Blue, had served him well for years, going back to the time when Tom was a real cowboy in the rodeos and Wild West Shows.

In 1917 Tom joined the Fox Studios. With the death of Old Blue that same year, Tom trained Tony to take over as his screen horse. It was during the eleven years Tom worked for Fox that he became the top cowboy star of silent films, deposing the formidable Western realist, William S. Hart. Tom's actionful, flamboyant representation of the Old West was more in tune with the Roaring '20s, as those years came to be known.

Tom and Tony were a screen team to reckon with: Tom, the daredevil cowboy stunt man who made it a personal creed to perform even the most highly dangerous stunts himself in films he designed for that very purpose; Tony, the saddlemate who worked as one with his master to thrill the popcorn crowd. He and Tony, no doubles, could be seen performing giant leaps from one cliff to another or scaling down a steep land crevasse, dangerous on foot much less on horseback. The highly schooled Tony seemed to take in stride the strenuous film stunt demands as well as the standard mouth work of untying Tom's hands or loosening his reins from the hitching post to find the captured Tom. Several times Tony was called upon to save his master from fire—a burning barn or forest fire. Seemingly unpossessed of the usual equine fear of fire, Tony would enter the fire area to save Tom. Only on the most dangerous stunts would Tom use an understudy for Tony. Less often — several years later when he was too big a star for the studio to allow him to risk his neck—he would allow a double for himself. The result of Tom's caution-be-damned attitude was various broken bones and other often severe injuries that left him fidgeting briefly in hospital beds.

By the early 1920s, Tom was making a reported $17,500 a week, living in a quarter-of-a-million-dollar mansion in the Hollywood hills, and sporting the flashy Western attire that would later become a fixture with such stars as Gene Autry and Roy Rogers. When in 1925 Tom and Tony toured Europe, they were mobbed by enthusiastic fans wherever they traveled.

But the times they were a-changing. By 1928 Fox Studios was reassessing its film output. Westerns were in a decline and seemed headed for even harder times with the coming of sound. How were these strange new microphones going to pick up sound in the great outdoors? It was suggested, too, that Tom's voice might not record well. For these and other reasons, Fox decided not to renew Tom's contract in 1928.

Too left Fox and went over to Joseph P. Kennedy's F.B.O. Company and made six last silent pictures by the end of 1929. It was reported that he received $1,000 each day he worked in front of the camera. Sadly, though, the pictures were greatly inferior to the Fox pictures and somewhat ofan embarrassment to the cowboy star.

Tom is seen here astride Tony, Jr.

And then came the Wall Street crash in 1929 to close the decade. Tom Mix had reached his professional peak during the first quarter of the decade only to see his fortunes—professional and financial—left in disarray as the decade slunk to a close. His Hollywood mansion was soon gone, an Arizona ranch lost, about a million dollars in stocks dissolved into nothingness and his picture career languished.

But Tom bounced back as the star attraction with the Sells-Floto Circus and toured the country with great success. Because Tony was beginning to get up in years, Tom bought and trained (or had trained) the horse he was to call Tony, Jr.—a Tony Senior look-alike except for the four white socks rather than two. Within a short time it was reported that Mix's circus earnings were approaching $20,000 per week—plenty to buy oats and hay for his horses and to live the good life.

In early 1932, with sound pictures now firmly entrenched and outdoor sound problems overcome, Tom joined Universal Pictures for a series of nine pictures. (Tom had worked diligently with a voice coach while with the circus so that he might overcome his acting and microphone concerns.) The nine pictures were filmed in only about a year's time—a grueling assignment under any circumstances, but particularly exhausting for a fifty-two-year-old star whose body was literally wired together as a result of horse falls, failed stunts and just plain reckless living. And arthritis had settled into his body—an old man's disease, he believed.

Tony, Jr. and the aging original Tony were both used in the Universal series. In October 1932, riding Tony in a film sequence at Lone Pine in the Mojave Desert, Tom gingerly guided the old horse along a treacherous five-foot embankment. Suddenly Tony lost his footing, tumbled headlong down the embankment and then rolled over on his side, pinning Tom beneath for several agonizing moments and leaving him unconscious. When Tom came to, it was discovered that his right leg and side were badly injured. Tony, now twenty-three, was badly shaken by the accident and was finally retired for good by Tom. In December of that same year—his Universal contract completed—Tom again retired from pictures, too.

It was back to the circus tents for Tom. Presently, he bought his very own circus, plunking down $400,000 to seal the deal—The Tom Mix Circus! But he chose the wrong time to invest in circuses. The audiences were turning to other forms of entertainment during the middle to late Depression years. Before long Tom began to lose money with his circus, then he lost a lot.

To patch his financial tatters, Tom agreed to make one last film, a serial for Mascot Pictures called *The Miracle Rider* (1935), a fitting title for the veteran cowboy actor who really was a true cowboy, first and foremost. But age had caught up with Tom Mix and in the serial he was a stiffened shadow of the screen star he had been in the vintage years of the 1920s. Longtime Mix fans of today warn viewers of his later films, that they are seeing only a small portion of the screen magic that Tom and Tony could muster on film in their prime.

When Mister Death finally visited Tom Mix in October 1940, he was mercifully quick in claiming his cowboy hostage. On a deserted Arizona highway, Tom, alone, raced southward in his custom-built roadster, heading for Phoenix. The accident must have been a montage of blurs for him—the sudden road crew, the detour swerve, the firm roadway giving way to loose dirt, the impotent brakes, the flip downward into the dry wash, the scrape of the heavy metal suitcase as it began to crash forward, neck pain, death.

Two years later to the day after Tom's death, old Tony joined his master.

Black Beauty

Certainly the most enduring horse story in book and visual media terms has been Anna Sewell's late-19th-century episodic novel *Black Beauty*. The travails of this pitch-hued steed (as related in the book by the horse himself, autobiographically) have moved producers to film action repeatedly, if not often effectively, over the years. As far back as 1921 the filming of the late-Victorian novel was a major production of the Vitagraph Company. Jean Paige, a popular actress for Vitagraph during the silent days of motion pictures, starred in the film, with former Vitagraph juvenile, James Morrison, playing opposite her.

As reported in *The Big V, A History of the Vitagraph Company*, this seven-reel version of Anna Sewell's novel changed the storytelling focus from the horse to a combination approach utilizing both the horse's-eye view of the story and the girl's. *Photoplay* (April 1921), in reviewing the film stated, "There is, therefore, the 'inside' story of the humans and the 'outside' story of the horses, and they dovetail so well there is no break in the interest and no resentment at the frequent changes from one to the other." The *New York Times* reviewer was not so kind, however, referring to the "inside" story as a "conventional melodrama, using the familiar stupid-but-beautiful heroine; the well-dressed, black-mustached, heroine-clutching villain; the up-to-the-last-minute baffled hero; and other odds and ends from the stockroom of fiction."

Surprisingly, Ingmar Bergman in his book *Bergman on Bergman* comments that this version of *Black Beauty* was one of the first films he ever saw, and he was so moved by it—particularly the sequence involving the horse in a barn fire—that it stirred his interest in films and was one of the great influences that caused him to go into filmmaking.

An interesting sidelight on this first filming of *Black Beauty* is a *New York Times* report from March 22, 1921, regarding a bogus claptrap film version of the story distributed by the Eskay Harris Feature Film Company in 1921 on the tail of the expensive Vitagraph production. Incensed by the interlopers, Vitagraph complained to the Federal Trade Commission that the Eskay Harris Company had merely taken an old film called *Your Obedient Servant*, shot some new footage designed to coincide with the basic Beauty story and released it as *Black Beauty* on the heels of Vitagraph's extensive ballyhoo of its own production. Ultimately the Harris version rode off into the sunset with little loot and threat of much litigation.

In 1933 the first sound version of the *Black Beauty* story was filmed. Lovely Esther Ralston (for a time billed as "The American Venus," after the title of a silent picture she had starred in) played the heroine in a low-budget version filmed by one of the most undistinguished of the movie companies, Monogram Pictures. It seems that Miss Ralston, under contract to MGM at the time, was rather uncooperative with production head Louis B. Mayer who, according to one report, had eyes for more than her talent. As a consequence, she was loaned out to various lesser studios in roles that were unlikely to further her career. The *Black Beauty* picture was but one example of this and one is hard pressed to find any record of the film today.

A little more than a decade was to pass before *Black Beauty* trod across the silver screen again. This time in 1946 in a B-grade production released by Twentieth Century-Fox. Independent producer Edward L. Alperson gathered together a competent cast of lesser film stalwarts (Richard Denning, Evelyn Ankers [Denning's real-life wife], Arthur Space) to act out the, by now, familiar tale—although great liberties were taken with the original source material, as was true in all of the film versions. Young Mona Freeman played the girl in this version and a horse by the name of Highland Dale played the title role. This filming of *Black Beauty* suffered at the time in comparison with *Smokey* by Will James, another popular horse story that had been filmed and went into release just prior to *Black Beauty*.

Another decade was to pass before *Beauty* again made it into motion-picture theatres, this time with a story line even more remotely related to the original. *Courage of Black Beauty* (1957) was another low-budget Edward L. Alperson production for Twentieth Century-Fox. This time the story took place on a San

Young Mark Lester is astride Black Beauty in the 1971 internationally produced film of the famous horse story.

Fernando Valley horse ranch and concerned father/son conflicts with Black Beauty ultimately being the catalyst that brings the widower father (John Bryant) and his son together in time for the final fadeout. Young Johnny Crawford, who would soon play *The Rifleman's* son on television for several years, portrayed the son in this film intended primarily for the youthful Saturday matinee crowd. As the *Variety* critic commented, "... it's an infantile offering for infantile audiences ... for the old folks (this) horsey tale may be a yawn."

It wasn't until 1971 that *Black Beauty* found a return path to the screen — this time by way of a British, German and Spanish production which starred young Mark Lester (of *Oliver!* fame) and rotund character actor, Walter Slezak. By this time some six-million copies of the novel had been sold in some seventeen languages, making, certainly, for a pre-sold audience, but again the producers failed to break the storytelling problem in their attempt to make the film have international appeal. As *Variety* commented, "In their attempt to please all audiences, in too many different lands, the filmmakers had to ride off in all directions at once ... to some extent, this charming horse saga emerges as a roughriding Western."

In 1972 *Black Beauty* galloped into television in a color syndicated series beautifully produced in England by Fremantle International and London Weekend Television. The producers were at least faithful to the background of the original story set in Victorian England and the series met with critical and audience acceptance—really for the first time other than in its original novel form. The half-hour series ultimately consisted of fifty-two episodes which revolved around the household of a Dr. Gordon (William Lucas), a widower who left London to set up practice in the countryside. Along with the good doctor there were his daughter, Vicky (Judi Bowker); his son, Kevin (Roderick Shaw); his housekeeper, Amy (Charlotte Mitchell); and a magnificent black stallion who, quite naturally, played an important part in the lives of these people.

The Black Beauty stallion of the 1972 television series.

Edward Albert and Black Beauty in a scene from the 1978 television mini-series of the story.

In early 1978 NBC-TV through Universal TV presented the most lavish film version to date of the *Black Beauty* story—a five-part mini-series with an all-star cast including Edward Albert, Cameron Mitchell, Diane Ladd, William Devane, Brock Peters, Forrest Tucker, Farley Granger, Clu Gulager, Kristoffer Tabori, Jack Elam, Warren Oates, Mel Ferrer, Don DeFore, Van Johnson, Ken Curtis and David Wayne.

As a television production, *Black Beauty* covered thirteen years in the life of the horse and was fairly faithful to the book, but the setting was changed from Victorian England to late 19th-Century Maryland—a modification that in this instance worked well for the story. Visually stunning, the production was filmed in Kentucky. While the mini-series failed to attract a huge audience (primarily due to stiff competition from the other networks), it nonetheless did well in the ratings and was a prestigious production for the network. Unquestionably, NBC and Universal's attempt to tell the *Black Beauty* story resulted in the finest version of Anna Sewell's novel—written over a hundred years ago and reputed to be the sixth best-selling book of all time.

My Friend Flicka
(and descendants)

Novelist Mary O'Hara's equine trilogy, *My Friend Flicka; Thunderhead, Son of Flicka;* and *Green Grass of Wyoming* comprises three of the most popular horse stories and films of modern times. During the 1940s, readers of Ms. O'Hara's moving and thoughtful stories were rewarded with screen adaptations which did justice to the source material—not always the case.

My Friend Flicka was the first of the threesome and it is felt by many readers and filmgoers to be the best of the lot. In late 1942 Twentieth Century-Fox gathered together a strong cast headed by young Roddy McDowall, Preston Foster, Rita Johnson and James Bell to film the *Flicka* story.

The screen version of *Flicka* stuck closely to O'Hara's original with only moderate cinematic sugarcoating. The plot finds West Point-disciplined father Captain McLaughlen (Foster) disturbed by his shiftless, irresponsible son, Ken (McDowall). Ken's greatest desire is to own and train his own horse. When he chooses a seemingly ill-bred, rebellious filly he dubs Flicka, Ken's father becomes even more exasperated with the boy. Young Ken, of course, wants to prove something to his father about himself as well as about the filly. Through the joy, discipline and heartbreak associated with rearing the filly, the father and son gain a better understanding of each other and grow closer together.

My Friend Flicka was a phenomenal success for Twentieth Century-Fox, causing the film company to immediately go into production on Mary O'Hara's sequel, *Thunderhead, Son of Flicka* (1945). All of the major cast members returned to their previous roles and just continued, basically, where they had left off in the previous story. Young Ken (again played by Roddy McDowall) still has some growing up and learning to do, and through his experiences with Flicka and her snow-white colt, Thunderhead, the boy edges ever closer to manhood—both physically and emotionally. The script calls for the boy to break the frisky colt to the saddle and to train him to be a racer. Ken succeeds to an extent, but his work with the horse comes to naught when in a county meet Thunderhead pulls a tendon. Crushed at the failure of his horse and himself, Ken thereafter uses the animal only as a saddlehorse. Redemption comes for Thunderhead when he saves his young master's life and the ranch's herd of horses from a wild albino stallion that has been terrorizing the countryside stealing mares for his herd. The to-the-death fight between Thunderhead and the albino is one of the finest horse fights ever staged for the screen—the scenes appearing excruciatingly real before the Technicolor lensing. Story poignancy is heightened during the horse fight through the knowledge that the wild albino is the sire of Flicka, Thunderhead's own mother.

My Friend Flicka and *Thunderhead* were both highly successful at the theatre box offices and filmgoers who saw both features enjoyed the sense of continuity—of a well-begun story continuing logically through a sequel. The audience could enjoy the maturing of both the horse and boy.

When I talked with Roddy McDowall about his performance in those two films, I mentioned that I was amazed at the horsemanship he displayed for such a youngster.

David Rothel: You seemed to be such an accomplished horseman. Were you really?

Roddy McDowall: Oh well, yes, I was, but I didn't really become one until the movie *My Friend Flicka*. I was very young; I was twelve or thirteen, and I loved horses. During the progress of two or three films that involved horses, I was trained to do everything—English, bareback, Western, to run a race. I ran a race, of course, in *Thunderhead*. I always thought I was wrong for those films, though, because I was still tremendously English.

David Rothel: How did you get rid of your English accent for the roles?

Roddy McDowall: I didn't really. In *My Friend Flicka* I think it's very prevalent. I'd only been here in the United States a year and a half at the time I made the picture.

Young jockey Roddy McDowall in a posed scene from *Thunderhead, Son of Flicka*.

Roddy McDowall is getting a little sympathetic advice from ranch hand James Bell about the injured Flicka in this scene from *My Friend Flicka*.

Although Roddy acknowledged that they were both fine films, he steadfastly felt that their success was due to something totally separate from their cinematic worth.

Roddy McDowall: The reason the film *My Friend Flicka* worked, historically, is that it was the first major piece about an animal that had been made in about ten years. *My Friend Flicka* and *Lassie Come Home* were made at the same time. In fact they had to stop *Lassie Come Home* until I finished *My Friend Flicka*. So for both of those films, one of the big reasons for their successes was the fact that they were the first for many years about animals.

David Rothel: The films were certainly very scenic, the Technicolor lensing adding a great deal to the beauty of the films.

Roddy McDowall: Actually *Lassie Come Home* and, I think, *Thunderhead* were the first films made that used monopack Technicolor, which was the one-strip color. The lights were excruciatingly hot to work under. The animals used to fall asleep. It was boiling under those lights.

David Rothel: Where did you shoot *My Friend Flicka* and *Thunderhead*?

Roddy McDowall: Kanab, Utah, Cedar City and Bryce Canyon in Bryce National Park—all in that area. Part of *Thunderhead* was done at the Noma County Track up in Oregon.

* * *

In 1948 the cycle of three films was completed when Twentieth Century-Fox filmed *Green Grass of Wyoming*. An all new cast was gathered for this final installment in the horse series. The youth interest was supplied by Peggy Cummins and Robert Arthur. Charles Coburn, Lloyd Nolan and Burl Ives lent strong support. The only tie to the previous films in the series was the horse, Thunderhead.

The *Green Grass of Wyoming* story is in two distinct parts, with each part taking place in a different location. The first part of the story concerns Robert Arthur, a Wyoming rancher, who buys a beautiful black mare and starts to train her as a trotter. Presently she is lured into the nearby hills by the wild stallion, Thunderhead. Rancher Arthur takes off after his mare and—after many stunning location scenes in Technicolor—returns with the mare *and* the now rather docile stallion.

Now the story shifts to an Ohio racetrack where in the big trotting event the black mare is nosed out of first prize by another horse driven by on-the-wagon alcoholic Charles Coburn, a Wyoming horse-breeding neighbor, harness-racing competitor and grandfather to Arthur's sweetheart, Peggy Cummins. Coburn is out to prove he can make a comeback from his alcohol problem and succeeds. All ends happily when it is discovered the mare's faltering in the home stretch was due to the fact that she is going to foal—thus maybe explaining why Thunderhead had returned to the ranch so docilely earlier in the film.

Of the three O'Hara stories, *Green Grass of Wyoming* was the most easygoing and gentle (perhaps explaining why it was the least successful at the box office of the three films). In *Green Grass of Wyoming* there is little of the life-and-death-struggle feeling that is so prevalent in *Flicka* and *Thunderhead* where there is constant threat of physical and/or emotional danger to horse, boy and father. All three of the films based on the Mary O'Hara horse stories represent some of the best work done on the screen with animals. The stories were all heartwarming and sentimental, but there was also a sense of sincerity and purpose behind them that kept them from the saccharine mire of so many horse-and-boy stories. Despite the obvious possibilities for maudlin sentimentality in the stories, the acting and direction remained true throughout. All three films could qualify for the comment of the *New York Times* critic regarding *My Friend Flicka:* " . . . it has a quality perhaps best described as 'heart.' "

The O'Hara horse stories were put out to pasture after *Green Grass of Wyoming*. It wasn't until 1955 and the entry of several successful animal series on television—*The Adventures of Champion, Fury,* and *Rin Tin Tin,* etc.—that Twentieth Century-Fox ventured for the first time into videoland with thirty-nine half-hour adventures of *My Friend Flicka.* Since the series was the first for Twentieth, a big budget was allocated and it was produced in color—a rarity for a mid-1950s television series.

The *My Friend Flicka* series remained fairly faithful to the Mary O'Hara original in character and animal content, if not in story quality or adult appeal. Twentieth was obviously looking for a family audience, but the program—as with so many of the animal-centered series — ended up appealing primarily to the pre-teenagers.

An attractive and appealing cast was gathered for the television series. Twentieth Century-Fox production head, Buddy Adler, brought his wife, Anita Louise (a former film star), out of semi-retirement to play the mother role of Nell McLaughlin. Tall, lumbering Gene Evans was cast in the original Preston Foster role of the father. Evans' main film appearances previous to the *Flicka* series were leads in two war pictures, *The Steel Helmet* and *Fixed Bayonets.* His deep voice and hearty manner worked well for him as the father figure in the series.

Johnny Washbrook essayed the role of the son, Ken, in the series. Few would place young Washbrook in the child actor league with Roddy McDowall, who starred in the *Flicka/Thunderhead* feature films of a decade or so before, but the boy was appealing even if he did look a little uncomfortable and out of place (a little too "citified," perhaps) around the Goose Bar Ranch and horses.

Johnny Washbrook was only ten when he signed for the *My Friend Flicka* series. Hailing from Toronto, Canada, he already had three solid years of show-business experience when the role of Ken was offered to him. He had appeared in more than two hundred television and radio shows in Canada, and on the stage in a summer-stock production of *Life With Father* in which his older brother Donald and his mother also performed.

"I discovered during *Life With Father* that Johnny was really meant to be an actor," commented Mrs. Washbrook. "One day the curtain went up and Johnny was missing. It turned out he'd had some trouble getting his coat on because it had gotten torn and before he knew it, the curtain was up. After a couple of minutes, picking the right spot, Johnny just sauntered onto the set and sat down. The audience never knew he was late.

"I asked him later if he wasn't frightened when he found the curtain up and himself in the wings and he said, 'No, I just figured the boy might be upstairs or something and might just come down after all the others were in the room.' I thought if he had all that presence at that age then there wasn't much doubt about his being an actor."

In April 1955 Johnny was called to New York to do a *United States Steel Hour* television show called *Roads to Home,* starring James Daley and Beatrice Straight. It was at this time that Twentieth Century-Fox TV was looking for a youngster to play the part of Ken in *My Friend Flicka.* One of the executives saw Johnny on the *Steel Hour* and called him to Hollywood to test for the part.

Here on the Goose Bar Ranch set are the *My Friend Flicka* starts Johnny Washbrook, Wahama (Flicka), Anita Louise and Gene Evans.

The Flicka horse featured in the television series was a four-year-old Arabian sorrel mare named Wahama. Except for the fact that it was Arabian, the horse somewhat resembled Gene Autry's horse Champion, having white stockings and a partially blazed face.

My Friend Flicka premiered on the CBS network on February 10, 1956, and only lasted for one season in first run. The series did, however, have a rather extraordinary existence in reruns (helped along no doubt by the fact that it was shot in color), appearing on all three networks at one time or another between 1957 and 1965 (on NBC in 1957 and 1963, ABC during 1959 and 1960, and then again on CBS in 1961, 1964 and 1965). After 1965 the series went into general syndication.

Johnny Washbrook, now grown, remembers the *My Friend Flicka* series fondly—particularly his work with the horse. After the series ended, he lost touch with Wahama and does not know what became of the horse. Whatever became of Johnny, himself? According to author Richard Lamparski, tracer of lost celebrities, Johnny is alive and well on the East Coast, acting in occasional Off-Broadway plays, repertory companies and dinner-theatre productions.

Fury

On October 15, 1955, the Saturday morning kiddie television ghetto of jerk-step cartoons was intruded upon by a gentle, contemporary Western series which resembled nothing more or less than an equine version of *Lassie*. It was, as the producers advertised, "The story of a horse and the boy who loved him." The series was called *Fury*.

The name of the black-stallion star of the series was somewhat of a misnomer since there was little that was furious about the horse or the series. In truth, from 1955, when the series debuted on NBC, until 1960 when the production ceased, the series really presented 114 half-hour black-and-white morality plays for young viewers.

The National Parent-Teacher magazine summed up the warm and winning qualities of the *Fury* program in a review they published soon after the program went on the air.

> A Western setting complete with outlaws and sheriff; a small boy and his rancher dad, valiantly upholding the cause of law and order; and a magnificent black horse that gives the series its name—*Fury* is evidence that these elements can be shaped into a thing of artistry, human sympathy and excitement.
>
> The episodes are admirably constructed . . . each theme is brought out clearly and naturally, yet without overstatement or moralizing. . . . Here is excellent material for family discussion of such timely and universal themes as friendship, loyalty, care of animals, attitudes towards cultures (the Indians) and the meaning of courage.

The title star of the series was a black American Saddle Horse stallion whose real name was Beauty. The horse came from Missouri and was trained by the well-known horseman, Ralph McCutcheon. Before the *Fury* series came along, Beauty was quite active in feature films, having appeared in *Black Beauty* (1946) and in *Gypsy Colt* in 1954 (for which he won a PATSY award). He served as the beautiful steed for such top-ranked film stars as Clark Gable in *Lone Star* (1952), Joan Crawford in *Johnny Guitar* (1954) and Elizabeth Taylor in *Giant* (1956).

Roles in such major motion pictures as the above, plus the success of the *Fury* television series made the highly trained Beauty and Ralph McCutcheon very wealthy. It was reported that over an eight-year period the animal earned for his owner/trainer over $500,000. For *Fury* alone the tab was $1,500 per episode. You can buy a lot of hay and oats for that kind of money!

Exciting, heartwarming adventure, starring Peter Graves, star of "Mission: Impossible," Bobby Diamond as *"Joey,"* and FURY, the wonder horse.

Beauty (alias Fury) was owned and trained by Ralph McCutcheon. In 1960 and 1961 Fury was the recipient of PATSY awards for his outstanding performance in the *Fury* television series.

The human stars on the series were Bobby Diamond, who played a youngster named Joey; Peter Graves as Joey's foster father, Jim Newton; and veteran character actor William Fawcett as Pete, the top hand on Jim's Broken Wheel Ranch. On the first program of the series (called *Joey Finds A Friend*) the relationships were established that would remain through the many episodes.

As the Independent Television Corporation press release summarized the story:

> Jim Newton, a widower, is the likable young owner of the Broken Wheel Ranch which specializes in capturing and taming wild horses found on the range. Jim lives there with his weatherbeaten old ranch-hand Pete, who serves as the place's chief cook and bottle washer.
>
> One day Jim goes to the city. There he sees a tough little city kid threatened by a shopkeeper. Jim goes to court to protect the boy and winds up offering him a home on the Broken Wheel Ranch.
>
> The boy Joey has some difficulty adjusting to life on the ranch. But as soon as he sees Jim's latest captive, a mighty black stallion named Fury, Joey senses he has found a kindred spirit.

Bellying up to the hitching rail are *Fury* cast regulars (left to right) Fury, Peter Graves, a young friend of Joey, William Fawcett and Bobby Diamond.

Bobby Diamond and his friend Fury are seen here on the set for an episode in the *Fury* series.

Bobby Diamond, who was twelve years old when he first signed for the series, struggled to keep his acting career alive after *Fury* went out of production in 1960. He miscalculated the future success of *My Three Sons*, turning down a son role in the Fred MacMurray hit series. For a time he had a running role on the *Westinghouse Playhouse Starring Nanette Fabray*. Then he played Duncan Gillis during the last season of *The Many Loves of Dobie Gillis*.

Bobby was shrewd enough to realize the vagaries of an acting career and so studied law. Since 1971 he has been a practicing lawyer in California, specializing in criminal and personal injury cases. Between court appearances he still pursues his acting career, albeit with very modest success thus far. Although he claims to have mostly happy memories of the *Fury* years, it would appear that he is seeking an adult image as an actor and does not wish to dwell too much on his childhood roles. My repeated calls and messages for a discussion of the *Fury* series were met with stony silence.

Peter Graves (the real-life brother of James Arness) played Jim Newton in the *Fury* series.

Peter Graves, of course, went on to the popular *Mission Impossible* television series and various feature motion pictures and television movie roles. Today Peter Graves smiles and acknowledges that the equine star outearned him during the run of the *Fury* series. Graves contends, however, that he never displayed nearly as much temperament as Fury, a trait that occasionally delayed shooting.

As Graves told a UPI reporter in 1978, "We made those in the days when nobody thought about taking a percentage of the profits of a series. We made them for $30,000 each for five years and then they ran for six years on NBC and then went into syndication [as *Brave Stallion*]. The guy who owned the horse asked for five percent and got it. Through the years I would see him and he'd say he just got another check for $90,000 or $65,000." Graves commented also that Fury lived to be twenty-nine, and was never allowed to breed for fear he "would never do his tricks again."

Probably the most-remembered bit from the many episodes was the closing scene when Jim and Pete would wax philosophical as Joey petted his four-legged black buddy. Jim and Pete would generally make a comment on life's blessings, Fury would nicker and they would all laugh.

"Yes, that was our tag line," Graves commented to UPI. "That's when I learned to laugh without feeling like it. That, my friend, is acting. But *Fury* was a series of little Aesop's Fables, timeless stories on the benefits of the outdoor life. Every show taught something; they were constructed that way, to always teach a little lesson.

"Years from now, your kids will still be watching *Fury*."

National Velvet

"Everyone should have a chance at a breathtaking piece of folly at least once in his life," rhapsodizes little Velvet Brown's mother at one point in the moving horse story, *National Velvet*. The "breathtaking piece of folly" in this case is the attempt by horse-loving Velvet and her young horse-trainer friend Mi Taylor to train a magnificent piebald (meaning a black-and-white pinto with large distinct patches) horse to qualify and run in the English Grand National Steeplechase, much less win it with little Velvet jockeying the horse home. This type of farfetched fancy, of course, has been the stuff and such of animal stories ever since writers discovered the human-interest sparks that could electrify readers: an appealing child and an affectionate animal juxtaposed in a sentimental and inspiring situation/conflict which tests both the child's and the animal's mettle.

Enid Bagnold created just such a story with *National Velvet* in 1935 and, presently, the powers at MGM shrewdly purchased the film rights to the story and populated the cast with three of its most popular child actors—Mickey Rooney, Elizabeth Taylor and Angela Lansbury—and featured another even younger scene-stealer, Jackie "Butch" Jenkins. Along wtih the kids, there was a supporting cast of superb character players including Donald Crisp, Anne Revere, Arthur Treacher, Reginald Owen and Arthur Shields. For some reason the piebald horse of Bagnold's story was changed to a sorrel gelding in the film, but still kept its name Pie.

Elizabeth Taylor was magnificent in the role of the engaging Velvet Brown—a classic matching of childhood talent to a role worthy of that talent. But Elizabeth remembers vividly the battle she had to wage to secure the role. As she comments in her autobiography:

> MGM had owned *National Velvet* for a long time and every once in a while they'd sort of dust it off. But they either couldn't find somebody of the right size or somebody who rode or somebody with an English accent. They began casting glances in my direction. Well, it was my favorite book, and I really was a marvelous horsewoman. At the age of three I could jump without a saddle. But when I came down to the producer's office, he saw that though I was eleven, I was only as tall as a six-year-old. He measured me on the wall and made a line with a pencil. He said, "I'm sorry, honey, but you're just too short. No one would ever believe that you could get in through the jockey's weighing room. You look like a child." And I said, "Well, I'll grow up." He laughed and patted me on the head.
>
> But I was absolutely determined. *National Velvet* was really me. I started riding every morning for an hour and a half before school. . . . I used to have two farm

The three youngest stars of MGM's *National Velvet* are collared here: Mickey Rooney, Elizabeth Taylor and Jackie "Butch" Jenkins.

breakfasts every morning at one sitting. For lunch I'd have steaks and salads, then swim and do exercises to stretch myself.

In three months I'd grown three inches. I went back to see the producer and said, "I did grow." He said, "You do look taller." He still had the little mark by the side of the door, and I had grown three inches. He kept that mark on the wall for years. And I got the part . . . I think Velvet is still the most exciting film I've ever done. And at the end, to be given the horse on my thirteenth birthday—well, it was one of *the* moments of my life.

The horse that producer Pandro S. Berman gave Elizabeth was a frisky animal named King Charles in real life. Elizabeth loved the horse, but most others gave it a wide berth because of its biting habits. Elizabeth had a way with the horse, though. As she remarked:

He was a splendid animal, grandsired by Man o' War, and I could jump him six feet bareback. But he was wild. He took a hunk out of the shoulder of the man who tried to train him to play dead for the film. Except for the jockey who did some of the jumps in the National, I was about the only person who could ride him—and bareback with just a rope around his neck. That horse used to follow me around the back lot like a puppy dog. He really was a lunatic. Just for the hell of it he once jumped over an automobile.

Mickey Rooney doesn't look too happy with Elizabeth Taylor's horse, Pie, in this scene from the MGM hit, *National Velvet*.

254 Thundering Hoofbeats

This is the "playing dead" scene for which the trainer, according to Elizabeth, lost a "hunk out of his shoulder" because of the horse's biting habit.

The Technicolor feature was directed by Clarence Brown, who was known for his ability to handle sensitive, emotion-charged films with a firm hand so that pathos and sentiment didn't turn to treacle. His other films included such memorable achievements as *Anna Christie* and *Anna Karenina* with Greta Garbo; *Ah, Wilderness; Edison the Man; The White Cliffs of Dover;* and (after *Velvet*) *The Yearling* and *Intruder in the Dust.*

National Velvet premiered at the Radio City Music Hall in New York in December 1944. It was a lovely Christmas present for wartime audiences looking for inspiration and a chance to spend a couple of hours believing that two youngsters could really accomplish the near-impossible during their "chance at a breathtaking piece of folly." The film proved so popular that over the years it has been repeatedly revived for new generations. In June of 1978, the CBS Television Network ran the now vintage tale as a two-part prime-time summer special. To this viewer the old magic remained.

Strangely, MGM did not see fit to sequel its popular horse story that had brought home the purse for the MGM coffers. It wasn't until 1960 that MGM, then just getting active in television production with such series as *The Thin Man* (with Peter Lawford and Phyllis Kirk) and the short-lived *Northwest Passage* (with Buddy Ebsen and Keith Larsen), decided to produce a *National Velvet* television series. It seemed a natural for family audiences that were enjoying the long-established *Lassie* hit series which was still drawing huge audiences. The popular horse series, *Fury,* had been on the air for five years and was at that time winding down. The way seemed clear to offer a new horse series that would have the wholesomeness of a close-knit family for general audience appeal and a beautiful horse and young girl off which to bounce the weekly story situations.

The *National Velvet* television series was surprisingly true to its original source material. The familiar characters from the novel and feature film were present, only with different actors, of course, essaying the roles. The cast included Lori Martin as Velvet, Arthur Space and Anne Doran as her father and mother, Carole Wells as Velvet's older sister Edwina, Joey Scott as Donald her younger brother and James McCallion as Mi Taylor. Mi, the young horse trainer played by Mickey Rooney in the feature, was more of a handyman on the Brown farm in the television series.

The series presented weekly half-hour episodes built around the family and the horse with the background theme remaining (as with the movie) Velvet's attempts to train her horse (called King in the television series) for competition in the Grand National Steeplechase.

Chestnut-haired Lori Martin carried the featured role of Velvet Brown in the series. Thirteen-year-old Lori was somewhat of an Elizabeth Taylor look-alike and like young Miss Taylor of some fifteen years before, Lori had been riding horses for as long as she could remember. She also shared with Elizabeth Taylor the difficulties associated with acquiring the role: Lori was chosen from among one thousand applicants for the role of Velvet.

Unfortunately, the role that had catapulted Elizabeth Taylor to stardom in 1944 failed to do so for Lori Martin, although she gave an excellent performance in the series. It was just that the series never had the impact of the MGM feature. The series format weakened the punch of the original source material and it evolved into a gentle, warm family series that was a little too lethargic for the kids in the audience and a little too juvenile for the adults. Even the fact that the family was English tended to diminish its wide appeal to American audiences.

National Velvet premiered on NBC September 18, 1960, and was successful enough to last for two years—fifty-eight episodes in all—before it moved into syndication and almost total oblivion—oblivion for the series and for the continued careers of the performers.

Velvet (Lori Martin) and King are pictured here on the *National Velvet* comic book which was inspired by the television series.

Tatum O'Neal is putting Arizona Pie through his paces in preparation for the equestrian Olympic competition.

The *National Velvet* story then lay dormant until 1977 when, with theatre screens gorged with blood, sex and devil doings (*Jaws, Shampoo, The Omen* et al.) MGM announced that it had contracted with Englishman Bryan Forbes to write, produce and direct a new version of the *Velvet* story to be titled *International Velvet*.

Everyone connected with the production was vehement in stressing that *International Velvet* was not going to be a sequel—at least not in the usual sense. "This is a different sort of sequel," Forbes insisted. "Our picture follows thirty years after *National Velvet*. There is no Mickey Rooney, no Anne Revere in our story; all of the characters have died except for Velvet. I was interested in her story as a study in what happens to people who win too early." It's interesting to note that the role of the now mature Velvet was offered to Elizabeth Taylor who declined.

In *International Velvet,* Velvet (Nanette Newman, Forbes real-life wife) does not appear to be a very happy adult. We discover from the dialogue that she has had an unsuccessful marriage, a painful divorce and is now living with a writer (Christopher Plummer), who is afraid of only one thing—"commitment."

Into their already troubled lives comes Velvet's orphaned niece Sarah (Tatum O'Neal) from Arizona. The girl is sullen and morose until she takes an interest in the last foal from Velvet's old horse, Pie. Sarah names the foal Arizona Pie.

Tatum and Arizona Pie are ready to compete at the Canadian Olympics.

In this up-to-date version of the story young Sarah soon becomes obsessed with the possibility of representing England on Arizona Pie in the equestrian competition of the Olympics. Under the training of crusty riding master Captain Johnson (Anthony Hopkins) she enters and (Would you believe it!) wins, thus becoming known as "International Velvet."

The film received enormously mixed reviews from the critics. The *Chicago Tribune* critic described it as "superior entertainment" that "couldn't have been made with more charm and finesse." *Newsweek*'s critic referred to the "syrupy script that plainly embarrasses the cast." *Variety* called the film "extremely fine." *New York* magazine probably had the most devastating comments: "*International Velvet* is truly dreadful—boring, genteel, saved from total worthlessness only by some lovely footage of horse and rider plunging over walls, fences and hedges."

Tatum O'Neal takes a hurdle on Arizona Pie in *International Velvet*.

Tatum O'Neal's reviews were as mixed as those of the film. Whatever this thirteen-year-old's reaction may have been to the critic's slings and arrows, she was able to well stuff her piggy bank with the salary she received for the picture: $400,000 plus a percentage of the profits, if any. Sadly, the film industry box office of the seventies was comprised mostly of boom-or-bust films and for the most part (Disney being the consistent exception) "family" pictures failed to find an audience. *International Velvet* was no exception.

And so the *National Velvet* story is again resting on the shelf, the magic of the original story and feature film eluding television and movie producers of other, later times. But life runs in cycles (as Frank Sinatra once told us in song) and certainly there will come another time for Velvet Brown to ride Pie in the Grand National—a time for us to again cheer her and the horse on to victory.

The Lone Ranger's Silver

One of the most popular horses of modern fiction has been the great horse Silver, ridden by the famous masked rider of the plains, the Lone Ranger. Ever since the creation of the tremendously popular series on radio in early 1933, Silver has been one of the classic animals of show business, supporting the Lone Ranger not only on radio, but also in novels, comic books, movie serials, features and television. The Lone Ranger's cry of "Hi Yo, Silver," is recognized around the world. Any child, asked to name a white horse, is bound to come up with "Silver."

The Lone Ranger's great white horse Silver had his own Dell comic-book series for several years. This issue is from 1960. Photo courtesy of Lone Ranger Television, Inc.

From the radio days on through the television and the film serial and feature picture years, there were a number of horses which physically portrayed Silver on the screen and in personal appearances. But the important thing about Silver was not so much the physical horse as it was the warm and trusting relationship that was established over the years, especially on radio, between the horse and his masked master.

On the radio series you came to realize that this was a horse like no other; that in time of crisis the horse was capable of unmatched stamina and courage—just like its master; that the great horse comprehended the self-proclaimed mission of its master to rid the West of wrongdoers and stood foursquare with (and beneath) the Lone Ranger in accomplishing this task. Corny? Sure. Absurd fantasy? Of course. But we were then a generation that wanted to believe such a camaraderie between man and horse was possible and the ethereal intimacy of radio *made* it possible to believe.

Seeing the horse and rider in the television series removed the opportunity to fantasize, and the great horse Silver of radio, for the most part, became just another television-and-movie horse—an outstanding beauty, but not the enchanted horse created in the theatre of the mind through the magic of a radio box.

Fran Striker, the head writer of *The Lone Ranger* radio series, created a fictional account of how the Lone Ranger came to acquire Silver which I recounted in my book, *Who Was That Masked Man?: The Story of The Lone Ranger*. The incident bears repeating here. As you may remember, the Lone Ranger, originally a Texas Ranger, was the only survivor of an ambush by the infamous Butch Cavendish and his notorious gang. Nursed back to health by the Indian Tonto, the lone survivor assumes the role of a masked avenger and calls himself the Lone Ranger.

While pursuing Cavendish and his gang, the Lone Ranger's horse is shot out from under him. He and Tonto then travel to Wild Horse Canyon where, it has been rumored, a great white stallion grazes with its herd. As I wrote in *Who Was That Masked Man*:

> As they reach the top of a rise leading into the valley, they are halted suddenly by a grisly sight far down in the valley. A great white stallion is in a death battle with a huge buffalo. The mighty stallion bravely lunges, rears and dodges as the gigantic bison repeatedly charges his smaller, tiring combatant. Convinced that the endangered white horse must be the wild stallion that has been spoken of so often, the Lone Ranger rushes to get within pistol range before the stalking beast completes a final death charge. Its strength gone, its silvery white coat blood- and dust-soiled, the magnificent stallion's muscles can withstand no more punishment. As the Lone Ranger races to the scene, he witnesses the once seemingly invulnerable steed stagger and then fall.
>
> As the shaggy brown beast draws back, head lowered for the final death charge, the valley echoes with well-aimed, thunderous explosions from the two guns, now smoking in the hands of the Lone Ranger. For a moment the monster stands motionless seemingly bewildered by this intruder, then falls in death.
>
> As Tonto had previously nursed him back to life, now the Lone Ranger works to save the life of the bruised and battered white stallion. Over the next few days the ugly wounds are tended and slowly heal under the gentle care of the masked man and his Indian friend. Gradually the unmatched strength and stamina of the mighty stallion return.
>
> "He's himself again," the Lone Ranger acknowledges. "I wonder if he'll take a saddle? Let's try."

The best-known radio Lone Ranger, Brace Beemer, is seen here with Silver and several young admirers. The photo was taken in 1947, two years before the television series began, but the tack being worn by Silver is that which was used in the television series. Photo courtesy of Lone Ranger Television, Inc.

As the Lone Ranger lifts the saddle to place it on the horse's strong back, a shudder runs through the wild stallion's body and he breaks fiercely away from his human benefactor.

"Let him go, Tonto," the Lone Ranger says. "I'd like to have that horse more than anything in the world, but he deserves his freedom; he fought for it. See how the sun reflects from his white coat."

"Yes, kemo sabe," the Indian replies. "Him look like silver."

"Silver, that would be a name for him." The Lone Ranger calls out to the white stallion, "Silver, here Silver!"

The mighty horse pauses on a rise a short way off and appears to study the masked man and Indian. The wild instinct possessed throughout the ages is challenged. This something within the stallion tells him to flee at once to preserve freedom, and yet he stands his ground. Some mysterious bond causes the silvery horse to suddenly bolt and gallop to the side of the Lone Ranger.

The saddle and bridle are quickly placed on the horse and the eager Ranger mounts cautiously, allowing the nervous animal to gradually feel the weight of a human body on his back. The man's voice speaks quietly and gently as the stallion grows accustomed to the saddle and rider. Silver seems to sense the desire of his gentle, yet firm, teacher and does his best to learn quickly. After several days of training, the intelligent Silver is ready for the challenges that lie ahead with the Lone Ranger and Tonto. They break camp and once again begin their mission to capture Butch Cavendish.

So for close to fifty years now the legend of the Lone Ranger and the fiery hoofbeats of his great horse Silver have thrilled generations of loyal fans all over the world — and I have a bulging file of letters from people who have read and commented on *Who Was That Masked Man?* and/or *The Lone Ranger* series to support that claim, as has Lone Ranger Television, Inc., a subsidiary of Wrather Corporation, the company which owns all copyrights to *The Lone Ranger*.

Silver is pictured here in the other set of tack that was used over the years. This tack was first used for the late 1930s movie serials [*The Lone Ranger* (1938) and *The Lone Ranger Rides Again* (1939)] and for personal appearances during the 1940s. To the best of my knowledge this tack and ringed saddle pad were never used in the television series. Photo courtesy of Lone Ranger Television, Inc.

Thunder

In the 1970s Saturday morning television programming was wallowing in a mire of stop-action super-hero cartoons and imbecilic live-action comedy series such as "The Far-Out Space Nuts." In the fall of 1977 a new live-action animal series entitled simply *Thunder* took to the air. Except for the up-to-date Western setting and the color photography, you would swear that the Fury series of the 1950s had been resurrected. This resemblance was no accident since *Thunder* was created by Irving Cummings and Charles Marion, the original writers/producers of the *Fury* series.

Thunder, a Marcum Production in association with Charles Fries Productions, took to the NBC television network on Saturday, September 10, 1977, at 11:00 A.M. with as much hoopla as the producers could muster — certainly they were not at a loss for words or for merchandising ideas related to the series. Their first *Variety* ad promised:

> THUNDER will be the finest young people's adventure series to come to NETWORK TV in a long, long time. It already has sponsors committed for the first twenty-six weeks and it should be on the air for many years.
>
> We have the first thirteen scripts and each one is a winner; filled with action-adventure, valuable information, lessons-for-living and containing no violence for the sake of violence.
>
> THUNDER, a beautiful black stallion with almost human intelligence, plays a major role in the lives of CINDY PRESCOTT and her school chum WILLIE WILLIAMS. These two lovable youngsters live on adjoining ranches. CUPCAKE is WILLIE'S irrepressible cookie-eating mule.
>
> CINDY'S mother, ANNE PRESCOTT, is a dedicated conservation- and ecology-oriented vet. CINDY'S and WILLIE'S dads are macho ranchers but very good guys.
>
> THUNDER is a perfect licensing property for logo and/or picture identifying the kinds of things that CINDY and WILLIE wear and use. The same applies to grown-up items like those worn and used by the PRESCOTT'S AND BY SAM WILLIAMS. And in the toy-and-game publications areas, THUNDER should be the answer to some fervent prayers.

The black stallion star of the *Thunder* television series. Inset are the human stars: Clint Ritchie, Melissa Converse and Melora Hardin.

The *Thunder* series, alas, was not to meet with the earlier success of the very similar *Fury* series. The series was certainly wholesome, non-violent, and suitable for all age groups. Unfortunately, it lacked a sense of freshness and style. The scripts were often too moralizing and almost pious in their execution—even for the most juvenile of viewers. The plot's "message" was often telegraphed from the opening scene exposition, leaving only the tedious how-it-would-evolve to take up the next twenty minutes or so.

The participants in the *Thunder* series certainly had good intentions and, heaven knows, good live-action adventure stories for youngsters are needed to quell the Saturday morning glut of plastic pap. *Thunder*, unfortunately, did not create an artistic or network-rating storm and, thus, after a brief shower of publicity and NBC exposure, evaporated into reruns and syndication.

Cindy (Melora Hardin) and Willie (Justin Randi) on their mule Cupcake in the *Thunder* series.

Francis and Mr. Ed—
The Talkers!

Why a talking mule and horse? Well, the mule worked out so well that it just seemed like a natural progression — natural, that is, if your mind works like that of a Hollywood producer. "If one talking animal is a hit, then certainly the public wants more talking animals — and maybe even a talking car that's really Jerry Van Dyke's mother." No, the public wouldn't be suckered in by the *My Mother, the* [talking] *Car* series, but it did like those talking animals, Francis the Mule and Mr. Ed (and, of course, Cleo the Bassett hound of *The People's Choice* series, which has already been discussed).

The cycle of loquacious quadrupeds began in 1949 when Universal Pictures bought the rights to David Stern's novel about a talking army mule named Francis. As with the later Mr. Ed, Francis (in the corncob-rough voice of veteran actor Chill Wills) spoke to only one person except under the most dire of circumstances. In the case of Francis, he only communicated with a rather trouble-prone, bungling type of fellow named Peter Sterling (played by Donald O'Connor in the film series). Why the wise and witty mule selected such a schnook with which to share his verbal verbosity can only be explained by the fact that it made it easier for the writers to set up comic situations between the two of them and other characters.

Critics generally refer to a series where the situation revolves around one basic comic ploy (in this case a talking mule) as a "one-joke show." The theory goes that the public soon tires of the one joke, stops laughing, and shortly thereafter stops watching. When the relatively low-budget movie *Francis* premiered in late 1949, the critics clucked in relative unison that the antics of the talking mule and Peter (O'Connor) were funny, that this one-joke film would be a crowd-pleaser, and would, thus, do well at the box office.

Little did the critics or Universal Pictures realize at the time what a smash hit this talking mule would prove to be with ticket buyers. There are those who claim that Universal (known in years past for its frequent boom-or-bust financial operation) was going through another bust period and was only saved from bankruptcy by the public's embrace of the raspy-throated mule. In any case, Universal was quick to try its luck again with the so-called one-joke premise. The result was *Francis Goes to the Races* (1951), another box-office winner which the public and even most critics found entertaining. The critics cautioned Universal, however, that this one-joke situation would soon wear thin.

Donald O'Connor and Francis the Talking Mule are seen here in a scene from the feature, *Francis Joins the WACs* (1954).

It did eventually wear thin, but only after seven films in seven years, and even then, it would be hard to determine whether it was the premise or the encroachment of television and the death of low-budget series films in general that brought the *Francis* series to an end.

For Universal the series was a financial bonanza. Shot on the backlot in black and white in just a couple of weeks, the films reaped huge profits and, as a side benefit, provided vehicles for Universal's starlets to get experience in front of the camera and widespread public exposure. Such under-contract ingenues as Patricia Medina, Piper Laurie, Lori Nelson, Julia Adams, Mamie Van Doran and Martha Hyer gained early screen credits in the *Francis* series.

Everyone was happy about the success of the series except Donald O'Connor, who rather quickly grew weary of being upstaged by a mule. Also, O'Connor in the early fifties was making it big as a song-and-dance man in such big-budget musicals as *Singing in the Rain* and *Call Me Madam*. He was also starring in the *Colgate Comedy Hour* television variety series. O'Connor wanted to shake loose of the public image of being a duncical straightman for a talking mule, but Universal had him under contract and kept cranking out *Francis* features each year.

Donald O'Connor is astride Francis in this scene from *Francis Goes to the Races* (1951). Francis became a six-time PATSY award recipient, winning more times than any other animal in motion pictures.

By 1956 Donald O'Connor had completed his Universal contract and refused to star in the 1956 edition, *Francis in the Haunted House*. Mickey Rooney (a seemingly likely successor to O'Connor) was cast in the lead human role (David Prescott) but the chemistry between Rooney and Francis did not seem to work as well for some reason—the situations did not play well and, consequently, the laughs were not there. Perhaps it was just that the public had grown too accustomed to Francis and O'Connor and would accept no replacement.

Ironically, about the time that Donald O'Connor got his longed-for freedom from the *Francis* series, the bottom fell out of the lavish film musical genre and O'Connor's television career also began to languish. While Donald O'Connor has successfully continued his show-business career over the years, his peak years as a film-and-television star ended with the demise of his participation in the *Francis* series.

In the spring of 1980 Donald O'Connor announced plans for a revival of the *Francis* series. Acknowledging that the *Francis* films were among the highest grossing films he ever made, O'Connor said he was looking forward to reuniting with Francis for the first time in some twenty-five years. The film is to be entitled *Francis Goes to Washington*.

During his discussion with reporters regarding the proposed new film, O'Connor reminisced about the original Francis. "There was only one Francis for the entire series," O'Connor recalled. "He was twenty years old and untrained when they got him. There was one stand-in mule and three others for trick shots." O'Connor added, "The original Francis died only a few years ago at age forty-seven, which is incredibly old."

A fellow by the name of Arthur Lubin directed all but the last *Francis* feature. When Universal wrote finis to the series in 1956, Lubin felt there was still some life in the one-joke premise and decided he would explore the possibility of a similar comic situation for a potential television series. It took Lubin four years (until late 1960), but finally his conception, *Mr. Ed,* made it to television. "Mr. Ed," a comedy series about a talking palomino horse, starred Alan Young as the horse's owner, a befuddled character named Wilbur Post. Connie Hines co-starred as Wilbur's sometimes perplexed and always scatterbrained wife.

Similar to the *Francis* series, the theme of the *Mr. Ed* television series was based on the dialogical (some considered it diabolical) companionship of Mr. Ed and Alan Young — for the horse would only talk to him. Again, as with Francis, the comedy routines revolved around the embarrassing situations into which Young became trapped and how he extricated himself from them—generally through the loquacity of Mr. Ed.

Now it was time for the television critics to step forward to prophesy that, while the series did offer some initial laughs, the public would soon tire of the one-joke premise of the series. A few critics also warned that all of those employed by the series' producer should be alert to other work since Mr. Ed and his series were doomed to the glue factory.

MR. ED

THE TALKING HORSE and HIS BARN FULL OF LAUGHS

starring:
ALAN YOUNG, CONNIE HINES

The popular horse, Mr. Ed, was a four-time PATSY award winner. He won the coveted award each year from 1962 through 1965.
©1961 Filmways, Inc.

Mr. Ed is seen here with his two co-stars, Alan Young and Connie Hines. The *Mr. Ed* series is still available for broadcast through Filmways Enterprises, Inc., a Filmways Company, in Los Angeles. ©1961 Filmways, Inc.

Mr. Ed prepares to go "down Mexico way" with Alan Young. ©1961 Filmways, Inc.

Five years and 143 episodes later the popular series left the CBS network to begin another long life in syndication. So much for the theory that one-joke situations fairly quickly lead to irrevocable failure in the show-business marketplace. In truth, the interesting/entertaining qualities of the characters involved in the so-called one-joke premises generally dictate the success or failure of such a series, not the gimmick—as in the cases of the talking animals. The public will grow fond of the characters and will want to revisit them for as long as they are interesting and entertaining in the series' story lines. The gimmick of the talking animal soon becomes relatively incidental and an accepted "natural" aspect of the series. This is not meant to gainsay the critics who are only "calling them the way they see them." On the surface Francis and Mr. Ed were only one-joke wonders. But what the critics could not possibly grasp on only an initial viewing or two was the general appeal of the actors and the animals together and the fact that the talking gimmick was only the take-off spot for the series' fun.

When the *Mr. Ed* series ended production in 1965, Alan Young kicked around show business for a few years, but found that his close identification with the popular *Mr. Ed* series hindered his chances at other roles. In 1967 he became a Christian Science practitioner. Finally, in 1970 he and his family moved to Boston where he spent four years as head of communications for the Christian Science Church. His responsibilities included making films for the Christian Scientists and supervising communications teams around the world as they filmed the activities of the church.

In 1974 Young was quoted as saying he felt "I'd done all I could for the church and could see it was not going to be a lifetime job for me." He returned to California to attempt to reactivate his show-business career. Young found the going rough upon his return to Hollywood. As he said, "When you leave show business nobody leaves a bookmark in the place you left so you can find your way back. It's like taking a stone out of a creek. Once you remove the stone the water fills the place. But that's not the worst—some people didn't even know I'd been away. That hurt!"

Alan Young's persistence paid off, though, and he began to get character roles in various series and occasional commercials to do. In 1977 he appeared in Walt Disney's film, *The Cat from Outer Space*.

According to a UPI story, Mr. Ed, the palomino star of the series, was purchased by Hollywood animal trainer, Clarence Tharp, shortly after the television series went out of production. For several years the horse toured with Tharp's stable of trained animals. In 1974 when his car broke down in Tahlequah, Oklahoma, during a tour, Tharp and his wife decided to stay there. Mr. Ed was retired to a Cherokee County farm near Tahlequah.

On February 28, 1979, the then thirty-three-year-old Mr. Ed passed on. According to Tharp, Mr. Ed's long life span equaled about 114 human years. He said Mr. Ed began losing his health about a year before. The horse had lost all his teeth and was restricted to eating baby beef formula for the last few months. Tharp told a UPI reporter that he buried Mr. Ed without a funeral or memorial service in the backyard of his trailer home.

Oh, yes, the voice of Mr. Ed was provided by former cowboy star Allan "Rocky" Lane — a fact which was, for some reason, a carefully guarded secret for some years.

The formal Mr. Ed. ©1961 Filmways, Inc.

7
The Cockatoo of the Walk

Fred the Cockatoo and his co-star Robert "Baretta" Blake.

Fred the Cockatoo

When the *Baretta* television series went on the air in January 1975, it appeared that it had at least two things going for it: a scrappy, talented little actor named Robert Blake to star and a milk-white cockatoo named Fred for comic relief. Blake was occasionally overly pugnacious as the plainclothes, street-wise cop, Tony Baretta: slamming mobster lieutenants against walls, ruthlessly "gathering evidence" by smashing a nose or cauliflowering an ear or two. But Fred the friendly cockatoo was always lovable, always ready to do a cartwheel, maneuver a fluttered perch on Bobby Blake's head, or some other delightful behavior to lighten the proceedings.

Within just a few weeks of telecasts on the ABC network, the *Baretta* series began to pick up rating's steam and gradually went on to be a big hit for three prime-time years. By the time the series went out of production in the spring of 1978, both Robert Blake and Fred the cockatoo were household names, stars of the first rank.

Interestingly enough, Fred was credited with starting a national craze to own birds as pets during the late 1970s. It seemed that just about everyone wanted a Baretta-like relationship with a bird. In July of 1979 *Newsweek* ran a feature on our "Feathered Friends." Frank Zamrock, a Los Angeles bird importer, was quoted as saying that, "The number one pet in America is still the tropical fish—but we're closing in on them." It was estimated that some twenty million people were breeding birds and that forty million owned at least one bird. As one might expect, canaries and parakeets were still the most popular, but with the emergence of Fred as a star on television, cockatoos and the other more exotic birds such as macaws, Amazon and African gray parrots, and toucans became very popular—especially among the rich. Prices for exotic birds rose drastically with the increase in demand. A gray parrot which sold for three or four hundred dollars in 1974 would now flutter in at close to a thousand. A pair of mated cockatoos reportedly sold for $12,000.

Fred, alone, was worth much more than that, of course, to the producers of the hit series *Baretta*. The bird (or at least his owner and trainer, Ray Berwick) was drawing a tidy weekly salary of $1,000. Berwick had "discovered" Fred in Hong Kong where the bird was born in 1967. At that time Fred was known as Lala. When Lala was only a few months old, Berwick bought him and brought him to the United States for training.

Robert Blake and Fred are seen here in a tender moment from one of the *Baretta* television episodes.

From that time on there was plenty of hard work for Lala, training to make him a show-business star. Lala was a quick learner according to Berwick, and before long had mastered the language (Lala, of course, had spoken only Chinese in Hong Kong) and learned a cageful of clever tricks.

When the bird call was put out for the *Baretta* series, Lala was ready, beating out a myna bird for the co-starring role and taking the screen name of Fred—a less cutesy name for the buddy of the bulldog-like Baretta. Now Fred became a television star. He even rated an understudy—a look-alike named Weird Harold, who specialized in flying stunts. Fred didn't talk much about his other stand-in who was stuffed.

By 1976 the awards started rolling in for Fred. In the annual PATSY awards for the year, Fred was named the First Grand PATSY Award Winner. In 1977 he again won the Grand PATSY Award. Also in 1977, *Photoplay* awarded a Gold Medal to Fred as the "Favorite Live Animal Star."

To get a look at the behind-the-scenes business of acting with a bird star, I talked with Fred's other co-star on the series, Tom Ewell, the highly talented Broadway and Hollywood actor. Tom in the years just prior to the *Baretta* series had slipped in the show-business echelon and was grateful to Robert Blake (actually upon the recommendation of Blake's actress wife, Sondra) for getting him back into the public eye. I asked Tom about working with Fred.

Tom Ewell: Well, I don't think there's an actor in the world that likes to work with an animal, because animals, in this case cockatoos, are not easy to work with. You have to adjust yourself to them and you have to watch them instead of trying to concentrate on your own performance. You have to concentrate on their performance because you can't use the take that you do until they get it right. This can be a very painful, long process. Offstage, they can be very friendly and very wonderful. Fred was very friendly—he only bit occasionally. As a result, I loved to play with him. Working with him, no; I've never liked working with animals, and I've never liked working with children—children are the same way. "Unless," as Bert Lahr used to say, "the kid's a heavy, you're dead working with children." It's the same way with animals. They are not actors or performers; they're personalities. And you have to adjust your work to them rather than share equally.

Fred used to get a lot of fan mail, and I used to read it, because he wasn't paying too much attention to it. I know he got several proposals of marriage.

David Rothel: Fred the cockatoo?

Tom Ewell: Oh, yes, from other birds that wrote to him. There was a bird, I remember, who wrote him from some place up in Maryland, some springs up in Maryland. He said, "I work for peanuts, how about you?"

David Rothel: (laugh) I think you're pulling my leg.

Tom Ewell: (seriously) No, I'm not. But the most touching letters we got for Fred were from children. We got many letters from children to Fred. It was always the kind of letter that indicated the child felt very close to Fred and felt that he was a friend. A lot of children in this world don't think they have friends. They either are in a large family or from families that don't particularly want children, but had them anyway. I never realized how many lonely children there are in this world until I started to read some of Fred's mail; it was very touching. One little girl I remember particularly, I remember her letter very well. She said, "I cry myself to sleep every night because no one loves me. But when I watch you, I know that you do love me, because I can see it in the way you look at me through the screen, and so that makes my life a little better." Letters like that touch you. For that reason I guess I don't mind so much working with an animal.

Epilogue

The PATSY Awards

Since the PATSY awards are mentioned frequently throughout the book, let me say a few words about these awards which are the animal equivalent of the Oscars presented to outstanding human actors each year. PATSY stands for Picture Animal Top Star of the Year and is awarded by the Hollywood office of the American Humane Association. The first PATSY award was made in 1951 to Francis the Talking Mule.

The PATSY award is the American Humane Association method for calling public attention to noteworthy performances by humanely trained animals in motion pictures. The awards recognize more than animal actors, however, and are an important annual event for the individuals who train the animals and direct their action before the cameras. In 1958 the American Humane Association added an identical set of honors for Performing Animal Television Stars of the Year, thus acknowledging television's equal importance as a media showcase for animal performers. According to the American Humane Association-published booklet, *Animals in the Film Industry,* "The PATSY awards signify skill and ability in animal handling and mark compliance with AHA standards in treatment of animals."

The impetus for the Hollywood American Humane Association work and the eventual PATSY awards goes all the way back to 1939 and the film, *Jesse James*, which starred Tyrone Power. In one particularly breathtaking scene the hotly pursued Jesse finds himself at the edge of a steep cliff as the posse of lawmen are closing in. Spurring his horse onward, Jesse and the horse jump off the cliff into the river many feet below.

To shoot the scene a greased plank was rigged out of camera sight so that when it was tipped, both horse and rider (a stunt man, of course) would tumble over the cliff and into the stream. When the stunt was executed for the camera, the stunt man lived, but the horse was killed. Word leaked out about the inhumane method used to get the effect on film. The public was outraged by the cruelty inflicted on the animal and, as a result, the American Humane Association decided to open a Hollywood office. Richard C. Craven headed up the office and sought the cooperation of the Motion Picture Association of America in establishing the policy of having an AHA representative supervise filmmaking connected with animal action in all future films. A code was soon agreed upon which stated:

> In the production of motion pictures involving animals, the Producer shall consult with the authorized representative of The American Humane Association and invite him to be present during the staging of such action. There shall be no use of any contrivance or apparatus for tripping or otherwise treating animals in an unacceptably harsh manner.

Over the years there have been many directors of the Hollywood office of the American Humane Association. When I called there recently, I was pleasantly surprised to discover that actress and commercial spokesperson, Carmelita Pope, is the present director. I asked her how the PATSY award winners are determined each year:

Carmelita Pope: Our AHA men who oversee the film productions keep records throughout the year of animals that have done a particularly fine job. We put that information in our PATSY file since we rely very heavily on their opinions. We also send nomination forms out to all the production companies with which we have worked, the animal trainers and handlers, the producers, directors, so forth—anyone involved in the productions which used animals who would be qualified to recommend an animal's performance. When we have received all of the nominations, we go through them to determine the animals that have the most votes. Then we contact the production companies and ask for film clips of the nominated performances.

After the film clips are received, we select a blue-ribbon panel, as we call it, to select the PATSY winners. The panel members may be people who are in the [motion picture/television] industry or out of the industry—it doesn't really matter as long as they are qualified. Every year, of course, there are different people on the panel, depending on who the director of the Hollywood AHA office is and who he or she wants on the panel. I try to get the least-prejudiced, the most open-minded group of people I can. I try to get people who are informed about the motion picture business—such as people from The Motion Picture Association or The Association of Motion Picture and Television Producers. These are just two examples of possible sources for our blue-ribbon panel. I like to have an odd number on the panel—either five or seven people.

The panel members review all of the film clips and they give us their individual written ratings which are compiled by our AHA representatives to determine the winners.

* * *

Over the years procedures and the animal categories have not been consistent. Ms. Pope explained that each new Hollywood AHA director tends to influence the PATSY award procedures, with changes occurring quite often. In recent years there have been four basic categories with occasional special awards. The four categories are canine, equine, wild animals and special. The special category includes unusual film animals such as ravens, goats, house cats, etc. The Hall of Fame Award is considered the highest special award; the Grand PATSY Award has been given twice—both times to Fred the cockatoo from the *Baretta* television series. Ms. Pope was hard pressed to distinguish the difference between the Grand PATSY and the Hall of Fame Awards, except to generalize that the Hall of Fame Award is considered more significant.

For the animal trainers, film producers and directors, the PATSY awards are very much like the Oscars—recognition from your peers for a job well done. And like the Oscars, they are greatly cherished by those who receive them.

Selected Bibliography

Aaronson, Charles S. *1963 International Motion Picture Almanac.* New York: Quigley, 1963.

Agen, Patrick. *Whatever Happened To—.* New York: Ace Books, 1974.

Amory, Cleveland. "Gentle Ben" Review. *TV Guide* (December 2, 1967).

Autry, Gene, with Mickey Herskowitz. *Back In the Saddle Again.* New York: Doubleday and Company, Inc., 1978.

Barbour, Alan G. *Cliffhanger.* New York: A & W Publishers, Inc., 1977.

Barbour, Alan G. *Days of Thrills and Adventure.* New York: The Macmillan Company, 1970.

Brooker, John. "Wrangler's Roundup." *Wrangler's Roost* (June, 1976).

Brooks, Tim, and Marsh, Earle. *The Complete Directory to Prime Time Network TV Shows.* New York: Ballantine Books, 1979.

Buxton, Frank, and Owen, Bill. *The Big Broadcast.* New York: Viking, 1966.

Canutt, Yakima, with Oliver Drake. *Stunt Man.* New York: Walker and Company, 1979.

Capra, Frank. *The Name Above the Title.* New York: The Macmillan Company, 1971.

Crail, Ted. "Yah, Yah, You Scene Stealer, You." *TV Guide* (August 10, 1968).

Davidson, Bill. "Bozo and Dan are an Item." *TV Guide* (June 11, 1977).

De Roos, Robert. "Making a Splash with 'Flipper.'" *TV Guide* (June 4, 1965).

Dunning, John. *Tune in Yesterday.* New Jersey: Prentice-Hall, 1976.

Essoe, Gabe. *Tarzan of the Movies.* New Jersey: Citadel Press, 1968.

Everson, William K. *A Pictorial History of the Western Film.* New York: Citadel Press, 1969.

Freeman, Don. "The Computer Labored—and Brought Forth a Bear." *TV Guide* (January 28, 1978).

"Girl on Horseback, The." *Newsweek* (September 26, 1960).

"Grizzly Adams and His Bears." *Western Frontier* (January, 1978).

Halliwell, Leslie. *The Filmgoer's Companion.* New York: Avon, 1971.

Hanley, Loretta, editor. *Series, Serials and Packages.* New York: Broadcast Information Bureau, Inc., Volume 15: Issue 2D, 1974.

Harmon, Jim, and Glut, Donald F. *The Great Movie Serials.* New York: Doubleday & Company, Inc., 1972.

Herz, Peggy. *TV Time '78.* New York: Scholastic Book Services, 1978.

Hintz, H. F. *Horses in the Movies.* South Brunswick and New York: A. S. Barnes and Company, Inc., 1979.

Horwitz, James. *They Went Thataway.* New York: E. P. Dutton and Company, Inc., 1976.

Janos, Leo. "Dog Star Benji's Best Friend." *US* (May 2, 1978).

Lamparski, Richard. *Whatever Became of . . . ? Fourth Series.* New York: Crown, 1973.

Lamparski, Richard. *Whatever Became of . . . ?* New York: Bantam Books, Inc., 1976.

McCarthy, Todd, and Flynn, Charles, ed. *Kings of the Bs.* New York: E. P. Dutton and Company, Inc., 1975.

McClure, Arthur F., and Jones, Ken D. *Heroes, Heavies and Sagebrush.* South Brunswick and New York: A. S. Barnes and Co., 1972.

Metz, Robert. *The Today Show.* Chicago: Playboy Press, 1977.

Michael, Paul, ed. *The American Movies Reference Book, The Sound Era.* New Jersey: Prentice-Hall, Inc., 1970.

Miller, Don. *Hollywood Corral.* New York: Popular Library, 1976.

Morhaim, Joe. "The Return of 'The Thin Man.'" *TV Guide* (October 26, 1957).

New York Times Film Reviews, 1913-1968, The. New York: The New York Times and Arno Press, 1970.

Parish, James Robert, ed. *The Great Movie Series.* South Brunswick and New York: A. S. Barnes and Company, Inc., 1971.

Ponicsan, Darryl. *Tom Mix Died For Your Sins.* New York: Delacorte Press, 1975.

Rothel, David. *The Singing Cowboys.* South Brunswick and New York: A. S. Barnes and Company, Inc., 1978.

Rothel, David. *Who Was That Masked Man?: The Story of The Lone Ranger.* South Brunswick and New York: A. S. Barnes and Company, Inc., 1976.

Slide, Anthony. *The Big V, A History of the Vitagraph Company.* New Jersey: The Scarecrow Press, Inc., 1976.

Torgerson, Ellen. "Wags to Riches." *TV Guide* (December 2, 1978).

Tors, Ivan. *My Life in the Wild.* Boston: Houghton Mifflin Company, 1979.

Tuska, Jon. *The Filming of the West.* New York: Doubleday, 1976.

Variety (Files from 1930-1979).

Weathers, Diane, with Janet Huck. "Feathered Friends." *Newsweek* (July 16, 1979).

Weatherwax, Rudd. *The Lassie Method.* Cooper Sales Associates, 1971.

Weisman, John. "A Star is Hatched." *TV Guide* (December 27, 1975).

Weiss, Ken, and Goodgold, ed. *To Be Continued . . . .* New York: Crown Publishers, Inc., 1972.

"Yo Ho, Rinty."*TV Guide* (February 26, 1955).

Zinman, David. *Saturday Afternoon at the Bijou.* New York: Arlington House, 1973.

Index

A

Aaker, Lee, 74, 76, 79, 80, 84
Ace (dog), 173
Adams, James Capen, 196
Adams, Julia, 271
Adler, Buddy, 241
Adrian, Iris, 153
Adventures of Champion, The, 214-15, 218, 241
Adventures of Rex and Rinty, The, 72
Adventures of Rin Tin Tin, The, 75-78, 80-81, 84, 86
Adventures of Rusty, The, 173
Adventures of the Thin Man, The (radio), 143
Africa Speaks, 31
After the Thin Man, 143-44
Agee, Johnny, 219
Albee, Joshua, 120
Albert, Edward, 235-36
Allan, Beverly, 181
Allen, Fred, 3, 9
Allen, Jed, 118-19
Allen, Rex, 208, 212
Allied Artists Pictures, 33, 162
Alperson, Edward, 232
American Broadcasting Company (ABC), 75, 120, 126, 199, 243, 280
American Humane Association, 135, 283-84
Amory, Cleveland, 186, 191
Andrews, Stanley, 153
Andy Griffith Show, 17
Animals in the Film Industry, 283
Ankers, Evelyn, 232
Annie Get Your Gun, 58
Another Thin Man, 143
Aquanauts, The, 40
Armstrong Theatre, 58
Arness, James, 214, 249
Arnold (pig), 135
Arthur, Robert, 240
Asta (dog), 91, 142-47
Astaire, Fred, 120
Atkinson, Eleanor, 101

Auten, Charles, 221
Autry, Gene, 208, 214-221, 228, 243
Ayckbourn, Alan, 146

B

Back In the Saddle Again, 215
Bad Day at Black Rock, 174
Bagnold, Enid, 251
Bailey's of Balboa, The, 188
Bannon, Jim, 214
Baretta, 74, 279-82
Barker, Lex, 24-25
Barnes, Frank, 77, 79-82, 174
Bearheart (dog), 79
Bearheart of the Great Northwest, 79
Beaudine, Jr., William, 121
Beauty (horse), 244, 246
Bedtime for Bonzo, 29-30
Beebe, Ford, 33, 215
Beebe, Lloyd, 198
Beemer, Brace, 176, 263
Beery, Wallace, 91
Bell, Book and Candle, 135
Bell, James, 237, 239
Ben (bear), 183 ff.
Benji (dog), 79, 128 ff.
Benji, 129-35, 137, 140
Benji's Very Own Christmas Story, 140
Benny, Jack, 4, 16-17
Bergman, Ingmar, 232
Bergman on Bergman, 232
Berman, Pandro S., 253
Berwick, Ray, 280-81
Beverly Hillbillies, 30, 135
Big Payoff, The, 72
Big V, A History of the Vitagraph Company, The, 232
Black Beauty, 231-36, 244
Black Sunday, 63
Blair, Frank, 12, 19
Blake, Robert, 72, 74, 279-82
"Blondie" (comic strip), 167
Blondie, 91, 135, 167
Blondie On a Budget, 167
Blue Sierra, 98

Bomba the Jungle Boy, 31-33
Bonzo (chimp), 29-30
Bonzo Goes to College, 29-30
Boots (horse), 221
Bowker, Judi, 234
Bozo (bear), 196-98
Bradley, Truman, 39
Brave Stallion, 250
Bray, Robert, 84, 118
Breslin, Patricia, 164, 166
Brickell, Beth, 187, 191-92
Bridges, Lloyd, 40, 63
Britton, Pamela, 168
Brooker, John, 214
Brooks, Rand, 74, 77-80, 84
Brown, Clarence, 255
Brown, James, 74, 76, 79-86
Browning, Ricky, 43-44, 51
Browning, Ricou, 38, 40, 42, 44, 49, 53, 56-57, 63, 188, 194
Browning, Rod, 140
Bruce, Nigel, 92-93, 96
Bruno (bear), 194
Bryant, John, 234
Buck (bear), 194
Bullet (dog), 148-49, 224
Burnett, Carol, 140
Burnett, Smiley, 222
Burton, Skip, 120
Buttermilk (horse), 149, 208, 224

C

Caesar, Sid, 3
Call Me Madam, 271
Call of the Klondike, 153
Cameron, Rod, 150
Camp, Joe, 129-33, 135-37, 140-41
Canutt, Yakima, 226
Capra, Frank, 88-89
Carson, Johnny, 135
Cat From Outer Space, The, 276
Cathy (dolphin), 45-46
Caw-Caw (crow), 33
Chaffey, Don, 121
Challenge of the Yukon, The, 176
Challenge to Lassie, 101, 103-104
Champ, The, 91

Champion (horse), 208, 214-21, 243
Champion, Jr., 216, 221
Chandler, George, 110-13
Chariot of the Gods, 196
Chase, Chevy, 140
Cheetah (chimp), 23-27
Chinook (dog), 77, 150 ff.
Clarence the Cross-Eyed Lion, 35, 184, 201-205
Clayton, Jan, 107, 110, 153
Cleo (dog), 135, 164-66, 269
Cleveland, George, 107, 110-11
Clyde, Andy, 113
Coburn, Charles, 240
Coca, Imogene, 3
Coffin, Tristram, 153
Colbert, Stanley, 42
Columbia Broadcasting System (CBS), 35, 72, 107, 118, 186, 188, 214, 243, 255, 276
Columbia Pictures, 29, 74, 91, 168, 171-73
Command Performance, 3
Como, Perry, 8-9
Connors, Chuck, 53
Cooper, Jackie, 72, 91, 164, 166
Corky (dog), 91
Corky and White Shadow, 162
Corrigan, Lloyd, 162
Courage of Black Beauty, 232
Courage of Lassie, 98-99, 102
Courtship of Eddie's Father, The, 188
Cowden, Jack, 38
Cowling, Bruce, 102
Cox, Monty, 193-94
Craven, Richard C., 283
Crawford, Joan, 244
Crawford, Johnny, 234
Creature From the Black Lagoon, The, 40-42
Crieder, Dorothy, 156
Crisp, Donald, 93, 96, 99, 101, 162, 251
Croft, Mary Jane, 164
Cronkite, Walter, 120
Crowther, Bosley, 92
Cruz, Brandon, 188
Culligan, Joe, 2
Cummings, Irving, 266
Cummins, Peggy, 240

Cupcake (mule), 266, 268
Curtin, Joseph, 143
Curtis, Barry, 214
Curtis, Ken, 40, 236

D
Daisy (dog), 91, 135, 167-70
Daktari, 35, 184, 186, 201-205
Dalbert, Suzanne, 160
Daley, James, 241
Dallas, 84
Damon, Les, 143
Davidson, Bill, 198
Day, Doris, 137
Dean, James, 10
Defore, Don, 236
DeHavilland, Olivia, 222
DeMave, Jack, 118-19
Denning, Richard, 232
Denver, John, 135
Devane, William, 236
Diamond, Bobby, 247-49
Diary of Anne Frank, The, 146
Dinky (chimp), 27
Disney, Walt, 101, 129, 131, 140, 260, 276
Dog of Flanders, 91
Donaldson, Ted, 172-74
Don't Give Up the Ship, 41
Doran, Ann, 102, 173, 255
Drake, Charles, 29
Drake, Tom, 98-100
Duncan, Lee, 66-68, 74, 77, 80
Durante, Jimmy, 16

E
Eagle Lion Pictures, 74, 172
East, Henry, 91, 135, 143
Ebsen, Buddy, 162, 255
Eight is Enough, 199
Ekberg, Anita, 19
Elam, Jack, 236
Ely, Ron, 28, 40
Essoe, Gabe, 23
Evans, Dale, 208, 224
Evans, Gene, 241-42
Ewell, Tom, 281-82

F
Fangs of the Arctic, 153
Fawcett, William, 247
Faye, Alice, 121, 125

Fay, Frank, 156
Ferdin, Pamelyn, 170
Ferrell, Todd, 113
Ferrer, Mel, 236
Five Miles to Midnight, 54
Fixed Bayonets, 241
Fiwzat, Allen, 133
Flame (dog), 77, 171-74
Flipper (dolphin), 38 ff.
Flipper, 37, 40, 45, 47-48, 51, 54, 58, 60-61, 63, 184, 186
Flipper's New Adventure, 45, 53-54
Flying Yorkshireman, The, 88
Flynn, Errol, 222
Fonda, Henry, 161
Forbes, Bryan, 257
Ford, John, 86
Ford, Paul, 188
Fort Apache, 86
For the Love of Benji, 137-38, 140
For the Love of Rusty, 173-74
Foster, Preston, 237, 241
Fox Studios, 228
Fox, Wallace, 150
Francis (mule), 42, 213, 269-71, 276, 283
Francis Goes to the Races, 269, 271
Francis Goes to Washington, 272
Francis in the Haunted House, 272
Francis Joins the Wacs, 270
Francis the Talking Mule, 42, 269-70
Franklin, Pamela, 52
Frawley, Pat, 196, 198
Fred (cockatoo), 279-82, 284
Freeman, Mona, 232
Fritz (horse), 214
Fury, 241, 244-50, 255, 266, 268

G
Gable, Clark, 244
Garbo, Greta, 216, 255
Garrett, Patsy, 133
Garroway, Dave, 3-4, 6, 12, 19
Gene Autry Show, The, 214, 216
Gentle Ben, 183 ff.
Gentle Giant, 183-84, 188, 191
Giant, 244
Gilbert, John, 72
Gillespie, Darlene, 162
Gleason, Jackie, 16, 54, 57
Gog, 39
Golden Boy, Jr., (dog), 77

Golden Cloud (horse), 223
Golden Idol, The, 32
Good Morning, America, 20
Goodrich, Frances, 146
Gorme, Eydie, 135
Gothard, David, 143
Graham, Fred, 149
Granger, Farley, 236
Grant, Kirby, 77, 79, 150, 152-62
Graves, Peter, 247, 249-50
Gray, Gary, 102, 105
Gray Shadow (dog), 77
Great Escape, The, 174
Green Acres, 135
Green Grass of Wyoming, 237, 240-41
Green Hornet, The, 176
Greenwillow, 54
Greyfriars Bobby, 101
Gulager, Clu, 236
Gunsmoke, 40, 154, 188-89
Gwenn, Edmund, 29, 93, 99-103, 162
Gwynne, Anne, 153
Gypsy Colt, 244

H
Hackett, Albert, 146
Hagen, Ross, 35, 205
Haggerty, Dan, 196-99
Hale, Monte, 153
Halloway, Jean, 121
Halpin, Luke, 37, 39, 44, 46, 50-52, 54, 57-64
Hammett, Dashiell, 146
Happy Days, 188
Hardin, Melora, 267-68
Harkins, Jim, 9
Hart, William S., 214, 228
Harty, Patricia, 168-70
Harvey (dog), 156, 158
Harvey, 156
Hayes, Ron, 120
Helfer, Ralph, 202
Henry, Mike, 27
Hey You (dog), 79, 81
Higgins (dog), 129, 133
Highland Dale (horse), 232
Hills of Home, 99-101
Hills of Kentucky, 72
Hilton, Les, 212

Hines, Connie, 272, 274
Hintz, H.F., 221
Hondo, 91
Hope, Bob, 14, 16, 86, 140
Hopkins, Anthony, 259
Horses in the Movies, 221
Howard, Clint, 183-89, 192-93
Howard, Jean, 188
Howard, Rance, 187-88
Howard, Ron, 188
Howdy Doody, 12
How Green Was My Valley, 93
Hudkins, Ace, 208
Hudkins, Art, 208-209, 222
Hull, Alexander, 102
Hutchins, Will, 168, 170
Hyer, Martha, 153, 157, 271

I
Ice Station Zebra, 174
Incredible Hulk, The, 84
Inn, Frank, 79, 129, 131, 134-36, 140, 143, 164, 167
International Velvet, 257-60
Ives, Burl, 240

J
James, Will, 232
Jarman, Jr., Claude, 104
Jeep (dog), 135
Jenkins, Jackie "Butch," 251-52
Jesse James, 283
J. Fred Muggs (chimp), 2 ff.
Johnny Guitar, 244
Johnson, Earl, 149
Johnson, Rita, 237
Johnson, Van, 236
Johnston, Ted, 180
Joyce, Brenda, 25
J-R (dog), 77, 79-82
Judy (chimp), 35, 201-205
Jungle Jim, 29, 33-35
Jupiter's Darling, 41

K
Katzman, Sam, 33
Kay, Mary Ellen, 153
Keller, Donald, 107
Kelly, Brian, 37, 47, 53-55, 62
Kelly, Paul, 102

Kentucky Jones, 189
Killer Leopard, 31
Kimbbo (chimp), 31
King (horse), 256
King Charles (horse), 253
Kirk, Phyllis, 143-44, 255
Knight, Eric, 88-89
Knight, Fuzzy, 161
Knight, Jere, 89
Koko (horse), 208, 212

L
Ladd, Alan, 57
Ladd, Diane, 236
Lady and the Tramp, 131
Lake, Arthur, 167-68
Lala (cockatoo), 281
Lamparski, Richard, 243
Lane, Allan "Rocky," 276
Lansbury, Angela, 251
Larsen, Keith, 40, 255
Lassie (dog), 29, 38, 79, 87 ff., 135, 162, 173
Lassie, 40, 75, 84, 107, 255
Lassie Come Home, 88-89, 91-93, 95-96, 98-99, 102, 121, 124, 240
Lassie Method, The, 91
Lassie My Lassie, 121
Lassie Productions, Inc., 122, 124-25
Lassie's Rescue Rangers, 120-21
Lassie Television, Inc., 87, 90, 106-108, 111-17, 119-21, 123, 126
Laurie, Piper, 271
Lauter, Harry, 153
Lawford, Peter, 96-97, 143-44, 255
Law of the Wild, 72
Leachman, Cloris, 110-11
Leigh, Janet, 99
Leonard, Herbert B., 74, 80, 82
Lescoulie, Jack, 12
Lester, Mark, 233-34
Lewis, Jerry, 41
Life (magazine), 54
Life and Times of Grizzly Adams, The, 196-99
Life With Blondie, 167
Lightning Warrior, The, 72
Lincoln Conspiracy, The, 196
Lindsay, Margaret, 173
Lindy (horse), 219, 221

Litel, John, 173
Little Champ (horse), 216
Little Trigger (horse), 211
Litvak, Anatole, 54
Livingstone, Charles D., 180
Lockhart, June, 96, 113
Loder, John, 72
Loesser, Frank, 54
Lone Defender, The, 69
Lone Ranger, The, 61, 176, 214, 261-65
Lone Ranger Rides Again, The, 265
Lone Ranger Television, Inc., 177-79, 181, 261, 263-65
Lone Star, 244
Look (magazine), 16, 54
Lord of the Jungle, 33
Loren, Sophia, 54
Lost Volcano, The, 31-32
Louise, Anita, 241-42
Loy, Myrna, 91, 135, 142-44, 146-47
Lubin, Arthur, 272
Lucas, William, 234
Lynn, Diana, 29
Lynn, Emmett, 153

M
McCallion, James, 255
McCutcheon, Ralph, 244, 246
MacDonald, Jeanette, 101-102
McDowall, Roddy, 92-96, 162, 237-41
MacMurray, Fred, 161 ff.
Mad (magazine), 16
Magic of Lassie, The, 95, 122, 124-26
Magnetic Monster, The, 39
Mahoney, Jock, 24, 26-27
Malibu Run, 40
Man and the Challenge, The, 40
Man Hunter, The, 72
Many Loves of Dobie Gillis, The, 247
Marion, Charles, 266
Martin, Lori, 255-56
Martin, Mary, 58
Martinez, Frank, 199
Marx, Groucho, 16
Mary Lou (snake), 202
Mary Poppins, 121
Mascot Pictures, 230
Mather, Aubrey, 174

Mattingley, Hedley, 202, 204
Maxwell, Robert, 106, 110
Mayer, Louis B., 232
Mazurki, Mike, 121, 125
Medina, Patricia, 271
Meeker, Ralph, 184
Mennella, Buddy, 4, 6, 7 ff.
Merey, Carla, 165
Metro-Goldwyn-Mayer, 53, 88-89, 91-93, 96, 98-99, 102, 105-106, 122, 126, 135, 142-44, 147, 173, 188, 202, 232, 251-53, 255, 257
Metz, Robert, 2, 12
Miami Seaquarium, 42, 44-46, 53, 55, 59-61, 64
Michael, Jay, 176
Mickey Mouse Club, 80, 82, 86, 162
Miles, Vera, 186, 191
Miller, Cheryl, 202, 204
Miller, Denny, 24
Miracle Rider, The, 230
Mission Impossible, 250
Mitchell, Cameron, 236
Mitchell, Charlotte, 234
Mitzi (dolphin), 43-45
Mix, Tom, 214, 219, 226-30
Moger, Stan, 80
Monogram Pictures, 31, 33, 153, 162, 232
Monroe, Marilyn, 120
Moran, Erin, 35, 205
Morey, Walt, 184
Morgan, Claudia, 143
Morgan, Frank, 98-99
Morrison, James, 231
Mr. Ed (horse), 212-13, 269, 273-77
Mr. Ed, 272-77
Mulberry Square Productions, 128-30, 132-34, 136-38, 140-41
Mulhall, Jack, 72
Munson, Lyman, 89
Murray, Jan, 27
Music Man, The, 54
My Dog Rusty, 173
My Dog Shep, 172
My Friend Flicka, 93, 211, 237-43
My Life in the Wild, 204
My Three Sons, 135, 249

N
Nader, George, 40
Nagel, Conrad, 173

Naked Ape, The, 16
Nakimba (chimp), 31
Nanette (dog), 66-67
Nanny and the Professor, 135
National Broadcasting Company (NBC), 2-4, 6, 8-9, 11-12, 27-28, 54, 72, 150, 164, 184, 189, 196, 199, 236, 243-44, 250, 256, 266, 268
National Velvet, 162, 251-60
Neal, Tom, 153
Nelson, Lori, 271
Newman, Nanette, 258
New York Times, The, 68, 92, 184, 232, 241
Nick and Nora, 144-45
Night Wind, 172
Nixon, Richard, 16
Nolan, Lloyd, 240
Norden, Tommy, 37, 46, 48, 54, 62
Northern Patrol, 153
Northwest Stampede, 172
Northwest Territory, 153
Novak, Kim, 19

O
Oates, Warren, 236
O'Connor, Donald, 269-72
O'Feldman, Ric, 45
O'Hara, Mary, 237, 240-41
Oh Heavenly Dog, 140
Old Blue (horse), 228
Old Man and the Sea, The, 174
Old Yeller, 91
O'Neal, Tatum, 256, 258-60
O'Sullivan, Maureen, 29
Otherwise Engaged, 93
Outer-Space Connection, 196
Owen, Reginald, 251

P
Padilla, Manuel, 27
Paige, Jean, 231
Painted Hills, The, 102, 105
Pal (dog), 91, 93, 95
Parsons, Lindsley, 153
PATSY Awards, 56, 85, 98, 119, 135, 137, 144, 164, 183, 204, 222, 244, 246, 271, 273, 281, 283-84
Peck's Bad Boy, 91

Peggy (chimp, 29)
People's Choice, The, 135, 164-66, 269
Perkins, Anthony, 54
Pernell, Larry, 40, 120
Perreau, Gigi, 29
Perry, Newton, 40
Peter Gunn, 144
Peter Pan, 58
Peters, Brock, 236
Petticoat Junction, 129, 135
Pflug, Jo Ann, 144-45
Phenomenon of Benji, The, 140
Phoebe B. Beebe (chimp), 18-19
Pinkham, Richard, 2, 9
Planet of the Apes, 93
Plummer, Christopher, 258
Pokey (dog), 107
Pope, Carmelita, 284
Powell, Dick, 172
Powell, William, 91, 135, 142-44, 146-47
Powers, Tom, 173
Power, Tyrone, 283
Preis, Jerry, 6, 15, 22
Prelude to War, 88
Producers Releasing Corporation (PRC), 72, 74
Provost, Jon, 110-11, 113, 115
Pyewacket (cat), 135

R

Ralston, Esther, 232
Randall, Glenn, 208-13, 215, 222
Randi, Justin, 268
Reagan, Ronald, 29-30
Rebel (dog), 214
Redford, Robert, 134
Reilly, Hugh, 113
Relatively Speaking, 146
Renfro, Rennie, 135, 167
Republic Pictures, 149, 222
Rettig, Tommy, 107-110, 113
Return of Rin Tin Tin, The, 72, 74
Return of Rusty, The, 173
Revere, Ann, 251, 257
Rex (horse), 70-71
Rhino, 39
Rhodes, Hari, 202, 204
Riders to the Stars, 39
Rifleman, The, 53, 234

Ringling Brothers and Barnum & Baily Circus, 219
Rin Tin Tin (dog), 66-86, 98, 241
Rin Tin Tin, Jr., (dog), 72
Rin Tin Tin VII (dog), 80, 83
Rin Tin Tin III (dog), 72, 74
Rip Cord, 40
Ritchie, Clint, 267
Robards, Jason, 69
Roberts, Lynne, 153
Roberts, Pernell, 121, 124-25
Robin Hood, 222
Robins, Peter, 170
Robinson, Jackie, 120
Rockwood, Roy, 31
Rogers, Roy, 148-49, 207-10, 213-14, 222-25, 228
Rooney, Mickey, 121, 124-25, 251-53, 255, 257, 272
Rothel, David, 7 ff., 57-64, 77-86, 93, 95, 146-47, 153-62, 173-74, 180, 208-13, 238, 240, 282
Roy Rogers and Dale Evans Museum, 149, 224
Roy Rogers Show, The, 149
Rusty (dog), 77, 171-75
Rusty Leads the Way, 173
Rusty Saves a Life, 173
Rusty's Birthday, 173
Ryan, Irene, 30

S

Safari Drums, 32
Salty (sea lion), 51
Santini, Milton, 43, 45
Sarnoff, David, 10
Saunders, Gloria, 153
Sawyer, Joe, 74
Schaffner, Franklin, 58
Science Fiction Theatre, 39
Scott, Gordon, 24-25
Scott, Joey, 255
Scotty (dolphin), 45
Screen Gems, 74
Screen Guild, 172
Sea Hunt, 38, 40-41, 63
Sells-Floto Circus, 230
Seven Little Foys, The, 14
Sergeant Preston of the Yukon, 161, 176, 178-81
Sewell, Anna, 231-32
Seymour, Dan, 153

SFM Media, 80
Shadow, The, 76
Shadow of the Thin Man, 143
Sharif, Omar, 140
Shaw, Roderick, 234
Sheffield, Johnny, 24, 31, 33
Shep Comes Home, 172
Shep of the Painted Hills, 102
Shepodd, Jon, 110-11
Sherman, Richard, 121
Sherman, Robert, 121
Shields, Arthur, 251
Sidney, Sylvia, 161
Silver (horse), 214, 261-65
Silverheels, Jay, 153
Simmons, Richard, 161, 178-81
Simms, Larry, 168
Sinatra, Frank, 260
Sing Along With Mitch, 54
Singing Cowboys, The, 216, 222
Singing in the Rain, 271
Singleton, Penny, 167-68
Skipper (dog), 33
Skippy (dog), 147
Skull and Crown, 72
Sky King, 150, 152
Slate, Jerome, 40
Slezak, Walter, 29, 234
Smith, Cynthia, 133
Smokey (bear), 186
Smokey, 232
Snow Dog, 153, 163
Sommers, Esther, 102
Song of Love, 39
Song of the Thin Man, 143, 147
Son of Lassie, 96-97
Son of Rusty, 173
Sorensen, Rickie, 25
Space, Arthur, 232, 255
Spoilers of the Plains, 149
Star Trek, 188
State Fair, 121
Steel Helmet, The, 241
Stern, David, 269
Stevens, Craig, 144-45
Stewart, James, 121, 124
Stone, Milburn, 153-54
Storm Over Tibet, 39
Straight, Beatrice, 241
Strawberry Roan, The, 216
Striker, Fran, 262

Strongheart (dog), 68
Studio One, 58
Sturges, John, 174
Sugarfoot, 168
Sullivan, Ed, 16
Summers, Yale, 202, 204
Sun Comes Up, The, 101-102
Sunn Classics Pictures, 196, 198-99
Superman, 106
Sutton, Paul, 176
Suzy (dolphin), 45-46, 49, 53

T

Tabori, Kristoffer, 236
Take Me Along, 57
Talbot, Gloria, 153
Tamba (chimp), 29, 33-34
Tarzan and the Great River, 27
Tarzan and the Hunters, 31
Tarzan and the Jungle Boy, 27
Tarzan and the Trappers, 25
Tarzan and the Valley of Gold, 27
Tarzan Finds a Son, 31
Tarzan Goes to India, 24
Tarzan of the Movies, 23
Tarzan's Desert Mystery, 24
Tarzan's Fight for Life, 25
Tarzan's Magic Fountain, 25
Tarzan's Three Challenges, 24
Taylor, Elizabeth, 92-93, 96, 98-99, 121, 162, 244, 251-55, 257
Tharp, Clarence, 276
Thin Man, The, 91, 135, 143-44, 146, 255
Thin Man Goes Home, The, 142-43
This Above All, 88
Thompson, Howard, 184
Thompson, Marshall, 202-204
Thunder (horse), 266-68
Thunderhead, Son of Flicka, 237-38, 240
Today Show, 2-4, 6-10, 12-13, 18-20
Today Show, The, 2
Todd, Zoe, 42
Tony (horse), 214-15, 226-30
Tony, Jr., (horse), 219, 221, 229-30
Toomey, Regis, 72
Tors, Ivan, 35, 38-42, 51, 54-55, 57, 62, 184, 186, 188, 193-94, 202, 204

Tough Guy, 72
Town Hall Tonight, 3
Tracked by the Police, 69
Trail of the Lonesome Pine, The, 161
Trail of the Yukon, 153, 160
Tramp (dog), 135
Treacher, Arthur, 251
Tremayne, Les, 143
Trendle, George W., 176
Trigger (horse), 149, 208-212, 214-15, 222-25
Trigger, Jr., (horse), 207, 211, 223-24
Tucker, Forrest, 236
TV Guide, 38, 54, 77, 140, 186, 198
Twentieth Century-Fox, 172, 232, 237, 240-41
Twenty Thousand Leagues Under the Sea, 41

U

United States Steel Hour, The, 58, 241
Universal Pictures, 29-30, 40-41, 84, 150, 172, 230, 236, 269, 271-72

V

Vallin, Rick, 153
Van Cleve, Patricia, 168
Van Doran, Mamie, 271
Van Dyke, Jerry, 269
Van Dyke, W. S., 146
Van Sickel, Dale, 153
Variety, 20, 69, 129, 133, 138, 140, 234, 259, 266
Verdugo, Elena, 153-54
Vitagraph Company, 231

W

Wahama (horse), 242-43
Waldo (dog), 135
Waldron, Roy, 4, 6-9, 15-16, 22
Warner, Jack, 68-69
Washbrook, Johnny, 241-43
Wayne, David, 236
Wayne, John, 120, 140
Weatherwax, Robert, 122, 126
Weatherwax, Rudd, 79, 89, 91-93, 105-106, 121-23, 126, 135, 143, 146, 167

Weaver, Dennis, 183, 186-92
Weaver, Sylvester "Pat," 3
Webb, Kathy, 122
Weintraub, Sy, 24, 28
Weird Harold (cockatoo), 281
Weissmuller, Johnny, 23-24, 29, 31, 33-34
Wells, Carole, 255
Werner, Mort, 9
Westmore, Bud, 41
When the North Wind Blows, 196
Where the North Begins, 68-69
White Cliffs of Dover, The, 93, 255
Whitty, Dame May, 93
Who Was That Masked Man?: The Story of The Lone Ranger, 262, 264
Why We Fight, 88-89
Wiggles (dog), 91
Wilcox, Fred, 91
Wilcox, Larry, 118, 120
Williams, Esther, 41
Williamson, Sam, 122, 156
Wills, Chill, 269
Willson, Meredith, 54
Wolf Dog, The, 72
Wolf Hunters, The, 153, 158, 161
Wood, Murry, 193
Woods, Donald, 72, 74
Word, Rob, 153
Wranglers Roost, 214
Wrather, Bonita Granville, 88, 121, 126
Wrather, Jack, 88, 110, 121, 126

Y

York, Duke, 156, 158
You Never Can Tell, 172
Young, Alan, 272, 274-76
Young, Chic, 167
Your Show of Shows, 3
Yukon Gold, 153-54, 158
Yukon King (dog), 176-81
Yukon Manhunt, 153
Yukon Vengeance, 153

Z

Zebra In the Kitchen, 184
Zimbalist, Stephanie, 121
Zinman, David, 167
Zippy (chimp), 25